Language Policy

Language policy is an issue of critical importance in the world today. In this up-to-date introduction, Bernard Spolsky explores many debates at the forefront of language policy: ideas of correctness and bad language; bilingualism and multilingualism; language death and efforts to preserve endangered languages; language choice as a human and civil right; and language education policy. Through looking at the language practices, beliefs and management of social groups from families to supra-national organizations, he develops a theory of modern national language policy and the major forces controlling it, such as the demands for efficient communication, the pressure for national identity, the attractions of (and resistance to) English as a global language and the growing concern for human and civil rights as they impinge on language. Two central questions asked in this wide-ranging survey are how to recognize language policies, and whether or not language can be managed at all.

BERNARD SPOLSKY is Emeritus Professor at Bar-Illan University, Israel, and Senior Associate, the National Foreign Language Center at the University of Maryland. His previous publications include *Conditions for Second Language Learning* (1989) and *The Languages of Israel: Policy, Ideology and Practice* (1999). He has published over 200 journal articles, is Editor-in-chief of *Language Policy* and was founding editor of *Applied Linguistics*.

KEY TOPICS IN SOCIOLINGUISTICS

This new series focuses on the main topics of study in sociolinguistics today. It consists of accessible yet challenging accounts of the most important issues to consider when examining the relationship between language and society. Some topics have been the subject of sociolinguistic study for many years, and are here re-examined in the light of new developments in the field; others are issues of growing importance that have not so far been given a sustained treatment. Written by leading experts, the books in the series are designed to be used on courses and in seminars.

Already published in the series:
Politeness by Richard J Watts

Forthcoming titles:
World Englishes by Rakesh Bhatt and Raj Mesthrie
Analyzing Sociolinguistic Variation by Sali Tagliamonte
Critical Discourse Analysis by Jan Blommaert

Language Policy

BERNARD SPOLSKY

CAMBRIDGE
UNIVERSITY PRESS

CAMBRIDGE
UNIVERSITY PRESS

University Printing House, Cambridge CB2 8BS, United Kingdom

Cambridge University Press is part of the University of Cambridge.

It furthers the University's mission by disseminating knowledge in the pursuit of education, learning and research at the highest international levels of excellence.

www.cambridge.org
Information on this title: www.cambridge.org/9780521011754

© Bernard Spolsky 2004

First published 2004
8th printing 2013

A catalogue record for this publication is available from the British Library

Library of Congress Cataloguing in Publication data
Spolsky, Bernard.
Language policy / Bernard Spolsky.
    p.   cm. – (Key topics in sociolinguistics)
Includes bibliographical references and index.
ISBN 0 521 80461 2 (hardback) – ISBN 0 521 01175 2 (paperback)
1. Language policy.   2. Language planning.   I. Title.   II. Series.
P119.3.S666   2004
306.44'9 – dc21   2003053295

ISBN 978-0-521-80461-5 Hardback
ISBN 978-0-521-01175-4 Paperback

For Elisheva, Yonatan, Eliahu (the language manager), David and Yair as they negotiate their own family language policy

Contents

Tables

Preface

There is a special challenge in writing about a comparatively new field. Language policy has been studied for at least fifty years, with growing interest and publication over the last two decades, but no consensus has emerged about the scope and nature of the field, its theories or its terminology. I will therefore venture definitions, present first efforts at a theory, attempt to do justice to other opinions and develop, where it seems needed, my own terminology.

There are two matters that I want to mention at the outset. At least since Thomas Kuhn raised the matter, the problem of a scientist's personal point of view has been widely recognized. Especially in the social sciences, it is hard to conceive of a scholar who is strictly neutral. Can one write about economics without an opinion about the morality of the division of resources and the growing gap between rich and poor? Can one write about political structures without taking a stand on the value of democracy and the danger of totalitarianism? Can one write about language policy without a personal view about the desirability of linguistic diversity? In an introduction to the field, however, my assignment is not to advocate but to attempt to understand and explain. As a pragmatic liberal, I acknowledge the need to distinguish between advocacy and neutrality and believe that the knowledge developed in this way will contribute to the social purposes I, too, share (see the essay on "The Social Science Project: Then, Now and Next," by Kenneth Prewitt in *Items*, vol. 3, no. 1–2, spring 2002).

One critical limitation of the field is our tendency to what I call linguicentrism, a term I coin to mean "language-centered" because "linguacentric" has taken on the meaning of "looked at from the point of view of one language only." This is a book about language policy, so that it is proper that its attention be focused on language and languages. At the same time, language policy exists within a complex set of social, political, economic, religious, demographic, educational and cultural factors that make up the full ecology of human life. While many scholars are now beginning to recognize the interaction of economic and political and other factors with language, it is easy and tempting to ignore them when we concentrate on language matters. Looking for basic data about the nations whose policies I was trying to study, I was suddenly shocked into reality by a note that kept turning up. The CIA *World Factbook* (updated annually, it can be found on the web at http://www.cia.gov/cia/publications/factbook/index.html) gives the latest population figures, but in a frighteningly large number of cases, a note explains that the estimate takes into account "Excess mortality due to AIDS." Should we be wondering about the official use of French and the role of the vernaculars in a country with excess mortality? Or about the prospects for Bosnian when so many of its speakers were recently massacred? But my expertise is in language policy – not syntax or semantics or AIDS or ethnic cleansing. Reminding myself of this serves, I hope, to keep a sense of proportion, a realization of the limitation of our understanding of human society.

My position, then, is that language is important and that any studies of societies that exclude (as they too often do) language are limited, but that language and language policy need to be looked at in the widest context and not treated as a closed universe. Language is a central factor, but linguicentrism (like ethnocentrism and linguacentrism in its regular sense) imposes limited vision.

The second matter is the question of debt to my predecessors and colleagues. Because the field is so new and I am writing this book close to the end of my own career, I am acquainted with and account as friends a large number of the colleagues whom I am quoting (or arguing with – my disagreements with Tove Skutnabb-Kangas and Robert Phillipson should not disguise my admiration for their work and the fundamental questions they raise). The citations and the list of references should make my debt clear, but there may be many cases where I have unconsciously absorbed points of view, terms, phrases even, that I no longer recognize as originating with others. Should this happen, I apologize in advance.

While this is my first attempt to describe the field of language policy as a whole, I met regularly with Robert Cooper during the time he was writing his by now classic *Language Planning and Social Change* (Cambridge University Press, 1989) and I owe a special debt to him.

My academic and personal contacts with Joshua and Gella Fishman over the years have taught me more than I can say about the relation between the academic and the personal in this field. Among the other scholars who have regularly stimulated and corrected me, I want to list Richard Lambert (whose invitation to the National Foreign Language Center introduced me to the notion of language policy), Elana

Shohamy (who worked with me to design an Israeli language policy), Richard Brecht and the late Ronald Walton (for exciting discussions especially about US policy), Christina Bratt Paulston (who keeps raising fundamental questions), John Trim (who has already thought through most of the issues I mention) and Ellen Spolsky (whose pioneering work on cognition, skepticism and literary theory challenged me to make similar sense of my own interdisciplinary field, and who has provided the fundamental support needed to continue my work). I want also to thank my students, whose enthusiasm for the topic when I taught my first course on language policy encouraged me to continue to study it.

I am grateful to Andrew Winnard for the suggestion that I write this book, to Helen Barton for her help in preparing it for publication and to the anonymous reader for the press who pointed out a number of errors and infelicities.

Jerusalem
April 2003

1 Language practices, ideology and beliefs, and management and planning

A fifty-six-year-old Turkish woman was refused a heart transplant by clinics in Hanover on the grounds that her lack of German (common among *Gastarbeiter*) made the recovery process dangerous. The clinic defended the decision: the patient might not understand the doctors' orders, might take the wrong medicine and might not be able to get help if there were complications. The state minister for health said (*Sunday Telegraph*, August 27, 2000) that in future in similar cases they must find a more practical solution. Doctors and hospitals make language policy when they decide how to deal with language diversity.

Many stories deal with similar cases. Some involve public signs, outward evidence of language policy. In the Old City of Jerusalem, there are trilingual street signs, with the changing order of languages (English, Arabic or Hebrew at the top) tracing the recent history of the city (British Mandate, Jordanian or Israeli rule). But other Israeli cities have signs only in Hebrew and English. After years of litigation, the courts recently ruled that street signs in cities with a mixed Jewish–Arab population should include Arabic. Half a world away, Transit New Zealand agreed to add Māori to English road and place signs (*The Dominion*, March 2, 2000; for more on Māori and New Zealand, see the section beginning on p. 200). Quebec law requires that all public signs be in French, permitting the addition, in smaller letters, of a translation into another language. In Wales, Carmarthenshire County Council decided that place and road signs should be in Welsh only. Swansea City Council disagreed: "As a council we have a policy of bilingual signs . . . if we are going to make Swansea a tourism centre we have to attract people of all nationalities" (*South Wales Evening Post*, March 3, 2000; for more on Welsh, see the section beginning on p. 81).

The language of public signs may seem a trivial local matter, but language issues can lead to major conflicts. At the end of June 2001, with the fighting in Macedonia continuing, the Council of Europe urged the Macedonian government to grant ethnic Albanians "the use of the Albanian language in Macedonian courts, schools and administration" (Agence France Presse, June 28, 2001). A real language war was possible.

Perhaps languages do not often cause wars, but language has certainly been a major factor in what Horowitz (2001: 1) calls deadly ethnic riots, which he defines as attacks by civilians belonging to one ethnic group on civilians from another group. The riots may be communal, racial, religious, linguistic or tribal. Horowitz lists a number of recent examples of linguistic riots: Assam in 1960 and 1972, Sri Lanka in 1956 and 1958, Ranchi in 1967, Mauritania in 1966, Karachi-Hyderabad in 1972 and Bangalore in 1994. Assam, a state in the northeast of India, tried to make Assamese its official state language, in the hope that this would favor natives in obtaining positions (Horowitz 2001: 208f.). The 1960 riots came in the midst of the campaign. The Assam Language Act made Assamese compulsory. The learning of Assamese by Bengali immigrant Muslims partly vitiated the effect of the law, so that ethnic tensions and violence continue (Misra 2000).

National language policy is a regular topic. China recently passed a new language law that bans the use of foreign words and the misuse of Chinese. According to the law, Putonghua is to be the officially legal language of China, its standard spelling and pronunciation to be required of all radio announcers, teachers and civil servants (The Straits Times, Singapore, November 17, 2000). In August 2002, the Turkish Parliament, applying for admission to the European Community, had passed laws abolishing the death penalty and permitting the use of the Kurdish language in broadcasting and education. The same month, the US Supreme Court agreed to rule on a law requiring libraries receiving federal funding to use software to filter out pornography and obscenity. On November 15, 2002, the Russian Duma (lower house of parliament) easily passed a law, saying that the "alphabets of the Russian Federation's state language and the state languages of the republics of the Russian Federation are based on the Cyrillic alphabet" (Reuters). On November 14, 2002, the lower house of the Yugoslav Parliament passed a resolution urging all state and local self-government institutions, public companies and educational, cultural and media institutions to use Cyrillic (Tanjug News Agency). On November 21, 2002, Associated Press reported that Turkey's broadcasting authority had authorized up to forty-five minutes a day of radio broadcasting in Kurdish or other regional languages.

Because of the centrality of language to education, many of the stories concern the choice of language as the medium of instruction in schools. In November 2000, the voters of Arizona approved Proposition 203, based on an earlier initiative in California, which replaced bilingual education with immersion English education. In Malaysia, there was debate over a threat to existing Chinese-medium schools (Agence France Presse, June 23, 2001), a new plan announced by the Ministry of Education to improve the teaching of English (The Malaysian National News Agency, May 17, 2001), a new Islamic radio station which planned to broadcast twenty-four hours a day in English, Bahasa Melayu and Arabic (*New Straits Times*, July 7, 2001) and a bitter public controversy over a government decision to start teaching mathematics and science in English after twenty years in which they had been taught in Malay, with a compromise decision to teach the subjects in English as well as Mandarin in Chinese schools (*Malaysia General News*, October 29, 2002). In Ghana, the minister of education decided that the use of the vernacular in the first three school years should be abandoned and English used instead (*Africa News*, August 16, 2002). After three decades of debate, the Tanzanian Parliament decided to switch the language of secondary schools from English to Kiswahili (Xinhua National News Service, January 16, 2001). In South Africa, a provincial education department said schools could not refuse to admit English-speaking students because they would upset the language balance against Afrikaans (News24, South Africa, January 15, 2003).

Businesses, too, are involved in language policy. The Common Market for Eastern and Southern Africa supported Zimbabwe's policy that dairy imports from Zambia must have instructions on the packages written in Shona and Ndebele, the official languages of Zimbabwe (*Times of Zambia*, July 10, 2001). With increasing globalization, more and more translation engines are being announced giving multilingual access to the web; these include a platform called Prolyphic to make web translation faster (*Business Wire*, July 10, 2001) and a website platform originally in French and already available in English that is now planning to add capacity in German, Spanish and other languages (*The Gazette*, Montreal, July 9, 2001).

Churches are not exempt. A Roman Catholic priest in Wezembeek-Oppem, a town near Brussels in the Dutch-speaking Flanders region of Belgium where the large French-speaking community has special rights to use its language (see pp. 164ff.), was removed from his parish by the cardinal for refusing to allow French-speakers to celebrate Mass in his church (Associated Press, December 30, 2002).

While very current, the topic of language policy is, of course, not a new one; two stories in the book of Genesis fit the definition. Adam, it will be recalled, took on the task of naming the animals in the

Garden of Eden, a role now regularly assigned to national language academies. And God, faced with the behavior of the people at Babel, "confounded their tongues" and decreed (and implemented) individual plurilingualism and social multilingualism. As a general rule, I will use the term multilingual to refer to a society in which a number of languages are used, and the term plurilingual to refer to the usually differentiated skills in several languages of an individual member of such a community.

WHAT ARE THE DATA?

There is no shortage of stories about language policy, but how do they translate into data that might build a theory? I was speaking recently with a neighbor about the data in our respective fields. He is an archeologist who excavates sites, noting the location of every potsherd that he finds. After chemical analysis of the objects, he uses statistical techniques to determine the original source of the clay. He compares these quantified empirical data with information in the Talmud about Galilean villages and is then ready to make generalizations about the trade relations between contemporary Jewish and non-Jewish villages. I tried to explain the problems we face in language policy. Some countries record their language policy in their constitutions or in law; others do not. Some implement their written policies; others clearly do not. Some countries can provide data about the number of people who speak various languages. Others do not even ask that question in their national census. When the question is asked, it is asked differently. In the United States, for instance, the census asks how many people grew up in a home where a language other than English was spoken; in Canada, it asks how many people are proficient in English. How, given all this uncertainty about basic data, can we attempt to derive generalizations that reach the reliability that my archeologist friend would expect?

The first sociolinguists who tackled questions concerning language policy and planning were troubled by these questions, but were more concerned with solving the language problems of developing nations. Some of their work, such as the pioneering studies of the language situation in East Africa, made efforts to build databases. A second wave of scholars in the field became more concerned with developing models of linguistic human rights on the basis of which they could encourage international groups to adopt specific policies. What was missing, however, was a systematic attempt to gather usable data on language policies at all levels. This book takes advantage of the fact that such an attempt is now being made.

WHAT IS LANGUAGE POLICY?

Visitors to the Canadian city of Montreal in the early 1960s may have been puzzled by the apparent imbalance between the widespread public use of English in signs and large stores and the fact that 80 percent of the population spoke French. Forty or more years later, it is now obvious that French has achieved a more appropriate public use. The linguistic landscape is now overwhelmingly French. Behind this change in public practice, there was a determined and explicit policy change, a set of managed and planned interventions supported and enforced by law and implemented by a government agency.

Other changes in practices of language choice are harder to account for. In a tiny isolated village in Papua New Guinea, where the ninety inhabitants spoke Taiap, a language unrelated to any other, Kulick (1992) found that children under the age of ten no longer spoke the local language in spite of continued isolation. Instead, all now used Tok Pisin, a New Guinea English-based creole spoken by their bilingual parents. The adults were unaware that their own language-use pattern had changed over time, from monolingual Taiap to regular code-switching bilingualism between Taiap and the Tok Pisin brought back to the village by young men after work in distant plantations. In adult language practice, Kulick discovered, only Tok Pisin was used in meaningful communication with children, while Taiap was used only for meaningless baby-comforting talk. This case appears to be a change in practice that cannot be attributed to any explicit policy decision – the parents were amazed when they noted the change in their children's language practice – but rather to alterations in situation, conditions and pressures of which even the participants are unaware.

To make sense of these cases and others, a useful first step is to distinguish between the three components of the language policy of a speech community: its language practices – the habitual pattern of selecting among the varieties that make up its linguistic repertoire; its language beliefs or ideology – the beliefs about language and language use; and any specific efforts to modify or influence that practice by any kind of language intervention, planning or management.

Haugen (1966b) suggested that the field could be organized under four headings: the first two were selection of a norm when someone has identified a "language problem," and codification of its written (or spoken) form, its grammar and its lexicon. Kloss (1969) called selection "status planning" and codification "corpus planning". The other two headings Haugen proposed were implementation (making sure that a policy is accepted and followed by the target population) and elaboration, the continued modification of the norm to meet the requirements of modernization and development.

In Quebec, the language problem in the 1950s, as one could understand by looking at language practices, was that a French-speaking majority was required to learn English in order to communicate with the largely monolingual English-speaking minority, who effectively controlled the business life of the province. Taking advantage of their political power, the French-speakers set out to change this policy. A series of laws limited access to English-language schools and required the use of French in many public functions. Working through political and governmental agencies, a change in language practices was managed by interventions referring specifically to language matters, but which had major economic, political, social and cultural causes and consequences (see below, p. 195).

However, in Gapun, there was no explicit management that led to changes in language policy. Rather, it was associated with the return to the isolated village of young men who brought back with them from the plantations two sets of items of value: a "cargo box" of physical objects and proficiency in a new language that marked their added status. It was the new language that was most easily shared with the other villagers, for language is a special kind of economic good, something that is available to be learned by anyone exposed to it and that gains rather than loses value the more it is shared with others (see below, p. 89).

From these cases, it follows that language and language policy both exist in (and language management must contend with) highly complex, interacting and dynamic contexts, the modification of any part of which may have correlated effects (and causes) on any other part. A host of non-linguistic factors (political, demographic, social, religious, cultural, psychological, bureaucratic and so on) regularly account for any attempt by persons or groups to intervene in the language practices and the beliefs of other persons or groups, and for the subsequent changes that do or do not occur. Fishman, Solano and McConnell (1991: 28) pointed out that "it is easy to be misled and intellectually impoverished by studies that examine only a small handful of variables whereas the circumstances of the real world actually involve very complex interrelationships between much larger numbers of variables." A simple cause-and-effect approach using only language-related data is unlikely to produce useful accounts of language policy, embedded as it is in a "real world" of contextual variables.

Linguistic ecology

A useful metaphor for the contexts is ecology, defined by Haugen (1971) as "the study of the interactions between any given language and its environment." Haugen himself recognizes an earlier use of the term in Voegelin, Voegelin and Schutz (1967) and also Voegelin and Voegelin (1964), which suggested that, "in linguistic ecology, one begins not with a particular language but with a particular area." The notion was foreshadowed in Trim (1959), who traced it back to Bloomfield (1935: 345) and Paul (1909: 37–45). People and societies are the environment. The metaphor of ecology must be handled very cautiously, as Michael Halliday remarked in his AILA Gold Medal address in Singapore (December 16, 2002), for it is far from clear what are the units of a language ecology, and there is no reason to argue from a need to preserve biodiversity to a need to preserve diversity of named languages.

Linguistic ecology needs to be looked at in a post-genome approach where nature and nurture are no longer artificially divided (see Spolsky 2001). Language forms a cultural system (building on certain basic biological components such as design features derived from body shape and structural features that are determined by brain structures), a system of unbelievable complexity and magnificent flexibility (anything I say can be and is interpreted and misunderstood in myriad ways, but we more or less get by). We acquire these language practices in constant "constructive interaction" (the term from Oyama 2000) with our social environment, both human and natural, so that changes in language variables (and so in languages) are most likely to be associated with non-linguistic variables.

Trim (2002) reminds us that the dynamic forces at work in the everyday activity of language communities are far more powerful than conscious, ideologically motivated policies. Language evolution is to be explained not just by small random variation strengthened by geographical isolation, but also by including functional and social selection. Nettle (1999: 79) proposes that different "ecological regimes favored different kinds of social networks, which in turn produce different-sized linguistic groups." The activating factor in his model is "ecological risk," managed by non-industrial societies by forming social networks that reduce diversity as people communicate with each other. The greater the ecological risk, the more interaction and so the fewer languages there will be in a country of given size and population. The change from hunter-gatherers to farmers and herders reduced linguistic diversity, as did European expansion and industrialization. It is changes in society that affect linguistic diversity, so that it is social policy rather than language policy that is needed to maintain it. Mufwene (2001: 17) reinforces this with a very striking metaphor: seen as a species, a language is parasitic, "whose life and vitality depend on (the acts and dispositions) of its hosts, i.e. its speakers, on the society they form, and on the culture in which they live."

Intervention (management, planning)

In studying language policy, we are usually trying to understand just what non-language variables co-vary with the language variables. There are also cases of direct efforts to manipulate the language situation. When a person or group directs such intervention, I call this language management (I prefer this term to planning, engineering or treatment). The language manager might be a legislative assembly writing a national constitution. About 125 of the world's constitutions mention language (Jones 2001), and about 100 of them name one or more official or national languages with special privileges of use. Or it might be a national legislature, making a law determining which language should be official. Or it could be a state or provincial or cantonal or other local government body determining the language of signs. It can be a special interest group seeking to influence a legislature to amend a constitution or make a new law. It can be a law court determining what the law is or an administrator implementing (or not) a law about language. Or it can be an institution or business, deciding which languages to use or teach or publish or provide interpreters for. Or it can be a family member trying to persuade others in the family to speak a heritage language.

But language policy exists even where it has not been made explicit or established by authority. Many countries and institutions and social groups do not have formal or written language policies, so that the nature of their language policy must be derived from a study of their language practice or beliefs. Even where there is a formal, written language policy, its effect on language practices is neither guaranteed nor consistent.

In all this, I assume that language policy deals not just with named languages and varieties but also with parts of language, so that it includes efforts to constrain what is considered bad language and to encourage what is considered good language (see chs. 2 and 3).

Language and language practices

Language practices is a term that encompasses the wide range of what Hymes (1967; 1974) called the "ethnography of speaking." Spoken language consists of concatenations of relevant sounds that form meaning-bearing units which themselves combine into meaningful utterances. Variations in the system may not change the meaning, but will be interpretable by listeners as identifying the origin or social level of the speaker (Labov 1966). This kind of variation has long been recognized in vocabulary; five hundred years ago, the first English printer wondered how to write the word for "eggs" and whether to prefer the southern *eggys* or the northern *eyren* (Caxton 1490). Speakers of American English wonder why Englishmen call a doctor's office a surgery, and Englishmen laugh that Americans walk on a side walk.

By language practices, then, I mean the sum of the sound, word and grammatical choices that an individual speaker makes, sometimes consciously and sometimes less consciously, that makes up the conventional unmarked pattern of a variety of a language. Varieties can be categorized and labeled. At the highest level is a language, an identified cluster of language varieties that we label English, or French or Navajo. Trying to be more precise, we might distinguish American English from British English and from Jamaican English, or New York English from Boston English. The process of categorization is not simple – almost all of the languages and language varieties named in Grimes (2000) have several names – but is deeply embedded in the social context. Language practices include much more than sounds, words and grammar; they embrace conventional differences between levels of formality of speech and other agreed rules as to what variety is appropriate in different situations. In multilingual societies, they also include rules for the appropriacy of each named language.

When members of a speech community (any group of people who share a set of language practices and beliefs) hear, or when sociolinguists analyze, a piece of discourse, they can identify not just the meaning, but also evidence of specific choices made in the course of speaking that characterize the age, gender, social class, probable place of birth and education, level of education and other facts about the speaker and his or her attitude, and provide clues to the situation and context. These choices are governed by conventional rules, not unlike grammatical rules, which are learned by members of the speech community as they grow up.

Language policy may refer to all the language practices, beliefs and management decisions of a community or polity. Consider a westernized primary-school classroom. Pupils quickly discover which language choices (and language items, too) are appropriate and which are discouraged or punished. They learn that the teacher has the privilege of determining who speaks and when and of judging how appropriate is the form of speech to be used, as well as the permitted topics. When these practices are spelled out by some external authority or taught explicitly by the teacher, this is an example of language management.

Levels

Language policy may apply at various levels of generalization. It might be at the level of an individual linguistic unit ("Don't use that ugly nasal vowel!" "Don't use that dirty word!" "Speak to me in full sentences!") or refer to labeled varieties which are clusters of units ("Don't use dialect!" "Say it in English!").

Language management may apply to an individual linguistic micro-unit (a sound, a spelling or the form of a letter) or to a collection of units (pronunciation or a lexicon or a script) or to a specified, named macro-variety (a language or a dialect). Given that languages and other varieties are made up of conventionally agreed sets of choices of linguistic units, a policy-imposed change at one level necessarily is connected to all levels; switching a lexical item is a potential step towards switching a variety. Many language purists consider borrowing a word from another language to be the first stage of language loss. But this is not necessarily the case – a receptive and flexible language like English probably benefits from its ability to borrow words.

Often, neighboring dialects are close enough to their neighbors to be mutually intelligible. Sometimes political borders divide this chain, so that mutually intelligible bordering dialects might be classified as belonging to two different languages, such as French and Italian. In the same way, political concerns regularly lead to disputes over whether a variety is one language or two. Using purely linguistic criteria and mutual intelligibility, linguists claimed that Serbo-Croatian was a single language, but Pranjković (2001) and other Croatian linguists had no doubt that Serbian and Croatian are as distinct as the Scandinavian languages. Urdu is intelligible to speakers of Hindi, but takes formal vocabulary from Arabic and Persian. Hindi, on the other hand, borrows vocabulary from Sanskrit. Here, too, the political aspect was critical in deciding how to categorize the varieties.

If we were to take a language, identified as such by having a distinct agreed name, as the basic unit of study, we would be forced to prejudge many central questions. If, on the other hand, we consider the basic unit to be the choice of a linguistic element from among available alternatives, then we avoid the need to attempt an artificial distinction between status planning and corpus planning. Of course, a great number of the issues in language policy deal with named language varieties, but as clusters of linguistic elements (e.g. those features that differentiate Hindi from Urdu, or those that distinguish American from British English). But they are also often focused on a more limited set of elements. For instance, the use of Ms. and the generic third person were key issues in the feminist movement's effort to manage language. Nettle (1999) argued that linguistic items, rather than languages, enter into the process of linguistic evolution.

Starting with linguistic items avoids the problems that arise from an unduly scrupulous distinction between status planning and corpus planning. Status planning refers to the appropriate uses for a named variety of language. Corpus planning refers to the choices to be made of specific linguistic elements whenever the language is used; it was corpus planning when the Serbians wanted the Croatian elements omitted. But obviously, as Kaplan and Baldauf (1997) noted, the two activities are virtually inseparable: "any change in the character of a language is likely to result in a change in the use environment, and any change in the use environment is likely to induce a change in the character of a language."

Language policy and policies

Language management refers to the formulation and proclamation of an explicit plan or policy, usually but not necessarily written in a formal document, about language use. As we will see, the existence of such an explicit policy does not guarantee that it will be implemented, nor does implementation guarantee success.

The first book in the Library of Congress to include "language policy" in the title is Cebollero (1945). The new field grew in parallel with sociolinguistics, a scholarly specialty that identified itself in the 1960s and included in its purview practical matters of language development. As time went on, the natural overlap with political science and public administration and education (especially educational linguistics) came to be recognized.

What does language policy look like? How do you recognize it when you meet it? The easiest to recognize are policies that exist in the form of clear-cut labeled statements in official documents. They might, for example, take the form of a clause in a national constitution, or a language law, or a cabinet document or an administrative regulation. About 125 of the world's constitutions express some policy about language, and about 100 of them name one or more official or national languages with special privileges of use. Nearly half (78) name a single official or national language, for example:

> The official language in the Republic of Albania is Albanian. (Constitution amended to 1998)

> Islam shall be the religion of the State; Islamic Sharia [Islamic Law] a main source of legislation; and Arabic the official language. (Bahrain Constitution 1973)

> The language of the Republic shall be French. (French Constitution amended to 1999)

In 32 of these 78 cases, the absolute statement is modified by a clause protecting other minority, national or indigenous languages, as, for example:

> La République gabonaise adopte le français comme langue officielle de travail. En outre, elle oeuvre pour la protection et la promotion des langues nationales. (Gabon Constitution 1997)

> El idioma oficial de Guatemala es el español. Las lenguas vernáculas, forman parte del patrimonio cultural de la Nación. (Guatemalan Constitution 1985)

> The national language of Indonesia shall be the Bahasa Indonesia or the Indonesian language. Regional languages that are well preserved by the people, such as the Javanese, Sundanese, Madurese, and other languages, will be respected and preserved by the state. (Indonesian Constitution 1945)

In 18 cases, there are two official or national languages named (in half with protection for other minority languages), in 5 cases there are three and in 4 cases four languages named.

> Pashtu and Dari are the official languages. (1963 Constitution of Afghanistan, in effect until a new one is written)

> The Belarusian and Russian languages shall be the official languages of the Republic of Belarus. Everyone shall have the right to use one's native language and to choose the language of communication. In accordance with the law, the State shall guarantee the freedom to choose the language of education and teaching. (1996 Constitution of Belarus)

> Belgium has four linguistic regions: the French-speaking Region, the Dutch-speaking Region, the bilingual Region of Brussels-Capital, and the German-speaking Region. (1970 Belgian Constitution)

> The official languages of the Republic of Cameroon shall be English
> and French, both languages having the same status . . . It shall
> endeavour to protect and promote national languages. (1996
> Cameroon Constitution)

The 1997 Constitution of the Democratic Republic of Congo names
four national languages (Kikongo, Lingala, Swahili and Tshiluba) and
two official languages (French and English). The new South African
Constitution lists eleven.

Many countries are without written constitutions and a good number of constitutions are without any mention of language, apart from
some human rights clauses saying that persons arrested or tried are
entitled to interpreters, or that there shall be no discrimination on
the basis of a list of characteristics including language. In some of
these countries there are specific language laws (like the Assamese
Language Act or the Official Māori Language Act in New Zealand).
France, a country with one of the most sophisticated and demanding
national language policies in existence, has recorded these policies in
many different laws since 1539.

Harder to locate are policies like those of Australia, which are written into Cabinet documents setting out priorities for funding. It is
even more difficult to define a national policy when there is a tension
between federal and local policies, as in India. The most difficult to
locate, describe and understand are countries where there is no single
explicit document. In such cases, as in England or the United States,
one must search for the implicit lines of language practices and beliefs in a maze of customary practices, laws, regulations and court
decisions.

Underlying this variation and complexity is the fact that language
practices and policies, like Topsy, tend to grow without overmuch official intervention. Only in special cases is explicit formulation necessary. Those writing constitutions for newly independent states are
sometimes forced to define the role of the competing languages,
although the American Constitutional Congress managed to avoid doing this. In such cases, the language-management process becomes
obvious, and is then easily studied. More often, any existing national
or local language practice has evolved piecemeal, with a combination
of law, regulation and custom. From time to time, a concerted political
effort is made to proclaim a new policy. This may be a law such as the
French Language Law of 1975, or that proposed by the English Only
movement in the United States, or it may be a government paper such
as the various forms of the Australian National Language Policy. It also

occurs when a Ministry of Education sets out to redefine the school-related aspects of language policy, such as the Dutch National Foreign Language Action Programme or the Israeli policy for language in education. But for the rest, the chore of deciding whether a country has a policy and what that policy is, is often first tackled by a sociolinguist and published in an academic journal.

Language ideology and beliefs

The members of a speech community share also a general set of beliefs about appropriate language practices, sometimes forming a consensual ideology, assigning values and prestige to various aspects of the language varieties used in it. These beliefs both derive from and influence practices. They can be a basis for language management or a management policy can be intended to confirm or modify them.

Language ideology or beliefs designate a speech community's consensus on what value to apply to each of the language variables or named language varieties that make up its repertoire. In most states, there are many ideologies, just as there are a number of speech or ethnic communities; one is commonly dominant. Put simply, language ideology is language policy with the manager left out, what people think should be done. Language practices, on the other hand, are what people actually do.

Language-management efforts may go beyond or contradict the set of beliefs and values that underlie a community's use of language, and the actual practice of language use. To describe language management, one may use a taxonomy derived from the question posed by Cooper (1989: 31) when he set out to investigate language spread and language change: "*who* plans *what* for *whom* and *how*." Considering these questions will provide us with a fuller notion of the nature of language management and how it should be differentiated from the general language practices and beliefs it is usually intended to modify.

(Policy) under what conditions?

Political scientists assume, Ager (1996: 11) noted, a policy-making system, a decision system and an organizational network, which co-exist in an environment with physical (geographical), political and socioeconomic components; in these components reside the conditions relevant to the policy development. Any attempt to limit the factors considered is likely to be soon challenged by a new case or by some unforeseen development. The widest perspective is needed, to avoid missing some vital factor. After a number of studies of Navajo language maintenance, for instance, Spolsky (1974b) suggested only half face-tiously that the best way to teach English on the Reservation was by building more roads. In point of fact, that explanation of Navajo language shift did not take into account the rapid spread of local television repeater stations a few years later.

The widest range of conditions can affect language policy. As Ferguson (1977: 9) put it, "All language planning activities take place in particular sociolinguistic settings, and the nature and scope of the planning can only be fully understood in relation to the settings." "Sociolinguistic setting" should be interpreted to include anything that affects language practices and beliefs or that leads to efforts at intervention. It is true that the 1960 Assamese riots focused on language, but the ethnic problems and violence that preceded and have followed them have been associated with a much wider set of concerns.

Governmental and bureaucratic structure is important. The tight central control that Richelieu aimed at and that was perfected after the Revolution by Napoleon makes it possible to conceive of the rigid structure that French language policy desires. The changes in Soviet policy that Lewis (1972) traced depended on changes in the balance between centralized rule (which favored strengthening Russian as the Soviet lingua franca) and encouragement of local pluralism and languages. In Spain, the post-Franco grant of autonomy to the regions allowed local authorities to change language policy. Similar granting of regional autonomy is supporting Welsh and Scottish Gaelic. In the United States, the constitutional authority of the states for education hinders efforts at centralized language policy (Lambert 1994). In each of these cases, political organization helps determine the possibility of forming and implementing language policy.

These major factors – the sociolinguistic situation and the attitude to it, the nature of political organization – help explain the main outlines of language policy, but many other specific reasons and motivations explain its complexity. Following the principle of starting with units of language rather than with languages, the next two chapters will explore language policies concerning bad language, good language and the associated topic of language purification and cultivation.

2   Driving out the bad

OBSCENITY, PROFANITY, BLASPHEMY AND OTHER BANNED LANGUAGE

The constraint on bad language is a common example of language policy. "Don't ever let me hear you say that word again!" the mother tells her child. "Watch your language! There are ladies present," the barman chides a customer. "You mustn't say 'ain't'!" the teacher nags her pupils. "That is not acceptable parliamentary language!" the Speaker admonishes the Member of Parliament. Basic to the process of correcting or trying to correct language usage is a widespread belief that parents or other caretakers have a responsibility to guarantee the successful socialization of their offspring by helping them to develop a variety of language that is useful for communication, by being intelligible, and that will lead to acceptance in desirable social settings, by not giving offense. Caretakers generally accept responsibility for helping their offspring to learn an appropriate or good variety of language.

RESPONSIBILITY FOR MANAGING BAD LANGUAGE

Generally speaking, interlocutors refrain from correcting the speech of others, but this principle may be ignored in an unequal social relationship, such as adult–child interaction (Schegloff, Jefferson and Sacks 1977: 381). This is extended to the teacher–learner situation, not just to deal with current misunderstanding but also to prevent future misunderstanding or keep the language "in good order within the speech community" (Jernudd and Thuan 1983: 80).

The notion of correct language remains at the core of an ideological debate, developing regularly especially in monolingual societies, with their concern for the form of the accepted standard language. Linguistic conservatives claim a kind of divine right for the correct form, however it may be established. On the other side, linguistic

16

liberals argue that all forms of language have equal validity, although some forms have picked up socially ascribed values in order to preserve the power of some elite group.

How common is the belief in the existence of a correct form of language? Many people are prepared to give judgments on how standard their own speech is and how best to teach the correct form of language to children (Niedzielski and Preston 2000). In most societies, caretakers correct children (Ochs 1986: 5). The details and starting age may vary in different speech communities, but it is generally considered appropriate "to speed the child towards communicative competence and adult norms of behavior" (Watson-Gegeo and Gegeo 1986: 19). The justification for language norms is intelligibility: "without them communication and understanding would not be possible at all" (Bartsch 1987: 140).

There is a general assumption that it is possible to control the use of bad language. Child development books give advice like, "Tell your child that swearing or crude language is not okay at your house." For US$130 you can buy a device which will filter out "foul" words in a television movie. Schools are expected to act for parents in controlling language. David Blunkett, education secretary in the British government (*The Times*, April 28, 2000) urged schools and parents "to eliminate foul and abusive language from our schools and homes."

Governments also take on the task of managing bad language. In the United States, obscenity is constitutionally left to state or local government, but the federal government has a law dealing with any obscenity that crosses or might cross state lines. The definition of obscenity or pornography is not determined in the law, but is decided according to local "community standards."

Many states and local governments in the USA have their own laws and regulations about bad language. The state of Georgia, for example, categorizes obscenity and what it calls "fighting words" as a misdemeanor. The city of Mesquite, Nevada, is concerned about the use of obscene or profane language in public places. These laws assume that language and action are connected: Blunkett thought that bad language led to acting like a thug, the state of Georgia believed that words can lead to fighting, the city of Mesquite associates obscene conduct and language. Disagreeing with the proverbial claim that "words will never hurt me," they all seem to believe that words can be violent, like "sticks and stones." They all exhibit a belief in the power (and so danger) of words.

The rules for the game of ice hockey include one banning profane language. The censorship or reviewing of movies and television tries to avoid language unsuitable for family viewing. With the rapid expansion of the internet, service providers set out their own language rules, in part to avoid giving offense and in part to avoid breaking obscenity laws.

All of these cases are language management, constituting an effort by someone with or claiming authority to modify the language used by other speakers. They derive from two fundamental beliefs, part of the common language ideology of many, if not all, societies. The first belief is that it can be done, that Canute can stop the waves, that speakers can be forced by law to avoid certain kinds of defined language. This is an *a priori* assumption in any effort at language management, though its truth turns out to be rarely borne out by the facts. The second belief concerns the nature of what should be controlled, what constitutes bad language. One common set of criteria for badness includes expressions that are obscene, profane, blasphemous, fighting words or sexual.

The Bible, like other religious texts, takes a strong position on the power of language. Creation in Genesis is the result of God speaking; and the Ten Commandments include one specifically concerned with language: "Thou shalt not take the name of the LORD thy God in vain; for the LORD will not hold him guiltless that taketh his name in vain" (Exodus 20: 7). The New Testament book of John opens with the creation theme: "In the beginning was the word." The Talmud has many strictures against inappropriate language and encourages euphemism.

Blasphemy, defined as "verbal irreverence towards God, or to sacred persons or objects," has meaning only within religion, and especially in religions like Judaism, Christianity and Islam, where the deity is viewed as a spiritual being with personal qualities (Pickering 2001). Blasphemy continues to be a crime in the UK, but only against the Church of England (Kermode 2002). In the USA, the First Amendment and the absence of a state church mitigated the severity of prosecution. In France, punishment was severe until the Revolution (Cabantous 2002). Islamic authorities banned Salman Rushdie and some contemporary Egyptian writers for blasphemy.

Traditional societies recognize the danger and power of language, and have taboos constraining the use of certain words. Traditional Navajos had a taboo against naming dead people lest they appear, and a similar taboo, especially in wintertime, against saying the word "bear" out loud. Chinese has strong taboos against the mention of death and has developed a great number of euphemisms (Hongxu and Guisen 1990). Euphemisms are common for body parts and actions. The phenomenon is probably universal, but the specific items are culturally determined and change over time.

There is an opposing ideology, that there is no such thing as bad language. It was expressed strongly by American linguists in the 1950s; you should "leave your language alone," to use Hall's (1950) phrase. The controversy over the fifth edition of *Webster's Dictionary*, which avoided saying that words were wrong and presented without judgment the words actually used by speakers of English, was between these two ideologies, the one that standards for language can be derived from criteria other than use, and the other that only usage determines standards.

MANAGING AND MITIGATING RACIST LANGUAGE

One form of language management, somewhat delicately labeled as "political correctness," has accompanied the growing liberal consciousness in many Western countries over the latter decades of the twentieth century. By the 1960s, American dictionaries were already cautious about racial and ethnic terms like "nigger." Negro was still unmarked, although pressure was already starting to replace it by Black or later Afro-American. Some forty years later, the term appears rarely: an eighty-three-year-old US senator talking about "white niggers" in 2001 not surprisingly drew reference to his Ku Klux Klan past, and two years later, another senator lost his leadership position for expressing racial intolerance.

One difficulty here is the flux in acceptable terms – Indians became Native Americans and now seem to be American Indians again. The American Psychological Association (Guidelines for Avoiding Racial/ Ethnic Bias in Language, http://www.apastyle.org/race.html) remarks: "Name designations of racial/ethnic groups change over time, and members of a group may disagree about their preferred name at a specific time." The Association also lays down specific style rules: Black and White are capitalized; Mexican American is not hyphenated; racial group names are capitalized. Care must also be taken in the use of adjectives; writing about "an intelligent Black student" might seem to imply that this was an exception.

There are a number of racist terms buried in place names and in scientific terms. Here, too, efforts are now being made to replace them. In 1997, the United States Bureau of Land Management reported that the California Geographic Board of Names had taken up the issue of derogatory Indian place names. There are also botanical name problems. Hunter (1991) regretted that a "number of racially offensive common plant names long ago slipped into the vernacular of gardening, and some have found their way into horticulture's most important reference books." He cited Niggerhead, Pope's Nose, Jew Bush, Digger Pine, and seventy-five South African plants with Kaffir in their common names.

Controlling personal names

Personal names might seem at first glance to be a private matter. Many of us have more than one: the official name registered with the government, the name used in religious ceremonies, the name our siblings used for us, the name by which we were addressed in school or in the army, the name that our spouse or other loved one selects for us and the "ineffable name" by which we know ourselves. All this seems to be a matter of language practices, but Jernudd (1995) noted that it was often controlled by governmental language policy. In Bulgaria, until 1989, ethnically Turkish people were obliged to avoid Turkish-sounding names and use Bulgarian ones. In Indonesia, there was pressure on ethnic Chinese to avoid Chinese-sounding names. In Japan, there is a limitation on the characters that may be used for writing names. In Singapore, parents are pressured to base Romanization on Mandarin rather than the Hokkien or Cantonese dialects that most of them use. In Sweden, since the beginning of the twentieth century, the government has been trying to persuade people to adopt family surnames rather than employ the older practice of using the father's first name followed by the suffix "-son."

Stamping out sexist language

A partly successful campaign to purge English of its inherent male chauvinism started in the US in the 1960s. The 1963 publication of *The Feminine Mystique* by Betty Friedan marked a new phase of feminist activism, which came to include language policy (Cooper 1989). Central was an attack on gender stereotypes in language. Androcentric generics became a primary target: the use of man for person, or of he for he or she. A phrase like "a poet who wants to reach his audience" suggests that poets are all male, and terms like chairman imply that only men hold this office. The clarion call to language management was an article by Lakoff (1973) that presented evidence of sexism in English.

Just as Blacks had earlier sought to substitute Black for Negro, so feminists sought to substitute neutral forms like person for androcentric ones like man. Manuals were written explaining how not to give offense, and professional associations and publishers were urged to require non-sexist usage. Guidelines were developed and enforced: the American Psychological Association started to refuse manuscripts that violated its guidelines. Cooper (1984) found a dramatic decline, from 12.3 per 5,000 words in 1971 to 4.3 per 5,000 in 1979 in the use of androcentric generics in US newspapers and magazines. Cooper wondered whether the change in language also led to a change in opinion and behavior.

Twenty years later, Pauwels (1998) analyzed the feminist campaign for language reform from the perspective of language policy. The first planners were individuals: women's groups, feminist collectives and ad hoc groups followed their lead and tried put pressure on publishing houses and professional associations. In a number of countries, government or agencies also implemented legislation outlawing sex discrimination. The reformers documented the existence of sexism in language, including the representation of the male as benchmark for all human beings, the invisibility of females and females as dependent, and stereotypical representations, the use of the masculine form for generic purposes, lexical gaps (in Italian, there is no female equivalent of *medico*, "doctor,") and gender nouns that carry different meanings when applied to men and to women (in Hebrew, an *ozer* is an assistant, but the feminine form *ozeret* is a household cleaner). The use of titles also showed discrimination: in English, before the invention of Ms, a woman's marital status had to be signaled but a man's was hidden. Experimental evidence showed the effect of these terminological differences on perceptions.

Non-sexist language reform, Pauwels suggested, has mainly been a grassroots activity. Style manuals now show how to avoid gender bias in English, Spanish and German. Like Cooper, Pauwels found that changes were taking place, and impacting on bureaucracy, educational publications, women's magazines and dictionaries and grammars. But Pauwels' (1998: 221) conclusions were pessimistic: "although there is still a paucity of research . . . so far the results have been not too promising." The waves remain difficult to control.

New targets soon emerged, and the American Psychological Association developed guidelines for avoiding heterosexual bias in language. Sexual orientation (not preference, which suggests choice), lesbian and gay male were to be preferred to homosexual; bisexual persons should be mentioned. The latest development is an attack on the use of discriminatory language against animals (Dunayer 2001).

From a language-policy point of view, these are efforts by groups to reduce the linguistic reflexes of ideologies and behaviors considered culturally unacceptable. The world in which violent language is banned appears on the outside to be no less violent; the reform in androcentric generics does not seem to correlate with any major improvement in the status of women; the avoidance of racist terms has not seemed to reduce ethnic hatred; and lesbians, gay men and bisexual persons are just as likely to be considered unacceptable when the terms are used precisely. But the language reforms serve to raise consciousness and can lead to needed action.

LANGUAGE PURISM

Bad language is considered dirty and impure. Clean, uncorrupt, pure language is highly valued ideologically. As a general rule in language matters, the past is believed to be pure and innovation is often suspected of corruption. The Zuni Indians did not allow foreign words in ritual performances, as part of their opposition to innovations in ceremonies (Newman 1955: 349). The Arizona Tewa had a similar ban (Kroskrity 1998); they also disapproved of language mixing. The hundred or so generally bilingual speakers of Tariana, an Arawak language in the Amazon region of Brazil, consider lexical borrowing "incompetent and sloppy" (Aikhenvald 2001).

Purism becomes important during a time of language cultivation and modernization (see ch. 4), providing a criterion for the choice of new lexicon. Purism favors native sources and tries to close off non-native sources (Annamalai 1989). It is closely connected with national feeling (Haugen 1987: 87). There are similar concerns to keep foreign influence out of music, literature and architecture.

Keeping languages pure by excluding foreignisms became an important management task in Europe in the seventeenth and eighteenth centuries, and was the central role of the language academies modeled on the Académie française: "The principal task of the Academy will be to work with all possible care and diligence to give explicit rules to our language and to render it pure" (Statutes and Regulations of the French Academy, February 22, 1735, p. 16). The motto of the Real Academia Español, founded in 1713 was *Limpia, fija y da esplendor* (cleanses, stabilizes and gives splendor). The academies shared the belief that language can and should be made or kept pure.

The goal of pure language is popular in language reform movements. During the revival of Modern Hebrew, the Pure Language Society, set up in 1889, aimed at "restoring to all of our people . . . a single, pure language, the language of our forefathers which is 'holy of holies' instead of the corrupted language they presently speak" (Saulson 1979). "Corrupted language" is a direct attack on Yiddish, often referred to as Zhargon, an illicit mixture of German and Hebrew and Slavic. The association of pure language and cleanliness was picked up by the founders of the City of Tel-Aviv, who in their 1906 prospectus claimed that the new town would be 100 percent Hebrew: "Hebrew will be spoken in this city, purity and cleanliness will be kept" (cited and translated by Harshav 1993: 143).

Language can be thought bad because it is corrupted by sexual references or obscenity, but other criteria are change of any kind and corruption by foreign elements. It is bad enough, some people believe, that languages are changing but even more serious when the source of that change is the intrusion of foreign elements. In the nineteenth century, Colombia was a leader in the pursuit of correctness (Niño-Murcia 2001). Spanish in Colombia was seen as less "contaminated" by indigenous words than in other Latin American countries. Language purity in Colombia came to mean the absence of *americanismos*, either words of indigenous origin or Peninsular words with new semantic reference. For different languages at different times, threats may come from different sources: for Dutch-speakers in Belgium, French is the enemy; for French, the rival is English; for Korean, it is Chinese and Japanese; for standard language it can be a non-standard variety (the spoken varieties of Arabic, creole in Haiti, regional dialects in England, *joual* in Quebec) (Weinstein 1989). A recent campaign to purify Brazilian Portuguese of its foreign borrowing captures the national chauvinism of much of the population; currently, the target is any word from American English; a century ago, there was similar concern about borrowings from French (Rajagopalan 2002).

Linguistic purity easily comes to associate with group membership including, in its stronger manifestations, with ethnic identity. The avoidance of obscene language, or of lower-class indigenous borrowings, marks a speaker as urbane or gentle. The eschewing of foreignisms proclaims linguistic and ethnic purity.

Purifying Turkish

One dramatic case of language purification occurred with Turkish under Kemal Atatürk (Lewis 1999: 2). Turkish language reform was intended to eliminate the many thousands of Arabic and Persian borrowings that had become entrenched in the language after the Turks became Muslim, creating a mixture of languages, called Ottoman in English, that served as the administrative and literary language and that was very far from ordinary spoken Turkish. Under nationalist pressure, the 1876 Constitution named the official language as Turkish and not Ottoman (Lewis 1999: 16). This was confirmed in the 1908 political program of the Young Turks. After reforming the alphabet, Atatürk began in 1928 a campaign to remove Persian and Arabic elements from Turkish.

Lewis blames the problems that followed on the lack of scholarship of the reformers. In their haste to throw out Persian and Arabic words, they sought replacements wherever they could find them. Especially attractive were dialect words. Army officers, schoolteachers and government officials throughout the country were asked to send in words in use among the people which formed the base of the language purification work. Some of this work was justified by the Sun-Language theory, which held that that Turkish was the first human language and therefore supported the borrowing of words from European languages on the grounds that they must have been borrowed from Turkish. Before he died, Mustafa Kemal realized that the campaign had not succeeded. In spite of this, the Language Society continued its work of purification (Lewis 1999: 70). More recently, the new enemy for the Turkish purifiers has been the invasion of words from English. After 1983, borrowed English words became the Society's main target. Lewis characterizes the reform, in the subtitle of his book, as "a catastrophic success," producing a gap between common speech and the language of the intellectuals and necessitating the translating of books by standard authors into modern Turkish. While not all agree with his judgment (Laut 2000), Lewis's account makes clear the difficulties of implementing language policy and the possibility of unanticipated results that need to be taken into account.

PURIFICATION — CONCLUSIONS

Many other languages have had their purification processes, including Estonian de-Germanization (Hennoste, Keevallik and Pajusalu 1999), Pilipino (Sibayan 1974) and the de-Sanskritization of Tamil (Schiffman 1996). Purism may be used as an argument for quite different goals: religious, ethnic, classicist and especially nationalist. The process continues: on February 5, 2003, the lower house of the Russian Parliament passed a law declaring Russian the state language of the Russian Federation, the TASS news agency reported. The law went further, banning the public use of invectives referring to race, nationality, occupation, social status, language, sex or religion, of obscene words and foreign words when there were Russian equivalents.

By looking at bad language, however defined, we have already seen important components of a model of language policy. Practices vary in different social situations and change under the influences of new demands and changing communication networks; beliefs and ideologies develop concerning bad language and provide a basis for both practices and for efforts at management; and management can be implemented at various levels of social organization, from family to nation state. While most commonly driven by an ideology of purity, the various criteria for defining language as bad are associated with a wide range of motivations: a moral or religious rejection of violence and overt sexual behavior, a religious concern for conformity and against blasphemy; a liberal objection to racism and sexism; a conservative objection to innovation; an ethnocentric fear of foreignisms; a state-supported movement for national identity. Even at the level of individual linguistic items, the full range of complexity in language policy is evident.

3 Pursuing the good and dealing with the new

LANGUAGE CULTIVATION

Some language policies aim to prevent people from using bad language and to have them avoid words or expressions assumed to offend because of their meaning, form or association with a stigmatized or foreign language or variety. The reverse side of the coin is made up of policies the aim of which is to improve the language variety itself, by cultivation or modernization.

Cultivation was the term coined in English by Garvin (1973) to translate *Sprachkultur*, to refer to establishing and modifying the norms of a literary or standard language. The norm must be based on "the average literary language practice over the past 50 years." It assumes the existence of an established, practicing literary elite who use the language in a consensually standard way. Garvin recognized other norms. A standard language was "a codified form of language, accepted by and serving as a model to, a larger speech community." An official language had gained its status by the formal recognition of a government. The term 'national' language could be neutral, referring to the language most widely used in a particular territory, or emotional, with an implication of serving as a national symbol. In practice – in constitutions, for example – the use of these terms is locally determined and one must be careful in interpreting them.

There are different views about standard languages. One ascribes to a standard language the mythical and emotional values of a higher species, seeing it as the representation of the spirit of the people and with a virtually divine mandate. Languages used for sacred texts – biblical Hebrew, Latin, Sanskrit, classical Arabic, Old Church Slavonic, for instance – gain this status from the religions they are associated with. National languages, like French and English and Israeli Hebrew and Malay and Indonesian have associated with them what Fishman called a Great Tradition, a set of beliefs about the relation of the language to the history of the people, in order to support their symbolic status;

26

such languages develop strong political and ideological support. A second approach sees a standard language as the "consensus . . . of what educated speakers accept as correct" (Quirk and Stern 1990). A third believes that all languages and all varieties of all languages are equally good. A fourth acknowledges that a standard variety has a higher status, simply because it is so widely accepted. A fifth view, associated with the self-proclaimed critical approach, believes that the superiority of the standard variety is a conspiracy of the elite establishment to maintain power.

Our focus in this chapter is on the form of a language. We ask what is needed to make a selected variety (however it has been selected) into a standard language, with the necessary defining characteristics of an agreed writing system and orthography, an institutionalized method of recording and disseminating the correct form of grammar, an acceptable and usable set of lexical items to handle all modern needs, a set of stylistic models suitable for all formal functions, and the tools and institutions to give speakers of the language access to all those characteristics. Underlying this urge to standardize is a belief in correctness, that there is a correct and desirable form of the language, distinct from normal practice. Languages are imperfect instruments, individuals learn and use them imperfectly, and therefore the variety that is most successful in communication is the one that is to be preferred. Nowak, Komarova and Niyogi (2002) propose the notion of communicative pay-off, the probability that the speaker of the language will be understood by someone else. Standard languages have the highest communicative pay-off.

While the development of a widely understood sound system is important, the first critical need for standardization is a writing system. In the case of an unwritten language with a sacred text or important high-culture texts, such as a set of genealogies or of folk histories, a preliminary step is an institutional method of maintaining the oral text, such as memorizers or poets, and a way of assuring accurate transmission.

ADOPTING, ADAPTING AND EVEN CREATING WRITING SYSTEMS

The evolution of language and the invention of writing were crucial signposts in the development of human society, language providing a system which "enables us to transfer unlimited non-genetic information among individuals," which in turn "gives rise to cultural evolution" (Nowak et al. 2002: 611), and writing furnishing a method of recording language and permitting communication over time and space.

The invention of writing systems is rare: adoption or adaptation is common. Most writing systems or scripts fall into the category of "something borrowed" rather than "something new." Writing as a system seems to have been invented independently only a few times, in or around Mesopotamia, in Egypt, in China and in Mesoamerica (Coulmas 2003). All other current systems are adopted or adapted from these original inventions.

A number of cases of exceptional innovation help us to understand the processes involved in creating or selecting a script. St. Stefan of Perm, the fourteenth century Russian Orthodox bishop, developed an alphabet for the newly converted Komi people (Ferguson 1968). Recognizing Komi opposition to the Russians, who were starting to dominate the region, he chose the previously unwritten Komi language for his missionary work and devised a new writing system.

The choices in such a case are straightforward: syllabary or alphabet, existing system or specially created one, diacritics or not, symbol sequences, punctuation, degree of morphophonemic information. Many languages preserve morpheme information even when the phonology changes. Contemporary missionaries (the Summer Institute of Linguistics, for instance) prefer to use the alphabet of the local national language as a base, adopting spelling conventions that will make transition to literacy in the national language easier. In contrast, both Soviet practice, which used Cyrillic for its minority languages, and Islam, which uses Arabic script, keep loan words in their original respective spellings. Until Stefan, the common practice in the Eastern Church, used for Gothic and Slavic, was to start with the Greek alphabet and add new letters as needed. The alphabet for Komi was new, with influence of traditional Komi decorative patterns. Stefan did not re-invent writing, but set out to design a new writing system appropriate for his purposes, enabling the Komi to take a proprietary interest.

There were similar cases (Cooper 1991): some twenty-one invented indigenous writing systems, fourteen of them produced in West Africa, including a syllabary invented for Vai in Liberia and Kikakui script, still used for Loma in Sierra Leone. Twelve of the twenty-one are associated with "supernatural inspiration or revelation," because scripts are so often associated with sacred texts.

The selection of a writing system (graphization) has been a major activity in the standardization of languages as a result of missionary activity. The Summer Institute of Linguistics (now renamed SIL International) has been involved in studying and developing literacy for

1,320 languages. The principles they have developed over fifty years involve selecting both a script and an orthography that pave the way for transition to literacy in the local national language.

There are conflicting criteria for judging the efficiency of writing systems. One set is technical and psycholinguistic, and includes ease of printing (now much less a problem with computers), ease of learning, ease of reading and writing and transferability to other languages. This latter consideration is important when initial literacy in one language is to be followed by transfer to a national official language. A major dispute regularly concerns the degree to which pronunciation or meaning is to be decisive. For a long time the consensus among US linguists was that an optimal writing system would be one that gave maximum representation to the spoken form (Berry 1958). This changed under the influence of transformational-generative grammar, especially as set out in Chomsky and Halle (1968), which assumed that there was an abstract level of representation of words that the grammar converts to pronunciation. The amount of redundancy built into written language makes it difficult to study experimentally the efficiency of different systems. Reading ability is highly correlated with socioeconomic background, masking other effects (Venezky 1970). Political and economic factors are often more important than linguistic and psychological ones.

As a result, the psycholinguistic-technical argument is often swallowed in a sociolinguistic one. When Young (1977) and his collaborators decided on the orthography of Navajo, they used the English alphabet as a base, but decided to mark vowel length, tone and nasalization. But was this efficient? Holm (1972) showed that Navajo was just as easy for a native speaker to read without diacritics added to mark these features, and much easier for native speakers to learn to write. But his proposal to modify the orthography led to vociferous objections, with an outright refusal of Navajo teachers to consider changing a system that in thirty years, partly by virtue of its adoption for the translation of the Bible, had achieved virtually sacred status.

This brings us to the second set of criteria for orthographies, namely the sociolinguistic and attitudinal, whether political or religious or ethnic. One of the strongest social factors affecting script choice is religious. Historically, Jews used Hebrew letters not just for Hebrew but also for Yiddish and Ladino and other Jewish languages. Non-Arab Muslims use Perso-Arabic script for their languages. Roman Catholic Slavs used Latin script while Orthodox used Cyrillic. Political motivation is also common. Distinct scripts support notions of independence, as noted in the West African invented scripts or in St. Stefan's work. Hindi and Urdu, closely related though they may be, seem much more distant when Hindi is written in "Hindu" Devanagari and Urdu in "Muslim" Perso-Arabic. The spoken varieties of Hindi and Urdu are close enough to be recognized as related dialects, but once they are written in Devanagari script or Perso-Arabic script, they appear profoundly different. The Soviet Union worked actively to persuade minority languages to choose Cyrillic script. With the disintegration of the Soviet Union, the Central Asian republics passed laws raising the status of their titular languages, and also became involved in alphabet reform (Schlyter 2001). In Uzbekistan, a revised Uzbek Latin alphabet was approved. In Kazakhstan and Kyrgyzstan, the changeover to a Latin alphabet is being discussed. In Tajikistan, debate continues between Latin and Arabic script. A Turkmen Latin alphabet was adopted in 1993 and includes some special letters.

One key component of the Turkish language reform described in the last chapter was orthography reform. In 1928, Mustafa Kemal Atatürk accepted the use of the Latin alphabet. Books in the old characters could no longer be used in schools. No new books were to be published in the old characters after the end of the year. All correspondence with government departments would have to be in the new alphabet within six months.

The Japanese writing system was reformed during the Meiji period (Coulmas 1990). Chinese characters pose interesting problems. Each *Hanzi* (character) stands for a syllable and a morpheme, so that once several thousand characters have been learned, it is possible to read and recognize new words made up by combining characters. Chinese vocabulary, written in Chinese characters, was borrowed over the centuries by Korean and Japanese. New Japanese terms, created by combinations of these Chinese basic characters, have in turn been borrowed back by Chinese (Coulmas 1991). The pronunciation of these words in each language is different.

There have been efforts to reform Chinese writing, starting with a Romanization movement and continued in a campaign to establish a practical orthography called *hanyu pinyin (hànyǔ pīnyīn)* using the Latin alphabet. Starting in 1954, a number of reforms were proposed and debated. Finally in 1986, the State Language Committee defined a policy of limited digraphia, with the traditional Chinese characters to be maintained as the "legally recognized writing system" and the "Scheme for the Chinese Phonetic Alphabet" (*Hanyu Pinyin Fang'an*) to serve as a learning aid (Peicheng 2001). To use the *hanyu pinyin* input system for computers, one needs to know Putonghua, standard Mandarin pronunciation. Thus, its full implementation depends on the success of the current campaign to teach Putonghua throughout China.

Fixing spelling

For those of us who do our writing on a computer, the regular appearance of words in red reminds us that we have somehow upset the spell checker. The spotted red pages are reminiscent of getting compositions back from the teacher. Now, as then, we sometimes wonder, "why does it matter?" Computers are over-literal and seldom make even the allowances that liberal or lazy teachers might. Given the amount of redundancy in normal speech, why should we be expected to achieve the degree of accuracy in spelling that might be reasonably demanded in measurement, to use the analogy for language standardization suggested by Cooper (1989: 131)? As long as language is restricted to communication in face-to-face situations, where there is non-verbal support for the message and the chance of immediately correcting misunderstanding, variation can be easily dealt with. It is when the communication is intended for an absent receiver that greater effort must be focused on accuracy and consistency.

The transmission of sacred texts was such an occasion for accuracy. Before these texts were written down, transmission was oral. It was concern for accuracy that underlay the development of Sanskrit phonetic theory by Panini in the fourth century BCE. When sacred texts were written down, complex procedures were developed to guarantee accurate transmission. The Jewish scribes who copy biblical scrolls for synagogue reading still follow elaborate rules governing the preparation of pens, ink and parchment, the form of letters and the layout of columns. Standardization of spelling was no doubt encouraged by the schools of scribes associated with ancient kingdoms; for modern languages, the practice developed through the activities of three institutions – government scribes, printing and schooling.

In England, the first step towards a standard orthography in the fifteenth century was when the Brewers' Guild began to keep records in English, and when, ten years later, the scribes of the Royal Chancery in Westminster started to send out official documents in it (Salmon 1999: 15). The growing numbers of literate laypeople were much less likely than the scribes to worry about standardization. When printing began in England, there were two types of orthography: a reasonably consistent national standard originated in Chancery followed by professional scriveners, and a local or regional private orthography. Printers generally followed the former, while less educated men and women wrote much more idiosyncratically. By the end of the sixteenth century, English writers were starting to complain about the problems produced by orthography influenced by local non-standard speech. Schoolmasters argued that children should be taught to pronounce English correctly so that they could spell correctly. By 1660, a large gap had developed between the traditional orthography of the printer and the freedom allowed to gentlemen and scholars. More and more textbooks and wordlists were published. The appearance of Dr. Johnson's dictionary in 1755 provided an authoritative model leading to eventual standardization, but he did not expect to "embalm the language."

Because the spoken language is not only always made up of a huge range of variations, but is always in constant change, any attempt to fix spelling once and for all is doomed to failure. The closer spelling is to pronunciation, the more frequent the changes will need to be. A spelling system that is morphemic or etymological will not need to change, but of course the learning of such a system will take a great deal of effort. It is a zero-sum game: simplified spelling is easy to learn (provided it is based on your dialect) but will need to change regularly, producing major problems with access to material written in the older system. Morphemic or etymological spelling is harder to learn, but is much more stable. These contradictory forces produce a tension that keeps spelling reform an open question. The issue of spelling, therefore, regularly emerges when language policy comes to public attention.

Fixing the spelling system

The question is not how to develop a standard spelling system, but how to deal with the problems that it has not solved. Traditionally, Hebrew was written without vowels. In printed Bibles, dictionaries, prayer books and books for young children, diacritic symbols are added above, below and inside the consonants to indicate the pronunciation. Reading Hebrew with vowels added is quite straightforward, but learning how to mark the vowels correctly is difficult, demanding detailed knowledge of Hebrew grammar. Over the years, a number of proposals have been put forward to reform the spelling system, including Romanization. In 1948, the Language Council published a set of proposals but it took twenty years for the Hebrew Language Academy to accept them, and neither the general public nor the newspapers have yet done so. Hebrew spell checkers offer three systems.

The Dutch, Geerts, Van den Broeck and Verdoodt (1977) claimed, have done better. In Belgium, a spelling system was accepted by royal decree in 1864, but it was rejected in the Netherlands. In 1954, a compromise proposal bridged the disagreements between educational establishments and the general public. A new commission appointed in 1963 came out with new proposals. Political parties and religious groups took strong and contrasting positions. Finally, in 1994, the two governments accepted a new reform.

If the Netherlands is an example of a long struggle over spelling, Norway has spent its hundred years of independence from Denmark going through several reforms that have left it with two systems still in flux. Haugen (1966a) traced the development of two opposing movements, each aiming to differentiate Norwegian from Danish, one choosing to base the new national language on the speech of educated city-dwellers, and the other choosing as model the folk speech of the countryside. Schoolteachers who taught the written standards were urged not to interfere with their children's spoken variety of Norwegian. Since 1885, Norway has had two official written standards, the one called *bokmal*, "book language," and the other called *nynorsk*, "new Norwegian." The orthographies of each have been regularly reformed, in part to reduce the gap between them. Enforcement of any kind, however, is restricted to schools and official users.

The Irish writing system was adapted by the end of the sixth century C E from Latin, producing a number of anomalies, such as different pronunciations for consonants in various positions, digraphs and vowels to mark palatalization and velarization (ó Murchú 1977). The system was fairly consistent and was codified in Dinneen's dictionary in 1904. When the Irish Free State was established in 1922 and Irish became an obligatory subject in schools, a movement for standardization of orthography was revived. Published in 1947, in spite of opposition from both conservatives and reformers, the new orthography has generally been accepted for dictionaries and school use. In general, Roman font has now replaced the Irish font used earlier.

Soviet minority language policy, too, applied to spelling. In the 1940s, the "Common Rule" was issued, requiring that all Russian words borrowed into minority languages be spelled in Russian, producing major gaps between spelling and pronunciation (Grenoble 2003). The rule was revoked in 1950.

German spelling rules were made official in a national orthography conference in 1901. In 1955, the education ministers of the German *Länder* declared the Duden reference publication to be official for spelling and punctuation. In 1986, an official commission was set up by Austria, Germany, Liechtenstein, Switzerland and other countries with German-speaking minorities which proposed some cautious changes – only 185 basic words were affected. In Schleswig-Holstein, voters passed a referendum against the reform, but the courts over-turned it. By 1999, most publishers and print media were starting to follow the new rules, but a year later the *Frankfurter Allgemeine Zeitung* went back to the old spelling.

There have been many efforts to reform English spelling. Three are particularly interesting. The first is the failure of nineteenth- and twentieth-century campaigns, including that mounted by and with money left by the writer, George Bernard Shaw, to simplify spelling and modify the shape of letters. Arguments for simplified English spelling continue to be made. The second is the slightly more suc-cessful US effort to develop a distinct and simplified US spelling of the language. There were many suggestions, a few of which were widely enough accepted to mean that word processors now require separate English and American spell checkers. Many of the innovations were proposed by Noah Webster, who published the *American Dictionary of the English Language* in 1828. The third is a proposal to simplify the learn-ing of English spelling by developing an initial teaching alphabet with one letter for each sound and one sound for each letter (Pitman and St. John 1969). While fashionable for a while in the 1960s, this attempt to reform English spelling failed to win popular support, but is still used in some schools in the UK, USA and Australia.

In general, spelling seems an ideal task for language management. Without regulation, practice can easily lead to endless variation, as writers attempt to represent their own dialect idiosyncrasies, or misre-member the etymologies underlying morphemic systems. Educational systems are ready and willing to teach spelling or new spelling systems, and publishers and printers are ready enough to correct and be cor-rected. At first glance, spelling seems to be a practical issue, resolvable by empirical testing of object criteria such as efficiency of use, ease of learning, transferability. But, even here, ideological considerations regularly interpose. Like other aspects of language variation, spelling can help identify. Switching scripts and alphabets can be associated with major changes in political affiliation. Any change is threatening to those concerned with the maintenance of even quite recent tradi-tions. Spelling can set up boundaries, not just between educated and uneducated, but also between people previously assumed to be speak-ing the same language.

Summing up, while the original basis for management efforts to obtain good language appeared to be pragmatic, here, too, ideolog-ical considerations came to play an important part. The criteria for good language, including writing and spelling systems, come to be con-cerned not just with a felt need for a common norm with consequent communicative efficiency, but also with the same issues of group identity, including nationalism, that became fundamental to criteria for unacceptable language. In context, language policy, even at the level of corpus planning, is political.

DEALING WITH THE NEW: LEXICON FOLLOWS CULTURE

Language-policy issues concerning innovation are regularly decided on puristic or political rather than pragmatic grounds. Left alone, most languages seem to find easy and comfortable ways to coin or borrow terms for new ideas or objects. Formal language management in this area may be pragmatic, as when the professionals in a particular area set out to establish acceptable terminology for a newly developed field of science. However, when ideological considerations determine criteria for new terminology, national language-planning agencies regularly attempt to manage terminological innovation to meet the criteria.

The example of Navajo illustrates many of the critical features of lexical elaboration (Spolsky 2002b; Young 1977). First, the need for elaboration develops when new concepts are introduced into a culture. Especially when the concept comes with a foreign term attached, there is a temptation to borrow the foreign term, making only the changes needed to fit native phonology. However, regularly, individuals will, if their language permits, coin new terms (or extend the meaning of old ones). In the course of time, these words will be disseminated and often shortened. From time to time, the process will move from informal to formal, and some group of individuals or organization will attempt to manage it. At this stage, ideological considerations, such as efforts to keep the language pure or native, will affect coining on the one hand and codification on the other. Formal management activities, however, are not assured of success.

Lexical elaboration: planned or laissez-faire?

In the 1970s, many linguists thought it was a mistake to attempt to control lexical elaboration (Fishman 1983). A decade later, many seemed to believe that all that was required in order to develop an acceptable new lexicon was a simple technical skill. What they failed to appreciate, Fishman (1983: 109) complained, was that successful management depended on understanding "the delicate and complex social context." Technical competence may be enough to create a nomenclature in chemistry, but it is certainly not enough to have the new terms accepted, liked, learned and used. The development of a new lexicon occurs in a sociocultural context where modernization contrasts with tradition, each bearing its own particular ideological weighting, and where there is tension between the imported concept and terms and the indigenous.

What is generally wanted in developing societies is not just an adequate terminology, but one that is identified also with the society. The Israelis, he suggested, want their chemical terms to be faithful to the oriental nature of the Hebrew language; the Hindi want them to reflect Sanskrit; the Filipino want them to be transparent, made up of morphemes that ordinary people can understand; the Arabs want them to reflect the language of the Qur'an; the supporters of Yiddish expected them to avoid Germanisms and so on. Successful modernization, then, must be responsive not just to universal needs of efficiency but also to the particularistic demands of localizing ideologies. In practice, the people attempting to develop a new lexicon are commonly either members of the educated elite, not necessarily sensitive to public feelings, or, leading to equal isolation, active leaders of the national-language reform movement. As a result, the process regularly leads to notorious failures.

Consider the choices faced by an individual or group undertaking the task of finding a new lexical item for a new concept. Assuming the concept or object came with a name or label attached, but in another language, a first obvious choice is simply to use the foreign term, modifying it if necessary or desired to fit the phonological orthographical pattern of the receiving language. The Soviet policy requiring minority languages to spell borrowed Russian words according to Russian orthographical rules is an example of an ideologically based refusal to adapt.

A second possibility is to take an existing word and extend it to cover the new meaning. Look up the English word "computer" in an old dictionary. The first meaning found is a person who computes: the term was later extended to machines with the same function. It is easy to make up a long list of new terms for computer use by extending meanings: virus, window, cursor, application, memory, hard drive, mouse pad, paste and backup.

A third possibility is to coin new terms, making use of the word-formation possibilities of the new language. English since its period of bilingualism with French has been happy to do this, not just using native roots but also regularly doing its technical word formation in Latin or Greek. As a result, its new words are commonly opaque to people lacking a classical education. Where German uses two common Germanic roots for "telephone" (*Fernsprecher*, literally "distant-speaker"), English speakers have either to know Greek or to recognize the productive roots in *tele*scope and gramo*phone*.

The International Research Project on Language Planning Processes (Fishman 1977), which lasted from 1968 to 1972, was the first major effort to describe and evaluate the work of language-planning agencies in this field. The study was carried out in India by Das Gupta, in Israel by Fishman, in Indonesia by Rubin and in Sweden by Jernudd, studying the specific issue of terminological development. The project gathered comparative evaluation data in three countries, India, Indonesia and Israel, finding differential learning among teachers, students and adults. Greater differences emerged between the populations (teachers, students, adults) than between the countries.

Vocabulary development was also felt to be central in Soviet planning, both to provide the new terms needed for the economic and social revolution and to rid Soviet languages of vestigial pre-revolutionary terms from languages like Arabic and Persian. The Soviet Union was a totalitarian society that was completely mobilized, with all social, political and economic activities coordinated to fill the needs of a national plan (Lewis 1972). Language management in the Soviet Union had to fit into the national plan for modernization. Urbanization and the development of literacy and schools went hand in hand. In many of the languages, efforts were made to use native resources and to eliminate undesirable foreign elements: in Armenia, for example, an effort was made to free Armenian from Arabic, Turkish and Persian influences. In the 1920s, Russian terms tended to be avoided, but gradually this changed so that by the 1970s most of the new terms were being borrowed from Russian. Russian was the intermediary for terms from English or French or German. Calquing from Russian was widespread and derivatives were formed from Russian using native affixes. Ozolins (1996: 187) points out the subsequent impoverishment of the republic languages: "Russian loan words, expressions, and other items were adopted to such an extent that even the syntactic patterns of republic languages began to change . . ."

There are very few national languages where some modernization is not going on. The modernization of Persian started in the tenth century, after two centuries of Arabic domination (Sadeghi 2001). Words were borrowed from Russian and Turkish, and later from French. In 1935, the new Iranian Academy set up eight committees charged with replacing foreign words with Persian words. In 1968, the Shah revived the activity under the Iranian Academy of Language. Twenty subject committees were set up and by 1976, 35,000 new Persian words had been proposed. The activities of the Academy paused after the Islamic revolution in 1979. In 1991, a new institution, the Academy of Persian Language and Literature, was founded, with an active word-selection committee.

The period between the two world wars was a busy one for language modernization in Estonia (Raag 1999). There were two institutions: the Estonian Literary Society, which supported the compilation of a dictionary, and the Academic Mother-Tongue Society, which sponsored nearly 200,000 new terms. During the period of the Soviet occupation, Russian became the main source of lexical elaboration but efforts were made to counteract the pressure. One hundred terminological dictionaries were published.

THE CONTAMINATION OF MODERNIZATION

These examples illustrate the ideological basis of criteria for cultivation. Those people who favor the old will oppose the introduction of novel cultural items of any kind, and even more the introduction of new names for them. The linguistic purist is normally conservative in other matters as well: in clothing, in food, in institutions and in technology. The only way to defend oneself against the diffusion of innovation is to build a physically or ideologically closed community, in the way that certain religious and ideological sects have tried to do. The Amish tried to keep electricity, engines and external education out of their lives, and to the extent that they succeeded were presumably able to avoid serious demands for new terminology. These, however, are the exceptions: more generally, with growing forces of globalization, very few societies have not been forced to accept technological, economic, cultural and, consequently, linguistic innovation.

Ensuring that linguistic innovation is controlled and does not introduce foreign words is a small but satisfying step to the traditionalists. Just as banning obscene language provides at least a surface appearance of chaste behavior, so avoiding foreign loan words makes it seem as though all is well.

Underlying purism is an understandable but ultimately harmful belief in the superiority of one's own tradition, nation, religion or ethnic group: understandable, because without it, one is cast adrift in a valueless system; harmful, whenever it is translated into action to cleanse one's society of otherness. The path from linguistic purity to ethnic cleansing may not be inevitable, but it is regrettably only too common.

4 The nature of language policy and its domains

TOWARDS A THEORY OF LANGUAGE POLICY

The analysis of language policy as it affects linguistic items like sounds and words provides a good basis for understanding the field. Such policies, based on various beliefs about language, develop within various social groups, and commonly result in efforts to manage the language practices of others. Pronunciations, spellings, words or kinds of language are discouraged or forbidden or punished or required, as obscene or sacrilegious or violent or impure or foreign or appropriate or modern. Much the same kind of forces will be found to underlie policies directed to named varieties of language.

There are four main features to the theory of language policy being developed in this book. The first is the tripartite division of language policy into language practices, language beliefs and ideology, and the explicit policies and plans resulting from language-management or planning activities that attempt to modify the practices and ideologies of a community.

Policy may be implicit, in which case there can be honest disagreement as to what is the real policy of a community. For example, there are those who argue that United States language policy is essentially monolingual, finding evidence in the low level of recognition of use of any language other than English, while others interpret the widespread use of other languages and the legal and official support of multilingual services as proof that it is really multilingual (see ch. 7). An explicit written policy may not be implemented. There is thus no obvious answer to the question of what the language policy of a specific nation is. In any social group, there may or may not be explicit and observable efforts at language management, but there will be generally one or more ideological views of appropriate language use or behavior, and certainly there will be observable, if irregular and not consistent, patterns of language practice. To study one component

39

of language policy while ignoring the other two will provide a very incomplete and biased view.

The second fundamental notion assumed in this book is that language policy is concerned not just with named varieties of language, but with all the individual elements at all levels that make up language. Language policy can apply to pronunciation, to spelling, to lexical choice, to grammar or to style, and to bad language, racist language, obscene language or correct language. It may apply to non-autonomous varieties of language, such as dialects like New York English, Afro-American English as well as to recognized, autonomous, standard languages like French and Russian. Questions of how to handle variation and of how to categorize varieties of language are at the very center of the study of language policy.

The third fundamental notion is that language policy operates within a speech community, of whatever size. The domain of language policy may be any defined or definable social or political or religious group or community, ranging from a family through a sports team or neighborhood or village or workplace or organization or city or nation state or regional alliance.

There is, of course, a good reason for the attention concentrated on political units, and that is the association of language policy with power and authority. In the modern world, states are an obvious locus of power, with a constitutionally established authority of governments over their citizens. In principle, and often in practice, a government can establish policy by constitution, law or regulation, and has the means to enforce or implement that policy. When the authority is divided, as in a federal system like India or the United States, the establishment or implementation of policy becomes much more complex. When the authority is delegated from a higher authority, as in a colony or other dependency, it is normal to look at the higher level for evidence of policy decisions.

The relationship between language policy and power is in fact two-way. The implementation of language policy requires power, but as Cooper (1989) illustrated so clearly in the case of France, Cardinal Richelieu's motivation in establishing the French Academy, with its role as initiator of language policy, was to provide one more means of bolstering centralization. As Stalin realized, a strong centralized language policy enhances the power of the central government, but as became clear after the breakup of the Soviet empire, once the central power is removed, the only forces keeping the former imperial language in place come from language practices and beliefs.

The fourth basic notion presented in the first chapter and illustrated in the next two is that language policy functions in a complex ecological relationship among a wide range of linguistic and non-linguistic elements, variables and factors. The relationship may well be causal, but that will often prove hard to establish. Even when we look at specific implemented language-management decisions, we often find either no result (the failure of preachers to eradicate blasphemy or of teachers to enforce grammatical correctness, for instance) or unanticipated results (the way that reversing language shift or language revival activities produce novel, undesired forms of language).

As in other social sciences, the concepts of language policy are fuzzy and observer dependent. On this basis, Sealey and Carter (2001) asked about problems inherent in the social categories with which sociolinguists generally work, such as gender, age, class and ethnic group. These, Searle (1995) argued, are not "brute facts" but categorizations dependent absolutely on the user. For example, while there is a physical and physiological dimension to age, any categorization, such as child, adolescent, adult, old person, will vary from society to society and even from observer to observer.

A notion like ethnic group is even more difficult, for it encompasses not just social aggregates (the term proposed by Greenwood [1994] for groups like the unemployed defined by virtue of a single feature they have in common), but also social collectives, groups defined by their acceptance of a set of conventions and norms. It is the very fuzziness of the categorization involved and the elements produced by the process that makes it unwise to expect that the processes and structures of the social world can be described with the precision and purity that mathematics offers to the natural sciences. Not just the elements, but also the interactions between them, are likely to be fuzzy. Causal direction will be slippery and difficult to ascertain. When we note that a certain pronunciation is associated with a certain social category, it is far from easy to decide which causes which. Do women speak the way they do because they are women, or do we decide that they are women because of the way they speak?

While the interaction between factors and policies is often expressed causally, it is wiser to think of it as a probable association or constructive interaction. Rather than saying that a given factor causes a specific policy, it is better to think of it as the probability relation of the form: "if situation S is true, then language policy P is more likely to occur." These situations, considered better as conditions (see, for example, Jackendoff 1983, Spolsky and Schauber 1986 and Spolsky 1989) are co-occurring and interactive, producing stronger or weaker probabilities as they interact constructively. At the most general level, in language policy the conditions are conditions for choice of a language element or variety (see for examples Spolsky and Cooper 1991).

DOMAINS

In this chapter, we make the transition from focus on the language items or varieties to focus on the social grouping. Though most studies of language planning and policy deal with states, here we follow the advice of Cooper (1989: 37–8) and start with the family unit: "The justification, it seems to me, is the same as that for including the decisions of institutions such as churches and schools, namely that the same processes which operate in macrolevel planning also operate in microlevel planning."

Essentially what we are doing is applying Fishman's view that language choice (the very core of language policy) is best studied in the context of sociolinguistic domains (Fishman, Cooper and Ma 1971). Domains, Fishman argued, are sociolinguistic contexts definable for any given society by three significant dimensions: the location, the participants and the topic. In his study of the Puerto Rican barrio in New Jersey, he established the local salience of the domains of home, church, neighborhood, school and work. A home is generally located in an apartment or a house; the normal participants, defined by their relevant social relations, are family members; and appropriate or unmarked topics are family activities. Bringing an individual from another domain into the home can change things: if it is a priest, for example, the other participants may switch to acting as congregants and other topics may be appropriate. Fishman et al. (1971) showed the interaction of domain with language choice; for New Jersey Puerto Ricans, Spanish was the normal language for home, church and neighborhood but English was normal for school and work. Domains, Fishman (1972) argued, are a useful way of making the connection between sociological (macro-sociolinguistic) factors and linguistic (micro-sociolinguistic) realizations.

Families

Domains must be established empirically for any given society. The domain labeled "home" varies in major dimensions: the middle-class, two-parent, 2.5-child home is quite different from the home of the millions of people who have moved from villages to the poverty of new urban centers or are barely surviving in hastily erected refugee camps.

Nonetheless, starting with what we have had come to consider a normal family enables us to consider the probable relevance of variation.

Just as in any other social unit, language policy in the family may be analyzed as language practice, ideology and management. Secondly, in any language-choice situation, the three major conditions affecting choice are the speaker's proficiency in language (zero proficiency normally preventing choice), the desire of the speaker to achieve advantage by using his or her stronger language and the desire of the speaker to derive advantage by accommodating to the wishes of the audience.

From these theoretical assumptions, it follows that in many families a monolingual language policy (observable in language practice) will be the result of the members of the family having proficiency in one language alone. Even here, though, policy will affect the choice of individual items (avoiding obscenity, for instance) and style ("Keep your street language away from the table!"). More complexity will arise when a second language comes into play, as a result of intermarriage or emigration or foreign conquest.

It is also likely that in many families, as in other social units, there will be no explicit language management but simply choices based on practice and ideology. Occasionally, however, there are clear cases of language management. My favorite is a story an acquaintance once told me about his grandfather. As long as the family lived in Morocco, he would insist on the use of Hebrew at formal family gatherings and meals. Once the family had emigrated to Israel, however, where all of them soon shifted to the use of Hebrew, he would insist on the use of Arabic (more precisely, Judeo-Moroccan) when the family was all together. Most of the knowledge that we have of family language policy derives from anecdotal accounts or from ethnographies of interesting multilingual communities.

In ethnographical studies, there are suggestions that distinctions between men's and women's language derives from original bilingualism. The Papua New Guinea village, Gapun, discussed in ch. 1, used Taiap, the indigenous language, for serious conversation among adults and meaningless comforting of babies, and Tok Pisin for casual conversation and for occasional instructions to children.

The bilingual home, with its bilingualism produced by intermarriage, is an obvious locus for the study of family language policy. We have anecdotal accounts of some carefully considered policies. An American-born linguist married to a native speaker of Serbian and resident in a French-speaking city in Canada agreed with his wife to speak German with the children, who would obviously (in North America) acquire English and equally obviously acquire French from their immediate surroundings (in fact, they developed three distinct varieties – educated French Canadian at school, Quebec vernacular *joual* with their neighbors and standard French playing with the children of the French consul). In a small pilot study of mixed language couples in Israel, we found as a general rule that the couple continued to speak to each other in the language that they had used together when they first met. A recent study of bilingual couples in Toronto (Noro 1990) showed effects of parental language use, family social position and children's schooling on the extent to which children continued to use Japanese at home.

Besides intermarriage, one of the main pressures on family language policy is immigration, whether to another country or to the city. In a simple model (see Fishman 1966), the first generation of immigrants starts to pick up the new language outside of the home, but generally do not switch until children start to acquire proficiency and commitment to the new language in school or in contact with their peers. The second generation then is bilingual, and the third, unless there is continuing contact with first generation monolinguals, tends to switch completely to the new language. In studies of emigrants from the former Soviet Union to Israel, we commonly found the main use of Hebrew to be associated with the children (Dittmar, Spolsky and Walters 2002). In other studies, the presence of a grandparent or another significant older person is often associated with maintenance of the immigrant language. Lacking empirical data, we cannot determine whether this is simply a matter of continuing language practice or the result of explicit management decisions ("Speak Xish when your grandfather is in the room!").

As part of efforts at Māori language regeneration, the New Zealand Ministry of Māori Affairs conducted a large-scale survey of Māori proficiency and use (Statistics New Zealand 2001), including a series of long interviews with fifty-six people. The study found four clusters of the factors that accounted for speaking or not speaking Māori in the home: knowledge, situation, motivation and critical awareness. Māori had often been acquired passively, was associated with negative experiences in school, was generally at a low level and was used with little confidence, especially because it was regularly criticized by older fluent speakers (see Spolsky 2002a). It was not so much real proficiency as perception of proficiency that influenced willingness to speak to language. Associated with situation were interlocutors, the monolingual practices in general society and the limitation of Māori use to ceremonials and older people. The components of motivation were identity, anxiety (related especially to inadequacy) and the lack of time and emotional commitment available to young people starting careers and bringing up children. By critical awareness, the study meant some knowledge of the nature of second-language learning, an awareness of the importance of natural intergenerational transmission in the preservation or revival of the language and appreciation of the need to make practical and implementable language-management decisions.

This Māori case may be compared with the revitalization of Hebrew. The first generation of Hebrew language users living in the Palestinian agricultural villages in the 1890s, whose children grew up to be the parents of the first native speakers, had a sound knowledge of the kind of Hebrew that their children were starting to speak, even if it was restricted to reading and writing. There were no native speakers to offer criticism based on their superior knowledge. Important also was the ideological intensity of that generation, who were living in a new land, developing new skills and professions, accepting new social and cultural patterns and at the same time encouraging their own children to speak a new–old language. And finally, there was obviously a "critical awareness" of what was involved; the societies in which these developments were taking place were strongly marked by frequent public debate on matters of ideology.

Among immigrant families in the Seattle area, Tuominen (1999) found that while the linguistic composition of the family predicted parental choice, "*the children usually decided the home language of the families*" (68, italics in the original). There were family "language rules" but the children had at one time or another challenged them; many of them protested against being forced to attend heritage language schools and they objected to using the home language in public; as a result, many parents compromised and ultimately gave in.

In an immigrant situation, it is common for the children to take leadership in the socialization process. The independent language development of immigrant children (including their common tendency to pronounce the heritage language using the phonology of English) is one of the main pieces of evidence cited by Harris (1995) in her claim that the child's peer group is more influential than the home in passing on social values.

The family is an important domain in which to study language policy, both to understand how external pressures are reflected in it and because of the critical relevance to decisions inside the family concerning the language or languages with which children should grow up. A decision to transmit or not to transmit the heritage language is a major influence in language shift or maintenance. Studies of the effect of reversing language shift (see ch. 12) usually take this decision as a critical measure of success or failure.

Moving beyond the family, a large number of intermediate social groupings, such as the church or other religious organization, the village or other immediate neighborhood, the various kinds of marketplaces and other commercial enterprises, the larger demographic units such as towns and cities, the multiple workplaces, the schools and other educational systems, the social and sporting and ethnic and cultural clubs and organizations, the political parties, the contacts with local, regional and national government, may easily constitute a reasonable domain for exploration of language policy.

School

Of all the domains for language policy, one of the most important is the school. Cooper (1989: 33) added acquisition planning alongside status planning and corpus planning as a third focus of language policy. Language acquisition policy, more commonly known as language education policy, will be found to be a crucial issue throughout this book. When and where schools exist, they take over from the family the task of socialization, a central feature of which is developing the language competence of young people.

There are a number of basic questions that arise regularly in language education policy. First and foremost is the decision on the language to be used as medium of instruction. It is rare for children coming to school to have control already over the language or languages that the school system will want them to know (Spolsky 1974a). Most commonly, children learn at home one (or more) of a number of local vernacular varieties or dialects, and are expected to acquire during their school years mastery of a selected official, national, religious or classical, standardized language. There are many factors that establish this gap between the language of the home and the language that the school wants everyone to acquire. The languages spoken in the home are usually unwritten and schools almost universally aim to develop literacy in a written form of language. This fact is seldom taken into account by advocates of mother-tongue instruction, who assume that because the home variety often has the same name as a written language, it is in fact the same. The language spoken in the home is likely to be a local variety, while the language of school will commonly be regional or national. Especially as an effect of urbanization and immigration, children coming to school are likely to speak a number of different dialects or languages, while the school commonly selects a single language as its desired goal.

Given this, the first task of the language education policy should be (but seldom is) to find a way to overcome this gap. The very first decision is about the medium of instruction: should teachers speak to the pupils, and expect the pupils to reply, in the language of the pupils or in the language that the school values? A central controversy in language education policy is over the issue of what is regularly referred to as mother-tongue education. Mother-tongue education assumes that, whatever the ultimate linguistic goal of the school, initial teaching should be conducted as far as possible in the language or variety that the children brought with them from home. There are obvious difficulties with this approach: the available teachers may not know the variety; the pupils in a single school or classroom may speak several different languages or varieties; the variety may not be written; and even if there is a writing system, there may be no teaching or reading materials in it (Khubchandani 2003).

The second related question is how early to begin teaching the school language, and how early to begin teaching in it. A large number of patterns exist. There are systems (the British colonial education system usually followed this model) that start teaching in the children's home language, that introduce the standard or official language in the first few years and move to instruction in the standard or official language at various stages – by the intermediate or secondary level commonly. There are systems (the French and Portuguese colonial models, a common pattern in urban situations, the spreading goal of the English Only movement in United States) that start teaching from the first day in the colonial or official standard language and assume that pupils will pick it up from simple immersion. In between these two extremes are a whole range of possibilities: schools that claim to be teaching in the standard language but in which the teachers and pupils continue to communicate in the local language, while using only material written in the standard language; schools that develop complex patterns of transition from the home language to the standard language; schools that attempt to maintain students' proficiency in the home language after moving them to the standard language.

A second aspect of language acquisition policy is the teaching of other languages in addition to the mother tongue and the school language. A country with a bilingual policy might be expected to develop students' proficiency in the other language. In Switzerland, for example, one would expect to find German taught in the French-speaking cantons and French in the German-speaking cantons. In most educational systems, it is common to teach at least one foreign language, usually a major international language or the language of an important neighboring country, and increasingly, English as the principal language of the globalized world. Sometimes, less now than previously, the additional language is a classical one. Sometimes, and there is the growing tendency towards this, the language selected is that associated with the traditions and heritage of an ethnic minority. Having selected the language (or languages), decisions have to be made about when to begin teaching it, how much time and effort to devote to the language, and what to set as appropriate proficiency goals. Most countries have language education policies that define foreign-language teaching.

The school, then, is a central domain for language policy, and language acquisition policy is, as Cooper (1989) argued, sufficiently important to be recognized alongside status and corpus planning.

Religion and religious organizations

Noting that a "far-reaching resurgence of religious movements has recently taken place in the contemporary world," Eisenstadt (2000) sees it as a restructuring of Western modernity rather than a coming clash of civilizations, and as a part of globalization. The interaction between religion and language policy is a rich area barely explored to date (Sawyer 2001). Ferguson (1982) claimed that religion has been one of the most powerful forces leading to language change and language spread. Cooper (1989) noted the language choices made by religions, such as the preference of both Islam and Judaism for maintaining sacred texts and prayers in a single original language. Kaplan and Baldauf (1997) call the spread of Christianity a kind of linguistic imperialism. Schiffman (1996) has a chapter on religion, myth and linguistic culture and notes many interactions.

In general, however, little scholarly attention has been paid to the close interactions between religion (whether beliefs or practices) and language policy. Although there have been few if any attempts to tie the two phenomena together, the descriptions of past and contemporary cases of language policy and planning provide basic data and careful observations that can readily furnish the basis for study. The aim of this section is to sketch the constructive interaction between specific religions and language policy.

Ferguson (1982) is the basic text on the relationship between religious and linguistic factors. He pointed out "the distribution of major types of writing systems in the world correlates more closely with the distribution of the world's major religions than with genetic or typological classifications of languages." Wherever Western Christianity spread, it introduced a variety of Latin script for writing previously unwritten languages; similarly, wherever Islam spread, it introduced Arabic script. Jews used Hebrew alphabets to write the many other mother tongues they acquired over the centuries (Yiddish, Ladino, varieties of Arabic and Persian and other languages).

A religion often preserves an earlier version of a language for public ceremonies, particularly when sacred texts are maintained in the original, even when they are also available in translation. Religious observances help maintain languages after immigration.

Ferguson also drew attention to the intertwining of missionary activity and colonization; for much of the world, the two activities took place together. Different patterns emerged: British-based Protestant missionaries favored translating the Bible into the vernacular and providing basic literacy in it, while French-, Spanish- and Portuguese-based Roman Catholic missionaries would teach the catechism in the vernacular but kept the Bible in Latin.

Ferguson assumed "that all religious belief systems include some beliefs about language." Some, like Hinduism and Islam, consider the sacred texts to be untranslatable. Hinduism is closely associated with Sanskrit. Hindu nationalism supports Hindi for all India, and Sanskrit as language of scholarship. The oldest South Asian religious texts, forming the Veda, are in Sanskrit. Because of the sacredness of the mantras, accurate transmission is required.

Islam is basically and strictly associated with Classical Arabic. Arab countries generally include in their constitution a statement that the state follows Islam and uses Arabic. While speakers of many other languages follow Islam, Classical Arabic dominates the religion linguistically. The Qur'an can only be read or recited in Arabic. There is dispute about the permissibility of translation. Prayers must be recited in Arabic. Only the Friday sermon may be given in the local vernacular in non-Arabic communities. Islam spread to North Africa in the seventh century and slowly moved into sub-Saharan Africa with kingdoms established in West Africa between the thirteenth and fifteenth centuries. While the introduction was often military, the main religious emphasis was on the word enshrined in the Qur'an. This guaranteed primacy for Arabic over the vernaculars, all of which were influenced by it. Muslim traders appeared in East Asia early. Works explaining Islam in Chinese were published in the sixteenth and seventeenth centuries. Typically, Islam was introduced into South Asia through Arabic or Persian. In India, Arabic was restricted to the religious sphere and Persian remained the medium of Muslim education, government and literature; it was replaced by Urdu, which developed into the standard language of Muslims. Some 60 million Muslims live in the Central Asian territories of the former Soviet Union. Suppressed during the Soviet period, when many local vernaculars were standardized, mosques have now reopened. There is a movement to use Arabic script for local languages. Islam was introduced peacefully to southeast Asia over several centuries; Indonesia is now the country with the most Muslim citizens in the world. Malay was often the medium (Kratz 2001).

Other religions, like Judaism, hold the language of the sacred text to be sanctified, but over time, have come to accept translation (Jews no longer observe the fast day set for the translation of the Septuagint). Aramaic, a Jewish vernacular during the period of the Second Temple, was used in a number of biblical books and developed into the major language for interpretation. Many sacred works were composed or translated in Greek. During the period of exile, Jewish community languages were used for religious teaching and much writing took place in them, although Hebrew maintained its central position as the religious and literary language.

Buddhism and Christianity, too, have encouraged translation, although branches of both have shown favor for specific translations. Buddhism has been willing to have its sacred texts translated into other languages. Texts were written in Sanskrit, Prakrit and Middle Aryan, and translated into Chinese; Buddhism entered Japan in the sixth century, written in Chinese. In Tibet and Mongolia, Buddhist texts are in Tibetan. Christianity, also, has regularly translated its sacred texts into other languages and often permitted the use of the vernacular for religious ceremonies. In Europe, the dominant language of early Christianity was Greek. Latin became the only liturgical language of Western Christianity until the Reformation, and continued in this role in the Roman Catholic Church until the Second Vatican Council. The Eastern Orthodox Church allowed Syriac and Armenian traditions and translation into Gothic, Slavonic and other languages. Copts in Egypt kept Coptic as their liturgical language after they switched to speaking Arabic. The influence of Christian missionaries has been enormous in the development of written forms of African languages. The nineteenth-century Protestant missionaries were ideologically committed to Bible translation. In almost every African language with a written form, missionaries introduced the writing system. Christian missionaries played a major role in the development of writing for surviving North American Indian languages, but in Latin America the Catholic Church was generally opposed to the Indian languages. The

work of various Protestant and Catholic missions in Zimbabwe produced different languages through the standardization of dialects of
Shona. In South Africa, the development and spread of a missionary
lingua franca that became Tsonga was accompanied by the breakdown
of traditional systems of chieftainship and kinship. In Madagascar, the
Bible translation and dictionary developed by the London Missionary
Society gave national significance to an elite local dialect.

Working in opposition to imported religions like Buddhism, Shinto
has tended generally to stress its specifically Japanese nature through
an insistence on linguistic purity. Zoroastrianism, a religion that developed about 1000 BCE in northeastern Persia, has been preserved by
a conservative priesthood. The original sacred texts were composed
in Avestan, interpreted traditionally in Pahlavi, which after the tenth
century CE was replaced by Persian written in Arabic script in Iran,
and by Sanskrit and Gujarati among those Zoroastrians who migrated
to western India.

Because language plays a part in so many aspects of religion, the
full sociolinguistic matrix of situations and functions for any specific
organized religious group can in fact be very complex. One obvious
distinction is between individual religious language practices (praying
alone, confessing, reading religious texts) and group activities (praying
in a group, singing hymns, listening to sermons, taking part in classes).
Given the make up of the particular religion, the language practices
involved may vary very considerably.

In multilingual communities, religion can play a special role in language choice. In St. Lucia in the West Indies, English is the official language but a French creole is widely used. In the churches in Liberia,
both English and Krio were used in services. Younger ministers were
expected to show their linguistic proficiency by making greater use of
English in the sermons than older established religious leaders (Breitborde 1983). In the Netherlands, the use of Frisian in church remains
controversial (Zondag 1987). Friesland adopted Calvinism in the sixteenth century and used the official Dutch translation of the Bible in
church, home and school. As part of the growth of Frisian nationalism, Frisian was sometimes used (if the minister managed to persuade
the local consistory) for hymns and sermons.

Complexities that arise when religions, languages and nationalities
come into contact and competition were revealed in the Northwest
Provinces (nowadays Lithuania and Belarus) after the suppression of
the Polish insurrection in 1863 (Weeks 2002). The Russian government
felt itself threatened by Polonization, expressed both in the spread of
Roman Catholicism in competition with the Orthodox Church and the

associated use of Polish in non-Latin parts of the service. The attempts to introduce Russian into the Catholic services were thus part of an effort to combat Polish influence among Belarusians.

From even this brief sketch, one can see the richness and complexity of organized religious practices as a site for the study of language policy. In the language policy of nation states, religion and religious conversion are regularly significant and deserving of study.

The workplace

There are many other social groupings that might be explored. Every institution and regular social group has its own language policy, certainly in terms of understood language practices, sometimes in ideological positions on language choice, and occasionally in explicit efforts at language management. Many of the language-management policies come from a higher level: the policy in units of the Canadian military to use French and English on alternate days, for example, derives from national policy on bilingualism, and the changing pattern of language use in a San Francisco hospital described by Macias (1997) followed the development of English-language policy guidelines by the US Federal Equal Employment Opportunities Commission in 1980.

Language policy in the workplace may also be locally determined. When Glinert (1995) surveyed private and public institutions in Israel for their response to the immigration of one million Russian speakers in the 1990s, he found no central policy, but a pattern of local adaptations involving hiring Russian speakers who could provide more efficient service to non-Hebrew-speaking clients. Strictly pragmatic considerations usually govern such situations. In their study of markets in Ethiopia, Cooper and Carpenter (1976) found that it is generally the seller who makes an effort to learn the buyer's language. In public and government institutions, however, there is generally no "buyer" and the functionaries often feel no obligation to ease access of new immigrants or others who do not know the official language; hence, the need for rights-supported language access policies.

Business firms often establish their own language policies. There have been many reports of multinational European firms that expect their staff to use English. Alcatel, a French communications business, was reported in the *Los Angeles Times* (April 9, 2000) to have made English its official language. Previously, only senior managers were expected to be able to use English in dealings with US customers, but under the new policy, all employees were to be offered English classes and product specifications were to be written in English.

Local government

In ch. 2, examples were given of laws that local governments use to control obscene language. In many cases, local governments are also responsible for public education, and may establish language acquisition policies. A third area in which local governments may be involved in language policy has to do with choice of language for public signs. Absent national policy concerning this, a local town or city council in a multilingual community may choose to establish or implement such a policy. With the growth of Welsh nationalism and responding to changes as a result of devolution, many local councils in Wales established a policy of bilingual signs (examples were given in ch. 1). In federal systems, subsidiary political units (states, provinces, autonomous regions) often have authority over education and language.

Supra-national groupings

While logically national language policy would seem to precede supra-national, there are reasons to mention the supra-national level first. In this section we will ask about the language policy made by various kinds of regional and international bodies (including the European Community and the United Nations) for their own administrative functions, but leave efforts to influence the language policy of their member groups to later (see ch. 8 on language rights).

In the internal bureaucratic language policy of supra-national organizations, tension follows the conflict between pragmatic and symbolic considerations. Pragmatic concerns favor parsimony, the use of as few languages as possible. National interests may accept this notion, but usually only on condition that a member's own national language is included in the minimal group. In 1995, the European Parliament passed a resolution firmly rejecting the French proposal to reduce the number of working languages from eleven to five, noting that such a change needed unanimous support. In 1999, a conference discussed European Union internal language policy. The pragmatic elements were clear: already, few meeting rooms with space for interpretation booths were available to handle all the current national languages of members. With plans to more than double the membership of the Union, the practical problem of providing interpreting and translating in all languages constituted a major problem. De Swaan (1999) showed that the member states would each support a proposal that included their own language, but oppose one that went further.

Before expansion, there were eleven working and official languages of the EC: Danish, Dutch, English, Finnish, French, German, Greek,

Italian, Portuguese, Spanish and Swedish (Nic Shuibhne 2001). Member states may write to the Union in any official language, and receive answers in that language; any communication from the Union to a state (or citizen) must be in the official language of the state. All regulations and official documents must appear in all languages. In practice, most internal working is in fewer languages – English, French and sometimes German. The costs of this policy and the implications of expanding membership are obvious. One requirement for new-country access to the Union was the translation of relevant Union laws and documents into the national language – including some 60,000–70,000 pages of basic legislation. In 2002 in each of the current candidate nations – Bulgaria, Cyprus, the Czech Republic, Estonia, Hungary, Latvia, Lithuania, Malta, Poland, Romania, Slovakia, Slovenia and Turkey – translation units with a staff of ten or so interpreters were reported to be hard at work. For its own working, the Union provides full interpretation for heads of government in meetings of the full Union, and attempts to provide documentation translated into all the national languages for all working groups and committees. Adding further languages will obviously strain efforts to implement the policy.

In the bureaucracy of the Union, de Swaan (2001: 171–3) noted that French had been losing ground to English. In 1991, 90 percent of candidates for jobs were fluent in French, 70 percent in English and only 16 percent in German. In that year, two-thirds of internal communication was in French and about a third in English, but de Swaan assumes the movement is towards English. In 1989, the European Community had 2,500 translators, 570 permanent interpreters and 2,500 interpreters on temporary contracts. In 1999 interpretation costs for the Commission amounted to 30 percent of the internal budget or EUR 325 million. In practice, in spite of the major efforts to maintain the status of the national languages, English is developing into the lingua franca of the European Union.

A second thrust of European Union language policy is improving the capacity of member nations and their citizens to collaborate across the borders established by their national languages. Pragmatically, this could be served most efficiently by selecting a single language as a lingua franca for the Union. In practice, this is tending to happen as most countries make English their first or major foreign language. If English were seen as neutral, it would be an ideal auxiliary language, but its historical association with both a single member of the Union (the UK) and with the country perceived as the main challenge to restoring European hegemony (the United States) means that non-pragmatic arguments continue to hold sway.

To try to counter the threat of English, a major effort to coordinate improvement in foreign-language teaching in Europe was a principal activity of the Council of Europe, now being integrated into the Union. It worked to develop a common framework for language teaching, a European curriculum and integrated methods of assessment of what it called plurilingual proficiency – the ability of individuals to function appropriately in their various languages. Among the innovations of the Council's work was a progressive reduction of the age at which foreign-language instruction began, emphasis on communicative proficiency, encouragement of teaching of two foreign languages to most pupils (a way to counteract the tendency to teach only English) and encouragement of programs for visits to other countries. Foreign-language teaching is an essential part of the Union's language policy; it shows up in reports of the accession process for new members of the Union, which are encouraged to increase the teaching of Union languages to officials and professionals.

The third thrust of European Union policy concerns for rights of minority languages. Having proclaimed ideological acceptance of multilingualism in order, no doubt, to argue for the recognition of their national languages by the Union, it was hard for the member nations to resist arguments for granting some rights to their own minority languages (this will be dealt with in a separate chapter, see pp. 113ff.).

Other supra-national organizations have their own language policies – the United Nations started with two working languages (English and French) and added to these Russian, Chinese and Spanish (and later Arabic) as official languages. But for a number of reasons – especially the underlying goal of unifying its members while not interfering with their sense of national identity – all the signs are that the European Union is developing a policy of particular complexity and interest, at its most ambitious expressed in a 1990 European Parliament adoption of the "principle of complete multilingualism" (Fishman 1995: 49). At the same time, the pragmatic constraints on successful implementation are considerable.

Nations and states (polities)

It is time to start looking in a more systematic way at national language policies. The policies at the national level interact with less studied and less obvious policies occurring at levels below and above the nation state. It is policy at the family level that finally determines language maintenance and loss, just as it is policy at the European Community level that is starting to become a major influence in one significant part of the world. Language policy studies that focus only on the individual nation state and its centralized language planning are likely to miss many significant features. However, because the study of language policy and planning began with concerns for newly independent nations or for societies seeking nationhood, and because nationalism has come to dominate language policy, the large majority of studies have been made at this level, which justifies the amount of space it receives in books on language policy.

5 Two monolingual polities – Iceland and France

TOWARDS PARSIMONY

Scholarly study of language policy started at the level of the state. In particular, early scholarship concentrated on the problems faced by nation states when they were first gaining independence, whether during the spread of national autonomy in nineteenth-century European countries, such as discussed in Haugen's classic study (1966a) of the development of the national language for Norway, or in post-First World War Europe with the new nations created by the Treaty of Versailles and their efforts to achieve standard languages through cultivation, or in the rapid burst of national independence following the collapse of European-based empires after the Second World War, or currently in the new nations produced by the breakup of the Soviet Union.

Each of these periods had different characteristics. Nationalism, with its search for national identity and Great Traditions, was a strong motivator for language management in the nineteenth century. Both the French Revolution and German Romanticism held a view of nationalism that assumed that a single unifying language was the best definition and protector of nationhood. Choosing an appropriate national language and purifying it of foreign influences was a major activity.

These ideas were still strong in language management after the First World War, but the major European powers assumed that newly created states established with the breakup of the Turkish and Austro-Hungarian empires would be happy to take on international languages alongside cultivation of their vernacular languages. There was also an emerging realization of the need to provide protection for those minority languages that had survived the population movements and territorial adjustments (more recently known as "ethnic cleansing") of the time.

After the Second World War, revulsion against the tragic effects of nationalism moved emphasis to protection of individual civil and

57

human rights, including rights concerning language, which started to challenge the continuing nationalistic tendency to use language policy for mobilizing identity. The breakup of the Soviet Union provided a fruitful theatre for playing out these contrasting forces, as newly independent countries tried to restore their titular languages while choosing, or being forced not to ignore, the rights of linguistic minorities. By the end of the millennium, a third force dominated the sociolinguistic repertoire of almost all nations in the world as the effects of globalization showed up in the increasing relevance of English as a universal auxiliary language. Whatever other issues a national language policy must confront in the twenty-first century, it must deal with the place of English.

I am not writing a history of language policy, but an introduction to the field. As a heuristic, I will organize my presentation using a model that attempts to correlate language policy with the linguistic and ethnic complexity of the state. This model, based on Lambert (1999) as modified by reading into it Fishman (Fishman 1969; Fishman, Ferguson and Das Gupta 1968), sets out three basic types of nation state: the monolingual (monoethnic), the dyadic (or triadic) and the mosaic or multiethnic. Lambert suggested that the various types of language-management activity are most likely to be found in association with particular types of ethnic composition of a society. He distinguished three types of countries defined by their overall sociolinguistic mix.

The first type is made up of countries that are ethnolinguistically homogeneous. Such countries, like Japan or China or the United States, may contain linguistic minorities, but these are perceived to be small and insignificant and are geographically or socially marginalized.

The second type consists of dyadic (or triadic) countries, which include two or three ethnolinguistic groups relatively equal in numbers or power. Prototypical examples are Switzerland, Belgium, Fiji and Canada.

The third group consists of mosaic societies, multiethnic states like Nigeria and India and Papua New Guinea, which contain a large number of ethnic groups. More than half the countries of the world, Lambert notes, have five or more substantial ethnic communities.

There are, Lambert claims, interactions between this typology and the kind of language policy the state adopts. The homogeneous countries usually assume that a national language has already been selected. They emphasize a normative concern for the form of the standard language, pay some attention to the learning of additional (foreign) languages and sometimes develop a policy to spread their own language outside their national borders. The second and third types of country are both usually locked into debate over choice of official language.

Lambert's typology of countries was based on the actual linguistic situation within the country. Following Fishman (1968, 1969), it seems better to consider not situations but perceptions. Fishman classed countries according to the number of Great Traditions or national ideological identities, that they recognized. Fishman (1971a) proposed three basic types of decision concerning language policy in developing nations. Type A decisions occurred in former colonies with no consensual Great Tradition, which accepted the Western colonial language as official or national language. Type B chose a single indigenous (or indigenized) language associated with a single accepted Great Tradition. Tanzania with Swahili was such a case. Usually, the indigenous language needed cultivation, and there might be a transitional period. Both these situations were fairly straightforward. A third cluster, which he labeled type C decisions, was required in situations where there was "a *conflicting or competing multiplicity*" of Great Traditions and languages. India was, of course, the prime example. While at regional levels it was often possible to arrive at a type B decision, selecting the major regional language, at a national level the selection of a single indigenous language would give too much advantage to its speakers, so that a common decision was to keep the colonial language as the working language.

While Fishman's model overlaps only partially with Lambert's (types A and B are both monolingual, and type C may be dyadic, triadic or mosaic), it adds the critically important dimension of ideological consensus rather than specific sociolinguistic fact. Table 1 combines these models.

This modified division will be used as a basis for organizing the complex patterns to be discovered in the language policy of polities. By taking self-proclaimed policies as a starting point, I am not suggesting that a constitutional or legal statement of policy is evidence of actual policy. Whether or not a country has a constitution appears unrelated to whether or not one can easily discern its language policy; in fact, there is regularly a difference between the constitutional statement and what actually seems to constitute the language policy of the nation state. For countries with a constitution, however, the inclusion of a language clause is evidence that at one time the issue of language policy was of sufficient salience or political relevance for an attempt to be made to make it explicit and fix it in the constitution.

Table 1 *Types of countries and language policies*

Type	Attitude	Ideology	Usual activity
I	One language is associated with the national identity; others are marginalized	Monolingual	Corpus planning (normativism), foreign-language acquisition, diffusion
II	Two or three languages associated with the national identity; others are marginalized	Bi- or trilingual	Status planning
III	No one language is seen as motivated by the national identity	Multilingual, with varying official status for several favored languages	Corpus and acquisition planning

PRESUMABLY MONOLINGUAL COUNTRIES

A number of countries are constitutionally monolingual. Others are more or less monolingual in practice or ideology. Those that claim in their constitution (Jones 2001) to be monolingual, with no mention of other languages and their rights, are Algeria (Arabic is the only language named), Andorra (Catalan), Bahrain (Arabic), Bangladesh (Bangla), Bulgaria (Bulgarian), Cambodia (Khmer), Cape Verde (Portuguese), Costa Rica (Spanish), Côte d'Ivoire (French), Egypt (Arabic), France (French), Honduras (Spanish), Jordan (Arabic), Kuwait (Arabic), Laos (Lao), Libya (Arabic), Liechtenstein (German), Lithuania (Lithuanian), Madagascar (Malagasy), Maldives (Dhivehi), Morocco (Arabic), Oman (Arabic), Portugal (Portuguese), Romania (Romanian), Saudi Arabia (Arabic), Syria (Arabic), Tunisia (Arabic), Turkey (Turkish), Turkmenistan (Turkmen) and Yemen (Arabic).

A third of this group is made up of Arabic Islamic states, the modern constitution of which regularly proclaims Islam as the national religion and Arabic as the national language. The exceptions to this among Middle Eastern countries are Iran (with Persian), Iraq (which recognizes Kurdish) and Lebanon (with special status for French). The three North African Arab countries, Algeria, Morocco and Tunisia, do not reveal in their constitutions either their Berber minorities or the widespread and well-established use of French. Many nation states which are Islamic or have an Islamic majority (e.g. Pakistan, or the largest Muslim state, Indonesia) do not have Arabic as their principal spoken language.

A second grouping is the Romance one, a list on which Spain would also appear alongside France, Portugal and Romania were it not for its post-Franco recognition of selected minority languages in autonomous regions. In fact, in many of the cases, the constitutional proclamation of monolingualism disguises much more complex practices and ideology, and is not necessarily the basis for language-management activity.

Absent the simple fact of constitutional proclamation, it is much more complex to determine whether or not a country is basically monolingual. Arguments can be made that the United Kingdom, apart from its recent recognition of the place of languages in the former Celtic periphery, is just as monolingual as France, or that the United States, in spite of its large and diverse immigrant and indigenous minorities, is marked by monolingual English hegemony. First, we describe the simplest polity.

Iceland as a monolingual polity

Looking at actual language practices, there are few countries that can claim virtually complete monolingualism. The most obvious is Iceland, whose population of 270,000 is reported to be monolingual in Icelandic. There is no mention of language in the Icelandic constitution. Vikor (2000: 125) stated "Iceland is practically the only example in Europe (and possibly in the world) of a linguistically homogeneous nation-state. 100 percent of the Icelanders speak Icelandic as their first language and use it as their dominant language in all spheres of life . . ." There are other languages in use: according to *Ethnologue*, there are 16,000 deaf who may know sign language, based on Danish sign language. English and Danish are widely understood and spoken.

Iceland was ruled by Norway and Denmark for six hundred years. It received limited home rule from Denmark in 1874, but after a volcanic eruption, the economy collapsed and some 20 percent of the population emigrated to North America. A new economy was slowly built up. In 1944, Iceland attained complete independence. Independence and geographical isolation have combined to maintain linguistic homogeneity, with only minor dialectal variations. Modern Icelandic is so close to Old Norse that the old literature remains easily accessible to contemporary readers.

According to Lambert, a monolingual country is likely to be concerned about the form rather than the status of its language. This is certainly true of Iceland. As early as the seventeenth century, speakers of Icelandic started to make systematic efforts to purify the language of foreign elements. It was not purity for its own sake, but rather in order to maintain and establish distance from a competing language, at that time Danish, which had become the language of business, and was spoken by upper-class Icelanders. The struggle for national independence was associated with the campaign to purge Icelandic of foreign, Danish elements. A second linguistic enemy emerged during the Second World War, when British and American forces occupied Iceland. In recent times, most common borrowings have come from English. To provide support for purification, the Icelandic Language Council was founded in 1964. In 1997, a word bank was initiated which includes glossaries in thirty-eight fields, a spelling dictionary and a dictionary of neologisms. The Council cooperates with other Nordic language councils. The main reason for the "persistent purist drive," Vikor (2000) believes, is that Icelandic identity, dependent on language, traditional literature and culture and isolation, has been threatened by Danish and English, both larger languages.

Monolingual nation states, Lambert suggested, also include in their language policy the acquisition of foreign languages. One of the principal features of the 1999 educational reform in Iceland, where modern languages are compulsory in elementary and secondary education, was a change in the relative status of Danish and English, the former delayed and decreased and the latter started earlier and increased. The change serves to downgrade the historical dominance of Danish and recognizes the growing importance of English in a global world.

Iceland is a nation state that is monolingual in practice, ideology and language management. As Lambert predicted, language management is concerned with the form of the language, with purism, but purism with a purpose. Good language is pure when it has been purged of foreign elements, of elements coming from languages seen as a threat to the survival of Icelandic language and identity. Thus, as I have been arguing, any attempt to keep studies of corpus and status planning separate would lose sight of the nature of and underlying motivation for Icelandic language policy. The Icelandic Language Council campaigned successfully in 1998 to persuade Microsoft to add Icelandic to the languages supported by Windows. In one way, this could be considered simply a pragmatic corpus management issue, but at the same time its symbolic value as regards the status of the language is clear.

Iceland, in practice and ideology monolingual, has developed a language policy influenced on the one hand by nationalism and on the other by the emerging challenge of English as a global language. Its language management, designed to purify the language, is motivated as much by nationalism as in any other nation state. If even the purist paradigmatic case of a monolingual nation state shows such strong evidence of concern for the status of its language, we should not be surprised to find in the reality of other ideologically monolingual but practically multilingual states much more complex blends of approaches to language management.

PRESERVING FRENCH IDENTITY

France is the paradigmatic case for strong ideology and management. According to *Reuters* (April 14, 2002), the major Paris newspaper *Le Monde* has come under attack for "undermining the French language and bowing to Americanization" by beginning to publish a weekly supplement of articles in English from the *New York Times*. While an earlier survey of readers favored the idea, letters to the editor were strongly negative. Although in earlier times the key concern of French language management was purification and diffusion of the language, for the last decade it has been, as the website of the French Academy acknowledges, fighting English (and especially American). The struggle continues, for in June 2002, the Académie des Sciences decided that its *Comptes Rendus* would in future give preference to articles in English, following the example of some other major French scientific publications.

Over the last few centuries, France has developed a vigorous language policy, the management of which is intended to support the ideological primacy of the French language in all of its glory and purity. In a plenary lecture at the 2002 Applied Linguistics Congress in Singapore, Ulrich Ammon suggested the underlying motivation of French language policy in a comparison between Germany and France. German policy, starting with Bismarck, aimed to build a united political unit that included all German-speaking areas. French language policy, on the other hand, since Richelieu, attempted to establish French as the unifying and sole language for the areas already under French rule. This straightforward principle helps explain the seriousness with which France has taken language policy.

The founding of the French Academy

For Cooper (1989: 3), the Académie française was a first and defining example of language planning. He emphasized its social and political context. France was in danger of disintegration when Cardinal

Richelieu was appointed first minister to Louis XIII in 1624. Two empires surrounded it, the Holy Roman Empire (Austria, Hungary and the German states) and a second empire ruled by the cousin of the Holy Roman Emperor (consisting of Spain, Portugal, the Netherlands, parts of Italy and the New World). These two Habsburg rulers constituted a serious external threat and internally, too, there were challenges to the power of the French king. Wars in the previous century between Catholics and Protestants had left a sizeable Protestant minority with virtual independence. In addition, the great nobles of France ruled their own regions independently, collecting taxes and maintaining armies; there were regular riots by peasants suffering from rising taxation and prices; and Louis himself was young, sick and hardly qualified to be a strong ruler.

Richelieu filled the gap and for eighteen years until his death worked to create a centralized modern state. His key mission was to establish order and to fight the disorder that threatened king, nation and God. To do this, he believed, the state must take authority over private behavior in all domains, including art. He supported ballet, painting, literature, sculpture and music, and expected support in return from artists and men of letters for the king and government.

The Académie française was mobilized for this purpose. With the centralization of the monarchy in Paris, in the late sixteenth century aristocrats and the artists that they patronized started to live in the capital city, and formed the core for the development of a small social and artistic elite. Only at the beginning of the seventeenth century were French children taught to read in French, and in 1637 the first major work of scholarship was written in the language. Richelieu himself was the first theologian to write in French. The first treaty written in French was in 1714. As a result of this increasing use of French in formal domains, a need emerged to develop and cultivate it. There arose a movement to cultivate and purify French by pruning it of obscure archaic and regional terms. At the same time, to satisfy the purists, the language of the common people, perceived as coarse and potentially indecent, was also proscribed. What resulted was an aristocratic, literary language, with high status and authority.

Richelieu, Cooper argues, saw this tendency as not just culturally and intellectually appropriate but also as a contribution to his goal of national unity. He invited a small, private club of intellectuals to form the Académie française. A year later, in 1635, the Paris Parlement recognized its responsibility for the French language and for judgment of books written in French. It was "to give explicit rules to our language and to render it pure, eloquent, and capable of treating the arts and sciences." This scholarly group, supported later by legislation and other management, was to develop the monolingual hegemony of the French language, first over France, and later over the French-speaking world.

The Academy now describes (on its website) its role as twofold: first, to guard the French language, and second, to make use of the many donations it has received, to act as a patron of the arts by awarding some eighty prizes each year. It was originally envisaged that the Academy would work on four products, a dictionary, a grammar, a rhetoric and a poetics, but in fact it produced only the first. The Academy consists of forty immortals, as the academicians have been called since the Academy was founded. The Academy elects its own members, who are poets, novelists, men of the theatre, philosophers, doctors, men of science, ethnologists, art critics, soldiers, statesmen and churchmen who have brought luster to the French language. Three of the current thirty-seven immortals are women. But much more active management was to follow the creation of the Academy.

Equality or liberty

The fate of French regional languages, Judge (2000) believes, was an effect of the centralization that started under Richelieu and continued after the French Revolution. The Constituent Assembly in 1790 had accepted bilingualism, passing decrees supporting translation into local languages and salary increases for bilingual teachers. In 1791, however, the Jacobins took power and called for the development of a centralized and uniform state. Education was to have a central role, and equality could only be guaranteed if everyone spoke the same language.

Equality emerged as of higher value than liberty. The Jacobins were convinced that equality of opportunity could only be provided in a uniform state. Condorcet wrote in 1791 that a person who was illiterate was not the equal of someone who had acquired education, and therefore could not enjoy the same rights. Education was one of the most important duties of the state. A common language would support communication on a national level. Standard French, the language of the elite thanks to Richelieu and the Academy, was the choice. Regional languages came to be associated with feudalism. French became the national symbol, and other languages were prohibited.

It took a long time to implement this policy; only in the 1880s did the Third Republic put into effect the Jacobins' policy by making primary education in French free and compulsory. The belief in the supremacy of French had as an unfortunate corollary an associated view of the inferiority of regional varieties (Judge 2000: 73). From the beginning of the Revolution, other languages were considered not to be patriotic. This ideological view has continued and is repeated in the Toubon Law of 1994 that states: "By virtue of the Constitution, French is the language of the Republic, and the French language is a fundamental element of the character and heritage of France."

With the hegemony of French enshrined in the Constitution and implemented by law, France was less reluctant to sign the European Charter for Regional or Minority Languages. The French government made clear its own interpretations of the Charter as not granting collective rights to speakers of minority languages or weakening the constitutional status of French. The reservations were expressed when France signed the Charter in 1999, seven years after the first signatures by other countries. According to the records of the Treaty Office on the web, it had not ratified the charter three years later. France would seem to still be some distance from accepting the rights of linguistic minorities or making any effort to raise their languages to equality with French.

French language management

The Académie française was one tool of language management, an organization with state authority to protect the French language. A number of major laws explicitly established French language policy (Ager 1996: 40–45). The edicts of Villers-Cotterêt in 1539 mandated that only French could be used in court, in legal documents and in judgments. Not unlike similar moves in Britain and elsewhere, this reflected the emergence of national languages and the beginning of the process by which Latin was replaced as the language of law and government.

During the French Revolution, the decrees of 1794 furthered the power of French, converting Church schools into state schools that were required to use French, banning German and Alsatian in Alsace and other regional languages, and requiring French for legal decisions. But there were not enough teachers to carry this policy into effect, resulting in a first unsuccessful attempt to set up an *école normale*. In 1881, the minister of education repeated that French must be used in all schools, which would be free, secular and compulsory. In 1925 the education minister attacked non-religious schools sheltering other languages. In 1972 President Pompidou said that "there is no place for regional languages in a France which is destined to play a fundamental role in Europe." The same monolingual policy was enforced in the newly conquered territories of the growing French empire.

Going beyond the school, a law passed in 1975 established that French must be used in commerce, in public places, in the media and in public service. This law had to be modified to conform to European law and was replaced, in 1994, by the Toubon Act, named for Jacques Toubon who was then minister of culture and francophone affairs. The law made French compulsory in consumer affairs, employment, education, audiovisual communication and colloquia and congresses held in France. Civil servants were required to use official terminology.

Much of the long parliamentary debate centered on the proposal to forbid the use of foreign words when a French word existed (Ager 1996: 161). The Constitutional Council said this limited individual liberty, but agreed that civil servants could be required to use official terminology. The law made the use of French for all products sold in France and for all government business obligatory. The prime minister told public servants that their "zeal for French" was to be taken into account in their annual evaluation. Anyone employed by the state (civil servants and teachers) had to follow the Constitution and use French, including all terms approved by their Ministry's terminological committee. Contact with foreign persons had to conform to the rules requiring the use of French in international relations (Ager 1996).

The management work of the Académie française has been reinforced by other agencies. The Office de la Langue Française was set up in 1937 and replaced twenty years later by the Office du Vocabulaire Français. In 1966, reflecting his neocolonial aspirations, President de Gaulle set up the Haut Comité pour la Defense et l'Expansion de la Langue Française and a Comité International de la Langue Française, to defend French and fight English at home and abroad. Another body established in 1973 was Le Comité de la Francophonie. Terminology committees in the various government ministries were strengthened, coordinated by central agencies. Their mission, restated in a decree of 1986, was to deal with gaps in French vocabulary in the terminology of the ministerial area of competence, to propose appropriate French words, and, since 1993, to disseminate official terminology.

There are more than a dozen other language-related agencies dealing with francophonie which have tended to reduce the role of the Académie française. The size of the enterprise and its complexity are impressive. No other national language has developed the same elaborate and well-financed network of government and semi-government agencies.

The other languages of France

While in ideology and management France is monolingual, in practice it is not. *Ethnologue* lists thirty-seven languages for France. Of them, seven have over 500,000 speakers: Alsatian, Basque, Breton, Italian,

Portuguese, Algerian Arabic and Kabyle (Berber). Another five have more than 200,000 speakers: Corsican, Gascon, Provençal, Moroccan Arabic and Tunisian Arabic. There are also over 100,000 speakers reported of each of Catalan, creole and a second variety of Berber.

In spite of this obvious diversity, the notion "one state, one nation, one language" is, Judge (2000) believes, acceptable to the majority of the French people. In French law, she notes, state and nation are synonymous. The common legal and administrative system and the common language together form the *cement* of the nation, the term regularly used in documents referring to the francophone world. This provision was only included in the French Constitution in 1992, just before the Maastricht Treaty took effect. Before that, the central role of the French language had come to be taken for granted, it seems, but with the development of the European Community, where the threat of English was already apparent, the language was thought to require constitutional protection.

There are no official figures on the number of speakers of the regional French languages, Judge points out, for there are no questions in the French census about language or religion. Seven regional languages are generally assumed to have survived: Alsatian, Basque, Breton, Catalan, Corsican, Flemish and Occitan. Occitan is sometimes classified as made up of several different languages; Corsican is sometimes considered a variety of Italian; Alsatian is sometimes considered a variety of German. Non-indigenous languages such as Arabic are not seen to be part of the "national heritage." Some other regional languages are sometimes mentioned: the creole languages from various former French colonies, Tahitian and Kanak from the Pacific colonies, and the various *langues d'oïl* including Picard, Gallo, Poitevin, Saintongeais, Norman, Morvandiau and Champenois.

Recognized in Spain as the language of the autonomous region (see pp. 197ff.), Basque in France is mainly a spoken language. Some immersion schools were set up in 1969, paid for by parents and opposed by the French government. Since 1994, the system (and other immersion schools in regional languages) has been recognized by the state and some support is provided.

Breton, the remaining Celtic language spoken in France, once had its own common national territory, history, culture and language. Its territory has shrunk over the centuries, and the number of speakers has declined. There were perhaps 700,000 speakers in the 1950s, and in the 1990s between 450,000 and 600,000 who could understand Breton and between 250,000 and 300,000 who could speak it. It was supported, Judge says, by the Church and by its associated educational system. The death in the First World War of a quarter of Breton male speakers and a major exodus from Brittany after the war (not unlike the nineteenth-century emigration of Irish speakers) led to a rapid decline. A movement to reverse language shift led in 1977 to the opening of the first Breton immersion school (*Diwan* schools, as they are called) and by 1997 there were 4,500 pupils in such schools and many other pupils receiving some instruction in Breton in other schools. Since 1994, the government has paid for some teaching positions. While older first-language speakers of Breton speak local dialects, both Judge and Jones (1998a) agree that the younger second-language speakers are using a standardized version that they have acquired in school.

There are still a few tens of thousands of speakers of Flemish in the extreme north of France, but the language has no official recognition. Alsatian is also in rapid decline, continuing as a spoken language but generally in a diglossic relationship with written German. Occitan and its varieties lost their status after the thirteenth-century crusade against the Albigensians. The areas where they were spoken were generally poor, and all education was in French, with regional varieties prohibited in school until the end of the Second World War. Only in Provence was the literary language maintained. There is a revival movement: by 1997, 12,000 pupils were studying Occitan in school. Catalan, like Basque, straddles the Franco-Spanish border. In Spain, it is the official language of an autonomous region (see pp. 196ff.). In France, there may be 200,000 mainly elderly speakers, although there have been schools since 1976, and by 1997 over 2,000 children were studying Catalan. Corsican is associated, Judge says, with nationalism and the separatist movement. Until the 1950s, there were probably monolingual speakers, but the Corsican language movements do not cooperate with the other political regional movements.

In recent years, the government has been tolerant of (or nervous of interfering with) regional language movements, and has tried to integrate the schools into the state system. Since 1951, a number of small concessions has permitted the teaching of some regional French languages. In that year, the Deixonne Law permitted the teaching of Basque, Breton, Catalan and Occitan for up to three hours a week as part of general education, but they did not count towards the overall grade awarded for the *baccalauréat* until 1970. Corsican was added to the list in 1974 and a number of other languages later. Since 1994, the state has been able pay teachers in Basque and Breton bilingual schools; however, a ruling in November 2002 annulled earlier decisions to permit bilingual education in regional languages.

Fishman (1991) does not mention France at all as a country involved in resisting language shift (although, of course, Quebec stars for its resistance to English), but Fishman (2001) includes articles that deal with Basque and Catalan. Discussing the case of Basque, Azurmendi, Bachoc and Zabaleta (2001: 236) pointed out that since the 1994 revision of the French Constitution, there has been no official recognition of any language other than French. As a result, any activity for the recovery of Basque depends on individual initiatives. In a perceptive and intriguing reference to French policy, Strubell (2001: 279) noted that it was not only supporters of reversing language shift who aimed to change family language practice.

> The dramatically successful language shift achieved by the French republicans broke the back of the so-called "regional languages" when the first whole generation of adult speakers of Occitan, Dutch, Breton or Catalan decided to speak to their children only in French.

But is this to be blamed on language policy? Tabouret-Keller (1968: 113) explained the loss of Occitan as a result of demographic rather than policy changes. It was a result of industrialization, the development of a mass communication network and the breaking down of rural isolation. In areas like Alsace, where farming remained profitable, regional languages were maintained much more strongly, but in the Midi, the need for both men and women to seek employment outside the villages was what transformed a previously bilingual situation into French monolingualism. It was not language policy (or language policy alone), but, as Bourdieu (2001) points out, the changing socioeconomic context that had the major effect.

Language acquisition management

Ever since the French Revolution, the state has been responsible for the teaching of French, with ministers of education issuing detailed instructions on the curriculum and publishing instructions on what is acceptable in examinations (Ager 1996: 67). To this, the Toubon Law added a requirement for mastery in French and knowledge of two other languages. The Ministry began a campaign in the European Union for a general requirement for two foreign languages, realizing that if only one language were to be taught, it would be English. From January 2000, all French primary school pupils were to start a foreign language at the age of ten; in certain areas, at the age of thirteen pupils may opt for a regional language instead of a second foreign language. "In practice and in response to demand," lycée pupils (fifteen to eighteen) include two foreign languages; students in science fields also take two languages after the age of sixteen (Eurydice 2000).

In the early 1970s, a program was begun to support teaching the language and culture of the country of origin of the growing number of immigrants. These programs were conducted by the countries of origin, the aim, Ager (1996: 87) suggests, being both to ease integration and to permit repatriation at the end of the period of the work permit. In 1994, a report by the Economic and Social Council condemned the program as inadequate and unsuccessful. Rather, support was to be given to French as a second-language program which would lead to more successful integration.

French diffusion policy

French language policy outside metropolitan France is one of the best examples of an active diffusion policy. The French language was spread to the peripheral regions by decisions affecting government and education (Chumbow and Bobda 2000). It was carried to neighboring countries like Belgium, Luxembourg and Switzerland through conquest and domination. It was carried to the New World, to Canada, Louisiana and the Antilles, by a wave of colonization. A second wave of colonization, in the nineteenth century, took it to Africa and to Indochina. In the European carving up of Africa, France dominated the north and the west.

The major characteristic of French colonization was, Chumbow and Bobda say, to attempt to assimilate the colonized peoples. The colonies were known as African French territories or as France overseas. All levels of administration, public life and education were in French (Alexandre 1963). It was "the official, explicit policy of the governments of the independent Francophone countries that literacy means literacy in French," (Armstrong 1968: 232), an ideology that they inherited from their previous French colonial rulers. Only by acquiring education and literacy in French could an African acquire the status of *civilisé*, "civilized." Failure to learn French showed low intelligence, and no aspect of black culture was worth maintaining. The second characteristic was recognizing this civilizing mission, spreading the superior French culture and avoiding the use of the languages of the "primitive peoples" (Chumbow and Bobda 2000: 42). At the same time, the educational system was strictly elitist, forming an educational pyramid with a few at the top. Regional schools in the capitals were intended to produce an elite of low-level functionaries – clerks, typists and teachers. There were also higher primary schools, essentially the top of the pyramid. The French that was taught, Chumbow adds, was pure Parisian, no regional variation was recognized. Finally, the local African languages were repressed except in religious settings.

These assimilationist policies were generally followed by the other Latin empire-builders: Portugal, Spain and Italy. Breton (1991: 155) noted that "a certain elite among the autochthonous dominated elements had theoretically a vocation to be promoted – not too fast, of course – to the level of the dominating ones, i.e., to receive the honor of entering the ruling nation." Only the colonial language, French, was recognized as a language; any other local variety was considered *patois*. This was echoed in the embarrassment felt by the various French ministries in dealing with the growing study of and action on behalf of the creoles, which became the spoken language of many former French colonies (Chaudenson 1993).

After the loss of the French colonies when independence was granted after the Second World War, the gap was in part filled by francophonie. Francophonie is an international language movement involving government and non-government elites in more than thirty countries where French is official or widely spoken (Weinstein 1989). Maintaining the official status of the French language is one goal. A second closely related goal is the cultivation of French and purifying it of unacceptable English (especially American) borrowings. The movement, Weinstein noted, started early in the 1970s and benefits mainly Quebec and France. As the French colonies became independent, France became conscious of its loss of empire and power, and the entry of the UK into the common market was seen as a threat to the existence of French language and culture. The French Academy of Sciences in 1982 saw a triple threat: the cultural and scientific dynamism of the USA, the laziness of speakers of French in maintaining the purity of the language and the burgeoning spread of English through the media and computers. The Academy insisted on the use of French in scientific publications and the translation of English articles into French.

In Quebec, the francophone movement was rapidly accepted as a method of maintaining identity and achieving autonomy. In Belgium, it offered support to French speakers threatened by the growing status of Dutch. In former French colonies, it offered protection to the elites developed during French rule and threatened by those who would rather use the local vernacular or English. Francophone summit meetings took place in 1986 and 1987. The work of purification of the language is mainly left to France and Quebec. Both have methods of enforcing their laws on linguistic purity, Quebec showing more zeal, perhaps, than France.

The motivation for French language policy

The differences in language policy in France and Britain can be accounted for, Ager (1996: 207) argued, in relation to four types of motivation. These are identity, image, insecurity and inequality. Ager (1999) finds the first three to be particularly relevant to France. Ager (2001) adds ideology, integration and instrumentality.

Identity, he argues (2001: 13), can be seen most clearly in the case of nation states; France is widely considered the inventor of the concept. Even before the Revolution, the establishment of the French Academy had attempted to reduce the power of the regions, but it was only with the French Revolution that this was seen as fundamental to the establishment of nationhood. The universal Rights of Man had to be expressed in French. As a result, he says, "a linguistic terror" was launched in Alsace and other parts of the country (2001: 17). The strongest attacks on regional languages and their virtual destruction began in 1881 with the establishment of secular, compulsory and free education.

By image, Ager (1996: 208) seems to mean external perception: "the belief that the nation's language needs to be spread abroad in order to create a positive image in the minds of those who do not yet embraced it as their normal means of communication." Here, the reference is clearly to diffusion activities, of which the notion of francophonie is the paradigmatic example of a method to attempt to restore the prestige of empire.

Language insecurity is "fear that one's language is inadequate for social needs (Ager 1996: 208)." This was strengthened by Quebec concerns about Americanism: Ager (2001) argues that the 1970 establishment of ministerial terminological commissions was a result of an earlier Quebec initiative in this area.

Efforts to reduce inequality were, Ager (1996) believes, a basic motivation for the 1981 literacy program. A second such initiative was the policy to permit immigrants to be provided by their country of origin with education about their language and culture of origin; this was the way to avoid responsibility to offer the alternative of integration by maintaining older identities. A third, the movement for spelling reform, was presented as a method of helping under-achievers.

There are, Ager (1996) notes, two alternative views of the role of correct language in social equality: efforts can be made to make it easier for people to achieve correctness, or correctness can be used as a barrier to social advancement. The French approach, with strong maintenance of an elite, appears to prefer the latter. In the late 1980s, an effort was made to modify French in order to deal with problems of sexism. There was an extensive and at times bitter public debate over proposals to feminize terms for professions. The proposal, presented in 1986 by a committee set up by the minister for women's rights, consisted of a declaration of principles and a list of proscribed and permitted forms. The committee was attacked in Parliament, and the French Academy published a letter of warning. In the end, a few mild recommendations were published, but have generally been ignored.

Has French language policy worked?

How effective has French language policy been? Considering that it has been fighting the regional varieties since before the Revolution, it is a wonder that they still survive at all. Two hundred years of active language management should surely have been enough to destroy them completely. This is further evidence of the powerlessness of language management. Tabouret-Keller (1968: 113) argued that it was demographic and economic changes that explained the loss of regional varieties rather than the active language-management policies of the central government. Similarly, the continued struggle to purify French from foreign influences, 250 years after Cardinal Richelieu gave the task to the Académie française, suggests that, like the labors of Sisyphus, it is a never-ending one. Moreover, the need for the Toubon Law and all the subsequent regulations suggests that it is no easier to defend French against other pressures than it is to develop a working economic policy.

Diffusion to the colonies was more successful. Chumbow and Bobda (2000: 44) described what happened in former French colonies: "the francophile leaders who took over from the French at independence pursued the language policy bequeathed by their masters. French continued to reign supreme even when all the conditions for the use of an alternative language were met." While there is an increasing recognition of African languages in West Africa, French remains the language of only a small elite even in so-called francophone countries. French continues to be associated with school and literacy, and there is considerable variation among the countries depending on the level of education, the existence of a competing language or lingua franca, the degree of urbanization, the dominant religion, profession, gender (women are generally denied formal education and do not know French) and domain.

The case of French thus produces a very difficult set of data for those who believe that language practice is easily managed. Clearly, there has been and continues to be a great deal of language management with quite disappointing results. True, French continues to be the dominant language of the national territory, but even in this there are signs of leakage. The regional languages, which should have been extinct by now, have taken advantage of the wedges driven into French hegemony by European Union mandates for minority languages (see pp. 121ff.). True, French has provided the rallying point for a new empire using the battle cry of francophonie, but in many of the countries that make up francophonie, there is strong pressure for recognition of autochthonous languages or of creoles, and perhaps even stronger pressure for recognizing the greater economic benefit of English. It remains to be seen whether English recognition of vernacular languages or French suppression of them will ultimately produce stronger allegiance to the colonial language.

MONOLINGUAL POLITIES – TENTATIVE CONCLUSIONS

With the possible exception of Iceland, monolingual polities turn out to be multilingual in practice, the monolingualism being evident in national ideology and government efforts to manage language; but there are competing forces. In both Iceland and France, globalization in the second half of the twentieth century meant that national monolingual hegemony had to fight against the threat of a spreading world language, English. There is internal resistance, too; in France, it was provided by the continued existence and ideological support for the peripheral languages, reinforced by a human rights concern for the speakers of minority languages, whether autochthonous or immigrant.

In these two cases, we have seen the effects on language policy of two main factors, sociolinguistic situation and national ideology. We have also seen signs of two other important forces, globalization and the associated spread of English on the one hand, and the growing tendency to recognize that language is a civil and human right. Before returning to the analysis of polities, we will explore these latter two factors in more detail.

6   How English spread

THE SPREAD OF ENGLISH

French language policy was driven by a desire to assert national unity, homogeneity and identity in the multilingual regions under developing political control. To start, the principal threats to the language were internal – the regional varieties that encouraged diversity and detracted from central power. After the Second World War, with the formation of the European Community, a new enemy began to emerge – English. While at first it might be seen as simply another European language, like German and Spanish, that needed to be kept in its place in the new supra-national organization, its invasion of French language space through borrowing and its growing global use as language of science, technology, sport, computers, popular music, trade and commerce, drove the French to major language management, including a constitutional amendment, a series of laws and regulations and a host of bureaucratic agencies. Thus, it is not unreasonable to suggest that in the latter part of the twentieth century, the threat of English became the main driving force for French language policy. The issue to be considered in this chapter follows from this. Was the threat itself the result of language policy? Did English become a threat not just to French but to many other national languages, as a result of successful language management by its supporters?

English, it is generally agreed, is today in a stronger position in the world not just than any contemporary language but also than any other historical language. Many other languages were successfully spread by military conquest (Aramaic in the ancient Middle East, Latin in the Roman Empire, Mayan with its Central American empire, Arabic through the Islamic conquest, Spanish in the New World, French throughout its African, Asian and Pacific empires). Even as recently as thirty years ago, the movement of English towards global dominance was scarcely perceived.

The contributors to the 1966 Airlie House conference on the language problems of the developing nations (Fishman et al. 1968) saw English as just another case of a language of wider communication competing with local languages. The participants saw their issue as a local application of the generalized choice between an indigenous local language and an introduced language of wider communication, and analyzed the factors involved. They spoke of the official support of the newly independent countries of North Africa for Arabic, and their continuing use of French, the conflict between Hindi and other Indian languages, arguments in Papua New Guinea relating to the choice between Pidgin and English. At a conference at the end of 1968, Fishman (1971a) saw no need to single out English as a special case. Even a decade later, at an international conference on language spread (Cooper 1982), the languages dealt with in single chapters do not include English but are Aramaic, Quechua and Aymara, Hindi, Arabic, Mandingo, Malay, English in Wales and Russian in the Soviet Union, Mandarin and Hungarian. English was still not seen as the driving force to be studied.

While in hindsight, the signs of globalizing English were already there, the process was slow enough at the time to avoid any sense of impending doom. Even professionals in the field of English-language teaching assumed that their target was small elite populations in countries where English was not the official language. Few predicted the speed and totality of change, but Fishman did. Realization of the new situation was starting to emerge, he wrote in the introduction to the first book reporting a detailed study of the spread of English (Fishman, Cooper and Conrad 1977: 6):

> the traveller returning to the United States from a vacation trip in Africa, Europe, or Asian is often heard to comment that nearly everyone he met seemed to be able to speak some English. To such impressionist accounts of the ubiquity of English as the world language, one might also add the clearly partisan evaluations of its importance as a lingua franca offered by the promoters of English.

Fishman's goal in the study was to find the evidence that would show the claim to be right or wrong. English was already the language of diplomacy (95 of the 126 members of the United Nations received working documents in English), the language of 70 percent of the world's mail, used by pilots to communicate with air controllers, the first language of nearly 300 million people, and the second language of probably many more. Fishman (1977: ch. 1) detailed the extent of the use of English, publications in it, and students learning it and learning in it, to prove that English had become a global language.

Causes of spread

Having accepted the fact, Fishman (1977: ch. 2) went on to consider the causes. Empires had previously spread languages that were sometimes maintained after their collapse. Brosnahan (1963) suggested that the three languages – Arabic, Greek and Latin – which survived their empires shared four characteristics: spread by military conquest, they became languages of administration; their rule lasted for centuries; they served as a lingua franca in multilingual areas; and knowledge of them brought material advantages to those who learned them. Generally adopted initially as additional languages, they ultimately became mother tongues.

In the modern world, Spanish fitted this imperial model most closely, for, in much of South America, it had largely replaced indigenous languages. English and French had been adopted as mother tongues in the former British, French and Belgian empires, but more normally, their role had been as an additional language. Fishman added more promising causes to Brosnahan's four: urbanization, industrialization, education, religion and political affiliation. Seeking empirical evidence, he studied 102 countries in which English was not the native language of a substantial proportion of the population in order to assess the contribution of the nine conditions as predictors of several criterion measures: English as medium of instruction or as a subject in schools, the percentage of the population studying English, and a composite score that included official status, English in administration, technology, tertiary education, as lingua franca, as first foreign language, English newspapers, English on the radio and books in English. He found that having once been a British colony was the single best predictor, but most of the other factors were partial explanations. Linguistic diversity was important, too. In a multiple-regression study, status as a former British colony, percentage of the population maintaining traditional beliefs, value of exports to English-speaking countries, and degree of linguistic diversity were significant. In other words, there was complex multiple causation.

Conspiracy theory

Ten years later, a fresh view was introduced. By now, the firm grip of English was being recognized in the emergence of distinct second-language varieties of English. At the same time, a much simpler explanation of the reason for the phenomenon was to be offered.

Skutnabb-Kangas and Phillipson offered a new concept, labeled "linguicism" which they defined as the intentional destruction of a powerless language by a dominant one. Linguicism involved granting overrepresentation to one language, just as racism and sexism gave overrepresentation to one race or one sex. They and others believed that larger, more powerful languages were driving out small, weak ones. They felt strongly the suffering of speakers of small languages, and the way that disadvantaged groups – the colonized, the immigrant, the conquered, the minorities – were everywhere confined to the bottom of the socioeconomic heap. As linguists, they chose to concentrate on language, developing concepts of linguistic imperialism and linguistic genocide, which shared in all the opprobrium of real imperialism and genocide. Both also assumed that these phenomena were not natural, not a complex result of a multitude of factors interacting with changing linguistic ecology, but the direct and simple result of planned intervention by identifiable human agents, that they were the outcome, in other words, of language management.

Phillipson (1992) applied this to English-language teaching, arguing that the spread of English was a result of linguistic imperialism, which was distinct from the economic, political, military, communicative, cultural and social imperialisms. It was the way that the elite of the center ("the powerful Western countries and interests") dominated the peripheries (underdeveloped countries) (Phillipson 1992: 52). Initially, these elites consisted of colonizing settlers or administrators; their rule was continued by indigenous elites educated through the colonial language. International organizations helped maintain the dominance. Essentially, Phillipson used the *cui bono* argument. To find out who is responsible for a situation, ask who benefits. "Most of the benefits and spin-offs of this relationship accrue to the Center, while the Periphery remains in a dependent situation" (Phillipson 1992: 57).

There was nothing controversial or new in Phillipson's recognition that English had developed into a dominant language in many countries, nor in the observation that this was most likely to happen in former British colonies. What was novel was blaming the diffusion of English on imperialism and suggesting not just a hegemony, the results of a complex set of interlocking conditions (as Fishman did), but the working out of some conscious policy on the part of governments, civil servants, English-teaching professionals and their elite collaborators and successors in the peripheral countries. Did it happen, or was it caused? Was it the unplanned result of the interaction of a number of factors, or the achievement of carefully nurtured bureaucratic

management? If the latter, we have here an outstanding example of
the success of a language policy.

Imperialism, linguistic imperialism and globalization

A first question is whether linguistic imperialism is, as Phillipson
claims, distinct from the general phenomenon characterized and attacked variously as modernization, westernization, globalization and
Americanization. Galtung (1980) thought not, subsuming language under cultural or social imperialism. If he is right, then we will not get
too far looking at the spread of English simply as a question of language policy. I have already expressed my doubts about linguicentrism
and suggested that language policy issues need to be looked at in a
much wider context.

The proponents of the conspiracy theory regularly cite Bourdieu. In
an essay published just before his death in January 2002, Bourdieu
(2001) summarized his view of globalization. The economic field developed, he argued, within the nation state, forming a mutual dependency with it. It worked towards unification and integration, with
the goal of monopolizing control of power and dispossessing part of
the population. National boundaries (customs duties, foreign exchange
controls) set constraints on continued expansion; the development of
a world economic field (globalization) provided a method to overcome
them. This involved the imposition of an economy "rooted in the historical particularities of the tradition of a particular society, that of
American society" on much of the world, to the benefit of the US
economy. It carries economic, political and military, cultural and linguistic, and symbolic advantages for the US model. In Bourdieu's view,
the spread of English is simply one more manifestation of a major
process affecting the world, its economy, and its culture. If this is the
case, focusing attention, as Phillipson does, on linguistic imperialism
as a separate force detracts from the more critical problem of dealing
with the social, economic, political and cultural causes and effects of
globalization.

The second question is whether there is evidence supporting Phillipson's claim that the basis for the spread of English was effective
management by the core English-speaking countries and their governments. Phillipson collected data on the practices, ideologies and
language management of many colonial administrators, their successors and many professionals in the field of English-language teaching,
but takes for granted the effectiveness of their management. One could
more easily make such a case for French, were it not for the comparative failure of three centuries of French language management, as set

out in the last chapter. What is the evidence for the spread of English being the result of a conscious policy of language diffusion? Can we find machinery for diffusion even more powerful than that described for France?

Tracking down language policy in the central core of English-speaking countries proves to be much more complex than it was in France. The United Kingdom has no constitution, and the US Constitution makes no mention of language. Canada has been forced by rising Quebec nationalism to accept bilingualism as policy, and South Africa, after a long period during which Afrikaans and English struggled for dominance, is now establishing a complex multilingual policy as it recognizes the multiethnic language situation. Australia continues to try to find a working definition of language policy: it has, over the last few years, produced a number of Cabinet-level documents asserting successively multilingualism, English dominance and economically driven second language proficiency in Asian languages. New Zealand, without prejudice to its unstated English dominance, has recently recognized Māori as an official language. Ager (2003) argues that the UK has only recently began to move towards explicit statement of underlying language ideologies, as the political parties take positions on purism and the role of English as marker of identity. At the same time, a policy of devolution has restored the status of Celtic languages in Wales and Scotland. In none of these countries can one find a clear tradition of centrally directed language policy – a consensual ideology and highly developed language-management bureaucracy – of the kind that was described for France.

English diffusion in the UK

The history of the UK shows the slow growth of English. English emerged a century after the Norman Conquest in conflict with officially used Latin and French. Just as in France, usage in the court and the legal world slowly moved to the vernacular, and was supported by a growing vernacular literature. Standardization depended on independent activities of civil servants, teachers, printers and self-appointed experts. In England, there was strong and successful opposition to plans to develop a language academy.

The slow acceptance of English is demonstrated outside England proper, in the periphery. The Welsh language was still strong for centuries after the 1536 Act of Union had made English the only language of law and government (Jones 1998b). Most of Wales was still dominantly Welsh speaking into the middle of the eighteenth century, when circulating schools under the auspices of the Society for the Promotion of Christian Knowledge brought Welsh literacy to half the population. It was only a century later, motivated by an argument that Welsh hampered material and moral progress, that public schools began to discourage the use of the language. The actual effects of this policy were not felt for some time. The language loss that did take place appears to have depended on a number of non-linguistic factors: an influx of English and Irish workers into Wales, population mobility provided by railways, losses of young men in the First World War and a decrease in religious observance. These social and demographic changes rather than any language management seem to have been critical.

The dominance of English in Britain and Ireland is comparatively recent: at the end of the eighteenth century, it had taken over Cornwall and a part of Wales, but not Ireland or the rest of Wales ((Barbour 2000: 25). Anglo-English remained diverse in dialect and the official (RP) variety was spoken by a small social elite (about 3 percent of the population), and rejected by many others (Barbour 2000: 29). From the nineteenth century on, educated at highly selective public schools in the south of England, the elite promoted standard English with its own prestige accent. Anyone outside the group was disadvantaged: anyone, that is, who was a non-English speaker, or a non-standard speaker or used a non-prestige accent or was a Catholic or a non-Christian or a nonconformist or poor or uneducated or educated in the non-prestige school or, we may add, a woman or graduate of a provincial university. This particular combination of non-linguistic and linguistic factors set the model for what was assumed to be good standard English. There was then no need for formal explicit language management; only now, as the power of the old elite is weakening, are there those, particularly in the Conservative party, who are working towards an explicit statement of standard language policy (Wallace and Wray 2002).

English in the colonies

This shows the absence of consistent language policy within the UK; we will find a similar pattern of inconsistency in the next chapter when we look at US language policy. How, then, might we account for the wide diffusion and eventual international dominance of English? Immigration to the colonies is one obvious answer. In the core English-speaking countries like Australia, New Zealand and much of Canada, the English-speaking immigrants began during the nineteenth century to outnumber and so easily dominate both autochthonous inhabitants and immigrants speaking other languages. The exceptions were South Africa and Quebec, where there was a large body of other immigrants speaking another European language with sufficient density of population to achieve some form of political independence or equality. In Australia, the autochthonous population was small and at best ignored; in New Zealand, once the number of colonists was greater than the number of indigenous Māori, a change in school language policy and Māori population movement from village to city eventually led to the loss of natural intergenerational transmission of Māori – something that has only recently been checked, but not reversed, by political activity. Thus, in the core countries English became the majority language in numbers as well as in power.

In other parts of the British empire, however, the number of English-speaking settlers was comparatively small, and establishing English was a much more difficult task. Throughout the nineteenth century, there was much debate about the policy to be followed in language and education. It was generally accepted that the responsibility of the colonial power was to educate the indigenous population, in order to modernize and westernize the country. The debate was over the language in which that education was to be given. In French, Belgian, Spanish and Portuguese colonies, the answer was simple: civilization depended on mastery of the European language, and only that language could be used and recognized for educational and official purposes.

There were some officials in the British East India Company and its successor Indian Civil Service who argued for a similar policy in India, and this was put into effect in a small number of elite urban schools. For mass education, however, what were called the orientalists in India argued for the use of the local languages. This policy of support of the vernacular language was followed by other colonial powers and appears to have had its strongest instantiation in policy restricting access in the colonies to Dutch to a tiny elite (Groeneboer 1998).

Out of a blend of the two extremes emerged a general British educational policy in the colonies of providing popular elementary education in the local vernacular, with gradual transition through bilingual to monolingual English instruction in the more selective higher levels. This policy of primary education in the mother tongue and secondary and higher education in a major language is accepted nowadays in much of the world as the implementation of basic human rights.

The colonial language policies, French, Dutch or British, shared a contemporary belief that the native population would be unlikely to develop a high level of westernization. All were paternalistic and imperialistic, assuming that the culture and language they had to offer would benefit the conquered people. But this was true of most empires. One important result differentiates French and British policies: at independence from British rule, there was commonly sufficient education and literacy in one or more of the indigenous languages for it to be a possible choice for national language, while at independence from French rule, a long tradition of official and educational use of French and banning of indigenous languages made such a choice rare, to be tackled only when there was very strong anti-French nationalist sentiment.

Phillipson's principal evidence for English linguistic imperialism comes from quoting arguments put forward by British and later by American administrators and English-language teaching experts in discussions of language policy. He cites a frequently quoted 1834 Minute of Thomas Macaulay, then a member of the Supreme Council of India. During the four years he was in India, Macaulay established equality of Europeans and Indians in legal matters, and set up a system of national education that was to be Western in character. He came down firmly on the side of the Anglicists in the dispute over the language of instruction. Evans (2002) believes that Phillipson overstated the importance of the Macaulay Minute, as the decision in favor of English education had been taken several months before he wrote it. Nor, Mohanty (2002) points out, was Macaulay's Minute the end of the matter. Debate continued, and the ultimate compromise was stated by Wood in 1854, with the vernacular used in the lower branches of education and English in the higher. English could be taught where there was demand, but it was not be substituted for the vernacular (Pennycook 1998: 70).

In India, what emerged was a combination of elite English education and popular education in a number of the major Indian languages. In Africa, too, there appears to have been variation in both theory and practice. The missionaries who introduced Western education to many parts of the continent were regularly attacked both for their emphasis on English and for their discouraging English by teaching local languages and establishing literacy in them. When the colonial governments developed their own schools, they, too, took different approaches, confirming the absence of a single central ideology and policy.

Phillipson was in fact as critical of colonial proposals to use mother tongues (as in the reports on African education prepared with financial assistance from an American philanthropic trust accepted in a 1925 British Colonial Office policy statement) as of the use of English itself, interpreting it as a result of American experience of developing separate education for the Blacks in the southern states. His linguicentric approach distracts attention from the central problem. It was not colonial language policy, whether to use the metropolitan or the local vernacular language as a medium in schools, that was the core issue; either could be interpreted positively or negatively. Rather, it was the colonial situation, whereby one nation came to rule another, that produced the underlying inequality that turned out to be virtually impossible to overcome. In other words, imperialism and not linguistic imperialism is the real issue.

A central portion of Phillipson's argument depends on his showing that the diffusion of English was a benefit actively sought by the English and American authorities. One of the key conspirators in his view was the British Council, established in the 1930s to combat German and Italian propaganda. It paralleled similar organizations established by major powers to work alongside cultural attachés in embassies. In the United States, the agents of language spread, according to Phillipson, were the publishers who exported books in English and the universities who accepted foreign students; in addition, starting in the late 1960s, a number of US agencies were responsible for teaching English. The Peace Corps was also slated by Phillipson as an agency for spreading English. Could this disparate group produce a conspiracy capable of more effective language management than the centrally directed French language establishment? On the face of it, it seems very unlikely, so that any active policy making or language management was likely to be no more than one of a multitude of factors associated with the spread of English.

Conrad (1996) attacked the assumptions of Phillipson's theories. First was its assumption that a language had power. For Phillipson, any learner of another language was assumed to be dominated by it. Conrad argued that learning a language increased the power of the learner, and it was this quest for empowerment that accounted for the enormous growth in demand for proficiency in English. Second was Phillipson's use of a conflict theory of social change. Cooper (1989) described conflict theory, which assumed equilibrium to be abnormal and change to result from the continuous competing interests of various parts of society. Marx presented this in economic terms. Conrad objected to Phillipson's assumption that because a language was associated with a colonizing power, it was automatically a method of maintaining the power of the rulers. Phillipson was equally critical when a colonial power chose to use the vernacular, arguing that this was just another way to maintain the separateness and inferiority of the local peoples. Conrad argued then that linguicism had no real place in the analysis; imperialism was the real enemy. Conrad was uncomfortable, too, with the way that the metaphor of language power led to the claim that English was busy spreading itself. It is not languages that are in conflict, but people who are using language to mobilize conflict with other people, or, from another point of view, individuals who are conflicted in their personal choice of languages to learn and use. Rather than gross generalizations suggesting that English is always dominant, we need more detailed studies of how it enters into the complex set of language choices made in a specific community.

To reject the strong form of Phillipson's linguistic imperialistic theory does not mean that study of language policy should exclude efforts to spread languages or efforts to persuade people to use one language rather than another. But we need to be clear in each case what actually constitutes the linguistic ideology and language-management efforts of a government and not assume, as Phillipson seemed to do, that continued English and American policy and English and American interests were all that was needed to account for the spread of English.

Empirical study of linguistic imperialism

Returning two decades later to the topic of English-language spread that Fishman first raised in 1977, Fishman, Rubal-Lopez and Conrad (1996: 3) sought empirical evidence of Phillipson's model of linguistic imperialism. They set out to answer three questions. First, was English still spreading? Second, if so, was the continued spread "directly orchestrated by, fostered by, or exploitatively beneficial to the English mother-tongue world?" Third, were there other forces that were contributing to the continued spread?

The questions proved to be difficult to answer. Rubal-Lopez (1996) analyzed data from 117 nations on 81 distinct linguistic, economic, political, military and religious characteristics. Between 1977 and 1996, there had been an increase in the number of foreign students studying in English mother-tongue countries. There had also been an increase in countries with English-language newspapers: fifty-five in 1977, eighty-four in 1996. There had also been increases in the circulation of English-language newspapers, with Africa leading. Many factors were associated with these changes: military, language, economic, well-being, developmental, political and religious. Linguistic heterogeneity was important in former colonies, where a difficult language choice could be resolved by selecting English. Economic factors were complex, but English was associated more with exporting to English-speaking countries than with importing from them; in other words, Rubal-Lopez suggested, it was the colonized rather than the colonizer that benefited. Another important economic factor was tourist travel from non-English-speaking countries to English-speaking ones. Countries with lower economic status were more likely to have students studying abroad. Various indicators of better developed health services also predicted more English, perhaps as a result of the required scientific and medical education. Overall, she found solid support, as had Fishman (1977), for two major predictors: linguistic heterogeneity in former colonies and calorific intake in non-colonies.

Fishman himself drew attention to "the sharp bite of local detail and unique historical experience" (1996: 623). Only five of the twenty former colonies were still conducting elementary education primarily in English, but the tertiary level remained highly anglicized. Book publication was more anglicized than newspapers, and other media more anglicized than either. Even in the three states most resistant to English (Quebec, Sri Lanka and Sudan), English was a normal language in upper-level and interregional economic and technical activities. In half of the countries, English was an official language or was legally recognized; in six there was de facto recognition. There was evidence in many other countries of the development of informal or localized use. This functional division, Fishman believed, might be true not just of former colonies but of the world as a whole.

Fishman (1996: 639) warned against misuse of terms like imperialism and neocolonialism:

> English in most former British and American colonies and spheres of
> interest is no longer as much a reflection of externally imposed
> hegemony (certainly not hegemony maintained by force, let alone by
> foreign forces) as it is part of the everyday discourse of various now
> substantially autonomous societies, all of whom are essentially
> following their own 'common sense needs and desires.'

In other words, the socioeconomic forces encouraging the spread of English are now indigenous in most countries of the world, and do not depend on outside encouragement or formal language-diffusion policy.

More doubt on the linguistic imperialism hypothesis is cast by the spread of English to areas without any British or US colonial past. Cenoz (1998: 175) described the growing importance of English in the Basque Country. Hoffman (1998: 145–6) noted that in northern Europe, English is virtually a lingua franca; and everywhere it fills a number of specialist functions. Even in currently or formerly francophone countries such as Tunisia or Cambodia or Vietnam, there is evidence of the growing spread of English. In Hungary, foreign-language studying is declining but English remains important (Dornyei and Csizer 2002).

The weight of the evidence shows that the spread of English currently is a result of forces not under the control of putative language managers. Language policy decisions were involved, but the major factors now affecting the spread of English are associated not with empires or with major campaigns for language diffusion such as those still being conducted by the French, the Spanish and the Portuguese, but come from the changing nature of the world and of its reflected language system. In part because it was already widely diffused, and in part because the major remaining superpower used it unselfconsciously, English was there to be grabbed as the most valuable hypercollective goods (see next section) available for international communication.

The global language system

Another theoretical explanation for the spread of English has been proposed by de Swaan (2001). It is individual plurilingualism, he argues, that holds humanity together; the speakers of its 6,000 different languages could not otherwise communicate. The non-haphazard connections between the various language communities constitute what he calls the global language system. Mutually unintelligible languages are connected by plurilingual speakers, forming ordered hierarchical systems. Most of the languages of the world are peripheral, used only for spoken communication locally. Connections between two peripheral languages depend on people who speak both, but such people are becoming more uncommon as communication increasingly tends to be not between adjacent villages but between villages and the regional capital. The speakers of peripheral languages thus tend to acquire the same second language, which becomes central to their region.

There are, de Swaan estimates, about a hundred languages that occupy a central position in the global language system. Together, these languages used by 95 percent of the world's population, are generally the medium of elementary and occasionally more advanced education, and are used in public media, administration and law. Some have been declared national languages and official for the state. Many of the speakers of the central language have plurilingual competence, in it and their local peripheral language, most commonly because speakers of peripheral languages learn a central language (the opposite process is rare). When speakers of a central language learn another, it is usually one on a higher hierarchical level, which constitutes the group of super-central languages: Arabic, Chinese, English, French, German, Hindi, Japanese, Malay, Portuguese, Russian, Spanish and Swahili. Each of these languages is central to its own larger constellation. Their diffusion can be traced historically, through the spread of empires in various parts of the world.

The dynamics of the development of the global language system can be accounted for by concepts taken from economics. In de Swaan's view, languages are hypercollective goods, which are not scarce, and not used up by use. While they require an investment to learn, they are available, in theory at least, to anyone to learn. Languages are also like standards, in that they are conventional, and like networks, in that they provide connections. From an economic point of view, choosing a standard or network or, as de Swaan proposes, a language, is an investment, and one that is the more valuable the longer it survives and the more other people use it. There is a special external effect common to networks (e-mail is an example) that the more users there are, the more an individual user benefits. Languages have an advantage over road or telephone networks, which can charge a fee and so exclude users. With hypercollective goods like language, stampedes may occur either towards or away from the goods. In the final stages of language death, the growing shortage of speakers is a cause for others to stop speaking it. In the rush to acquire a central language, the more speakers it has, the more people want to learn it.

De Swaan proposes a system of calculating the value of a language to its speakers and those who learn it. The worth or Q-value of a language takes into account its prevalence (the number of people within a language constellation who speak it) and its centrality (the number of people knowing another language who can use it to communicate). For example, within the Netherlands, Dutch is both prevalent and central, as speakers of Frisian and Sranan can use it to communicate with each other; at the European level, however, there are few people outside the Low Countries who speak Dutch, so that its centrality is low. In Europe as a whole, German has the most native speakers, so that its prevalence is high, but English, with many fewer native speakers, has the most second language speakers, which makes its centrality high. English serves as the central language in many regional systems, allowing Arabs to talk with Russians and francophones with Chinese.

This model, de Swaan suggests, underlies the global shift towards English. Globalization raises the system level at which Q-values are calculated to the top of the hierarchy, where English is the obvious choice. He argues that this was not designed, but "the mostly unintended consequence of a myriad of individual decisions (and the non-decisions, resignation and compliance) which completely ignored the aggregate consequences for the larger language constellation" (2001: 186). It was, he concludes, a blind process.

De Swaan's model provides a stronger explanation of the diffusion of a world language than does a conspiracy theory. It explains the power of attraction of central, super-central and global languages, which constitutes nowadays a major issue in the language policies of most nation states.

WAS OR DID ENGLISH SPREAD?

If the spread of English could be shown to be the result of the language policy of the core English-speaking countries, especially the United States and Britain, as Phillipson (1992) proposed, then it would be the major example of successful language management. However, there is no strong evidence for this claim. The spread of English and its development as the first genuine global language appeared to result rather from its being in place to take advantage of changes in the world language system over the past century. These changes, not so much linguistic as economic, technological, political, social, religious and structural, are where we need to look for underlying causes. They provide the centripetal pragmatic force that at each level of linguistic systems and networks works to raise the value, desirability and attractiveness of the language with the highest Q-value. Working against this force is an opposite trend, the centrifugal symbolic forces underlying efforts to establish or maintain ethnic or local or national languages. These are the source of resistance to English or other dominant languages, characterized now most generally by Fishman's term, reversing language shift (see ch. 12).

The development of English into a global language is not the simple end result of language management. Rather, it reflects local and individual language acquisition decisions, responding to changes in the complex ecology of the world's language system. Because it is not under management, it is hard to predict the next stage. So far, national-language management – such as laws and agencies in France and Brazil and Russia trying to keep English out – appears notably unsuccessful in checking it. The European Community is spending a great deal of time and money insisting on the internal use of the languages of its member states, but there is reason to suspect that unless cheap accurate machine translation suddenly develops, the interpreting and translating machinery will finally collapse under growing pressure, leaving the strongest lingua franca in place. Relieving some of the pressure for English, the growing use of other languages for electronic communication is a particularly important development, but it simply keeps a place for local languages in local communication. It is nonetheless a clear warning that the situation could change. English might simply develop into a neutral auxiliary language, more efficient and cultivated than Esperanto, but no more associated with its native speakers. Or some powerful new chip may finally, after forty years' work trying to develop machine translation, provide the long-awaited device that will permit each of us to speak to it in our own language.

In the meantime, two fundamental points have emerged for the understanding of language policy. The first is that the spread of English is not the direct result of either wise or self-centered language management. The second is that English as a global language is now a factor that needs to be taken into account in its language policy by any nation state.

7 Does the US have a language policy or just civil rights?

LANGUAGE IN THE US CONSTITUTION

Although the evidence shows that the spread of English is not the direct result of a successful policy for language diffusion, there remains the question of whether the UK and the United States actually have language policies? If so, in the absence of explicit constitutional statements of language policy, where does it reside and how can it be discovered?

Discussion of language policy has been rare in the UK; only recently have there been signs of a developing acceptance of the responsibility of the educational system to assure the maintenance of desired linguistic norms on the one hand and the granting of language independence to Wales and Scotland as part of devolution.

In the United States, in contrast, while there is a similar absence of an explicitly organized and implemented language policy, and while there was also traditional opposition to the notion of establishing a language academy or any other administrative body charged with its development and implementation, the issue of national language policy has arisen historically on a number of occasions. During and after the war of independence, the issue of a national language did come up but was left without any formal decision. Independence from British rule did not lead to seeking a new national language, although there were later moves to mark formally the distinctions of an American language (Weinstein 1982). Marshall (1986: 11) has no doubt: "The Founding Fathers of our country did not choose to have an official language precisely because they felt language to be a matter of individual choice."

Perhaps people understood that English was the language of the new Republic. Hernandez-Chavez (1995) argues that the choice of English for writing the Constitution began a policy of the imposition of English and the suppression of other languages. Newly added territories such as New Mexico and Louisiana were expected to add English to their repertoires. Apart from this, just as the control of education was not a function of the federal government but to be decided at the level of individual states, so it was assumed that individual states had the right to establish local language policies. Thus, the xenophobia of the 1920s may have represented a national ideological trend, but any implementation, such as the banning of bilingual education programs, took place at the state or local level. Efforts to establish a national policy for the teaching of foreign languages depended on non-governmental private or professional bodies.

From its colonial beginning, the American linguistic pattern was marked by diversity in language practices (Lewis 1980). The colonization itself was linguistically diverse: Spanish beginning in 1513, English in 1583 in Newfoundland, French in 1605 in Canada, Dutch in 1623 in New York and German in 1683 in Philadelphia. But it goes too far to assume that diversity in practice and the notions of individual freedom built into the Constitution and the Declaration of Rights were automatically allied with a firm acceptance of multilingualism. Just as mottoes of liberty, equality and fraternity in the French Revolution did not prevent the continuation of the campaign to destroy the regional languages, so there was no overriding commitment in the new United States to the maintenance of linguistic diversity. The colonizing groups showed limited tolerance for the languages that preceded them. In most cases, Native Americans were forced to adopt European languages. With United States conquest of other European colonizing groups, their languages in turn were submerged under the growing hegemony of English. Spanish ceased being a sovereign language in the United States after 1848 and German and French were slowly weakened. Their previous recognition helped French in Louisiana and Spanish in New Mexico, but this did not guarantee maintenance.

The nineteenth century was marked by rapid increases in immigration to the US, especially from Europe. The US population went from under 4 million in 1790 to over 211 million in 1974, with different linguistic and ethnic groups arriving simultaneously. Some of the groups attempted to establish independence; most attempted to fit into the dominant English-speaking culture.

Immigration to the United States

Fishman's (1966) study of the fate of the complex mosaic of languages brought to the United States records the results of this process of assimilation. His data reveal how in two or three generations the majority of non-English-speaking immigrants had shifted towards English. But this process was neither universal nor consistent, for it was balanced by an

opposite tendency: "Two processes – de-ethnization and Americanization on the one hand, and cultural-linguistic self-maintenance on the
other – are equally ubiquitous throughout all of American history,"
Fishman (1966: 15) concluded.

Kloss (1966) investigated the potential causes of language loss, and
found that most variables, such as size, level of cultivation or location,
had ambivalent results. Those languages that were established earliest
(French is the best example) seemed to hold on longest. Communities
that closed themselves off from social, political, religious, cultural and
economic integration with the general culture – the Amish and the
Hasidic Jews were the obvious cases – were successful also in maintaining their native languages. Fishman himself proposed a more general
thesis: non-English languages were most likely to be preserved in those
groups, autochthonous or immigrant, that were denied or that resisted
social mobility. From this, it seems reasonable to assume that US linguistic ideology assumed or accepted linguistic integration, the most
efficient solution to linguistic diversity in a community accepting the
importance of modernization and unification.

Some scholars have identified this ideology in statements made
regularly in the late nineteenth century (see, for example, Ricento
2001). Pavlenko (2002) described its development. The plurilingual immigrants were joining what was essentially a multilingual society. The
absence of any reference to language in the Constitution can be interpreted in two ways: as an absence of commitment to multilingualism,
or tolerance for multilingualism. During the nineteenth century at
least, tolerance was shown by the fact that California and Louisiana
officially recognized bilingualism and that there was a movement in
the nineteenth century to recognize German as the official language
in Pennsylvania and Ohio. Educational practices, too, accepted multilingualism.

The Fourteenth Amendment to the US Constitution, passed in 1868,
reaffirmed the principle of equal protection:

> Section 1. All persons born or naturalized in the United States, and
> subject to the jurisdiction thereof, are citizens of the United States
> and of the state wherein they reside. No state shall make or enforce
> any law which shall abridge the privileges or immunities of citizens
> of the United States; nor shall any state deprive any person of life,
> liberty, or property, without due process of law; nor deny to any
> person within its jurisdiction the equal protection of the laws.

Some groups were treated differently. There was forced integration and anglicization of Native Americans. Chinese and Japanese

immigrants were kept out of the regular school system. German-medium instruction was supported until the 1880s, when tolerance of diversity started to be weakened by the beginning of mass migration, the main source of which was no longer northern Europe but southern and eastern Europe. Many immigrants were Catholic or Jewish and they continued to attend mother-tongue parochial schools. They were culturally and linguistically different, and perceived as less educated and less intelligent. Efforts were made in the 1890s to speed up the assimilation process, especially by teaching English, but they were unsuccessful.

During the First World War, xenophobic feelings were increased by war-induced nationalism focused not just on learning English but also, driven by anti-German sentiment, on discarding allegiances other than to the United States. German books were removed from libraries; German theatres were closed; German music was banned; and the teaching of German stopped in schools (Pavlenko 2002: 179). Thirty states passed laws obliging aliens who could not speak English to attend evening schools, and thirty-four made English the only language of instruction in public schools. By the end of the period, positive attitudes towards bilingualism had been replaced by a widespread belief that it had little to contribute, and that the teaching of foreign languages in school was a bad thing, encouraging the maintenance of linguistic heritages. Bilingualism became associated with inferior intelligence and lack of patriotism. By the 1930s, Pavlenko believes that US ideology was firmly monolingual.

It is, however, a mistake to use the term ideology in talking about the United States, or any other democracy for that matter. The important US thinkers of the post-Civil War period, such as Oliver Wendell Holmes and Thomas Dewey, saw the fundamental notion of democracy to be a free market of ideas but not of ideologies. Democracy meant openness to different ideas, including ones with which one disagreed. The notion of academic freedom which developed at the beginning of the twentieth century attempted to capture the essence of this anti-ideological position: in a free society, unpopular ideas and minority opinions must be defended. At the same time, then, that there was a strong body of published opinion supporting monolingualism, important American thinkers like Thomas Dewey and Horace Kallen were starting to write in support of cultural pluralism.

The wave of arguments in favor of monolingualism did not interfere with the continuation of heritage-language loyalty, including home and community language use, the publication of newspapers, and the maintenance of bilingual programs into the twentieth century.

Lewis (1980: 366) described this earlier stage of US bilingual education: programs for Native Americans, the teaching of German in parts of the United States well into the nineteenth century, parochial schools in French, schools for Scandinavians, Dutch, Lithuanians, Poles and Slovaks that taught in the native language with English as a second language. These practices were, however, impeded by xenophobia. The result was nearly thirty years of English-only legislation, during which many states made English the only medium of instruction for public. Until the late 1960s, much of the United States was legally committed to a policy of public education in English only. Only private schools chose to ignore this, and there was no national enforcement of a uniform policy. When eventually a national policy began to emerge in the 1960s, it was to be generally supportive of multilingualism and multiculturalism rather than monolingualism and the melting pot.

Cycles like this, with no evidence of equilibrium, suggest that we are dealing with conflicting tensions; any action towards one end quickly produces a counteraction in the other direction. Such tendencies are common in political life. The surface support for individual rights in much of Europe over the last thirty years (see next chapter) seems suddenly to be disappearing in strong concerns about the effect of immigration. France, the Netherlands, Denmark and Sweden are all producing new right-wing parties that are winning elections on xenophobic platforms. Understanding the complex nature of national language beliefs, we can more easily understand the seeming inconsistencies and changes in positions. Reaffirming the notion of constructive interaction (Oyama 2000) rather than causality, we see why it is risky to assume that ideologies lead to policies. In fact, beliefs about language choices and values tend to be inconsistent and inconstant, to vary with changes in the ecology, and to be partially at least open to influence of language practices and management.

US language practice and beliefs

The question that we are trying to answer is whether the United States has a language policy. If we look at language practices, the answer is far from simple. While most private and public business is conducted in English, many individuals and communities continue to use other languages regularly in certain domains. It is true that it is generally easier to get by with English than with other languages, but there are enough exceptions to keep the question open.

The 1980 US Census revealed that 11 percent of the resident population over the age of five was reported to speak a language other than English at home; in 1990, this had risen to 13.8 percent and in 2000 to 17.6 percent. Many of these people were at least bilingual: in 2000,

25 million (out of 45 million) were reported to speak English very well and another 9 million to speak it well. Among speakers of Spanish at home, just under 50 percent could speak English very well in 1980; in 2000 the figure was over 53 percent. Considering other languages, too, language practice in the United States is not monolingual.

If we ask about beliefs about language rather than practice, the answer, too, can be complex. Many people believe that English was or should be the official national language, but about the same proportion believe that neither the teaching of foreign languages nor bilingual education is a threat to English. Forced to make binary choices, as in recent referenda in California, Arizona and Massachusetts, the voting public will come down on one side or the other, but the popular beliefs are sufficiently complex to allow for creative solutions.

If there is no clear answer to be found in practices or in beliefs, language management at various levels and times reveals an equally multifaceted situation. This can be seen by looking at policies in education and in legal decisions. They do not form a consistent and regular pattern; Fishman (1966: 30) notes that "only rarely has America taken steps to hasten the linguistic and cultural enfeeblement of its immigrant groups."

US language management

Attacks on policies permitting the use of other languages in US schools are certainly not new (Crawford 2000a). Benjamin Franklin was upset by the fact that German settlers in Pennsylvania were teaching their children in German rather than English. After the Louisiana Purchase in 1803, the new governor required that English rather than French be used for all public affairs, but the 1845 state constitution provided for bilingualism in the legislature. The 1849 constitution for California recognized rights for the Spanish language, including bilingual publication of laws, but this was reversed by the 1879 constitution. Beginning in 1880, the US government put into effect a policy in the education of Native Americans of banning indigenous languages, religions and ceremonial practices, but this was temporarily relaxed in the 1970s. Similarly, in Puerto Rico, English was declared the official language of instruction immediately after the Spanish–American War; only in 1948 was Spanish restored. In Hawaii, English instruction was introduced in 1853 and became the sole medium of instruction in public schools in 1896.

While what Crawford calls the "conquered peoples" suffered from the colonializing rejection of their indigenous languages, up until the end of the nineteenth century most European immigrants were handled more tolerantly. They were permitted to run their own affairs in the enclaves in which they settled, often operating non-English schools. In 1839, Ohio authorized German–English instruction; others states passed similar laws. Kloss (1977) noted the use as medium of instruction of Dutch, Danish, Swedish, Norwegian, Polish, Italian and Czech, as well as German, French and Spanish.

The Americanization campaign that began around 1910 was driven by fear of the revolutionary potential of immigrant workers. Henry Ford wanted all his workers to learn English. Theodore Roosevelt believed that foreign-language-speaking immigrants remained divided in loyalty; he proposed setting up schools and sending anyone who had not learned English in five years back to their country of origin. Xenophobia grew during the First World War, and public use or teaching of German was widely banned. However, with the adoption of the immigration quotas in the 1920s, the flow of non-English-speaking immigrants slowed down, and the non-anglophone groups dwindled. Only a handful of rural and parochial schools continued to be bilingual. It was not until the 1960s that the issue became important again, with growing non-English-speaking immigration.

A series of local decisions, usually driven by local interest, but able to appeal to a rhetoric of linguistic uniformity, were the basis for national unity. When not challenged directly, the general consensus appears to have been tolerant of linguistic diversity, but language provided a focal point for any fears that might develop of threats from minorities, whether autochthonous or immigrant. The fact that education was outside the constitutional authority of the federal government, except when specific conquered groups like Native Americans and Puerto Ricans came under federal agencies, meant that, just as there was no consistent national ideology, there was no possibility of developing a uniform federal language policy.

LANGUAGE AS A CIVIL RIGHT

Even before the 1964 Civil Rights Act, US courts had on a number of occasions defended the rights of speakers of languages other than English. In 1923, the Supreme Court ruled in *Meyer* v. *Nebraska* (262 US 390) that while the states could require English as the medium in tax-supported schools, they could not do this for private schools. In 1926, the Supreme Court found that a Philippine Bookkeeping Act that prohibited the keeping of accounts in languages other than English, Spanish and Philippine dialects violated the Philippine Bill of Rights that Congress had patterned after the US Constitution.

An early focus of legislation to establish Civil Rights in the United States was on voting rights for Blacks, as set out in the 1957 Civil Rights Act and strengthened in 1960 Act and again in 1964. Title VI, (42 USC §2000d et seq.), was part of the landmark Civil Rights Act of 1964. It prohibited discrimination on the basis of race, color and national origin in programs and activities receiving federal financial assistance. Several important court decisions used Title VI to establish a need to deal with language discrimination. In 1971, the Federal Court for the US Eastern District of Texas held that the absence of a bilingual education program violated the Fourteenth Amendment and Title VI. In 1974, the Federal 10th Circuit Court of Appeals in *Portales* v. *Serna* also held that Title VI gave children with limited English-speaking ability the right to bilingual education.

Another landmark case, *Lau* v. *Nichols*, limited the range of the constitutional rights. It recognized that something had to be done to deal with the problems of students of Chinese origin, but did not stipulate that bilingual education was the only way to deal with their plight. The Office of Civil Rights surveyed 333 school districts and issued a document setting out other remedies that were available. Lewis (1980: 376) argued that this and other litigation which followed was to be expected, "in view of the traditional, and in some instances almost invincible prejudice against bilingual education among local educational agencies." Even in 1976, he noted, a dozen states still prohibited bilingual education and only seven made it mandatory under certain conditions.

What is important is that the 1964 Civil Rights Act provided a basis for the federal government to intervene in language management. For the next thirty years or so, however, most of the action and concern concerning language rights moved from Title VI to a law specifically intended to deal with the problems of those pupils described as linguistically disadvantaged.

The Bilingual Education Act

In a comment that attests to his years of experience as an HM Inspector of Schools in England and Wales, Lewis (1980: 369) remarks that "Policy is decided and determined by those who, reluctantly or willingly, are prepared to pay for it." This is what made the Bilingual Education Act of 1968 such a significant decision in the history of US language management. The Act, which expired on January 8, 2002 (see James Crawford's Obituary 2002c), provided funding for thirty-four years for educational programs that taught in languages other than English.

During these years, there was continuing controversy over the form and effectiveness of the programs.

The ambivalence is apparent from the very beginning. The original legislation was proposed to teach English to children from non-English-speaking backgrounds. It was in other words a direct continuation of Title VI of the Civil Rights Act, providing a remedy for discrimination against pupils who did not speak English. It was not intended, though it was sometimes used, to serve the additional goal of providing support for the maintenance of the languages of minority groups. It was this aspect of the program that raised, as Lewis (1980) argued, the anger of local education agencies and was used as justification, thirty years later, for the public campaign that attacked it. With the expiration of the Bilingual Education Act, teaching English is meant to continue under a new educational reform program called No Child Left Behind, and the work of the former Office of Bilingual Education and Minority Languages Affairs will be taken over by the Office of English Language Acquisition, Language Enhancement, and Academic Achievement for Limited-English-Proficient Students, now renamed the Office of English Language Acquisition.

This was the original motivation of the Bilingual Education Act, a political initiative that came from senators and congressmen from the states with significant Spanish-speaking populations – Texas, California, New York, New Jersey, Florida, Arizona and New Mexico, with support from Maine with its significant French-speaking minority. It was a continuation of the Civil Rights movement that was originally focused on the disadvantaged position of US Blacks. It provided a way of implementing growing concern for the teaching of English to non-English speakers. It also provided an opportunity for public discussion of the issue of language policy.

The Senate held five days of hearings in May 1967 and two more days in June and July (*Bilingual Education* 1967). The House for its part had two days of hearings in June (*Bilingual Education Programs* 1967). From the beginning, the difficult balance between bilingual education and teaching English was recognized. The first witness, Senator Paul Fannin from Arizona, agreed that Mexican and Puerto Rican students should be encouraged to speak Spanish, to develop "bilingual facility," and not to "shun their Hispanic heritage." He went on:

> But there is no logical reason why Spanish should be preferred over English, the native tongue of Americans and the language each of us most [sic] develop fully in order to compete effectively in our modern, highly technical society.

In the hearings, Senator Yarborough regularly stressed that his concern was with teaching English to Spanish-speakers. He disagreed with a suggestion of including languages other than Spanish, expressing a commonly heard argument concerning the languages of immigrants, that they were in the United States by choice and so had consented to give up their language.

The arguments presented in favor of bilingual education by educators included the value of bilingualism, its role in reinforcing respect for the home, its effect on self-concept, its personal value for technical and professional work in later life, and the need to conserve native competence in the languages of immigrants as a national resource. Only Joshua Fishman spoke for language maintenance as a goal. He argued in his evidence presented to the committee for the conservation of a "neglected national resource," languages other than English. In presenting a case for cultural pluralism, multilingualism and the maintenance of minority languages, Fishman was alone among the many witnesses heard in the congressional hearings on the Act to express a belief in government's responsibility to support all languages spoken in its territory. The other witnesses and the committee members and presumably, the members of Congress who enacted the Bill, saw bilingual education rather as one method of providing a satisfactory transition to English proficiency.

Speaking at a conference at the end of the first year of the implementation of the Bilingual Education Act during which 7.5 million dollars had been spent, Fishman (1971b) expressed his disappointment, and shared in the blame at the failure to turn the bilingual education program into more than something restricted to the Spanish-speaking poor. He drew attention to the huge gap between the authorization of funds ($15 million for 1968, $30 million for 1969, $40 million for 1970) and the actual appropriation (0 in 1968, $7.5 million in 1969, $21 million in 1970). There had been failure, he said, in convincing appropriation committees that bilingual education was not just a sectional matter or just another part of the anti-poverty program. He called for the development of effective lobbying groups, both professional and ethnic, who could establish "real bilingual education." In his account of the state of United States bilingual programs at the end of the first decade of the implementation of the Act, Lewis (1980) argued that the programs were generally considered remedial. The teaching of English often became the major priority, and there was no serious attention to maintaining the other language once this had been achieved.

The United States had no unified language policy, whether in practice, belief or language management, even at what is sometimes considered the high point of its acceptance of multilingualism and multiculturalism.

Testing

If we trace other aspects of US language policy, we find a similar lack of uniformity. One of the results of the xenophobia of the 1920s was a major reform in immigration policy, the goal of which was not just to control numbers of immigrants but also to give priority to immigrants from northern Europe, thought to be more suitable and more easily assimilated. The immigration act left a serious loophole in that it permitted automatic visas to foreigners who wished to study in US schools and colleges. Lacking the professional skills to assess the language proficiency of applicants for visas, the Commissioner of Immigration asked the College Entrance Examinations Board in 1929 to develop a test for this purpose (Spolsky 1995b). After the Second World War, with the foreign student business picking up, a second such request was made. In the early 1960s, problems with the security and validity of available tests led to State Department support for an initiative backed by the Ford Foundation to produce a new test. As the test was being developed, it turned out that the various branches of government that had supported the idea were unable or unwilling to provide any financial backing. Thus, what could have been a matter of national language policy was in fact left to private foundations and agencies to develop.

MANAGING LANGUAGE ACQUISITION

For many years, US foreign-language teaching policy was also left without central government guidance. The various professional bodies, such as the Modern Language Association, that attempted to encourage the teaching of foreign languages were left to persuade schools and state education departments of the potential value of knowledge of foreign languages. How unsuccessful this was became clear with the outbreak of the Second World War, when various defense and government agencies discovered the absence of a pool of proficient speakers of urgently needed foreign languages. Again, a non-government initiative conducted with Foundation support through the American Council of Learned Societies began the program of initiating teaching of the languages such as Japanese and Chinese and Arabic that would be relevant in a world war but that had been ignored in the educational system (Cowan and Graves 1944).

With the outbreak of war, various parts of the defense establishment did start teaching some of these languages. The Navy, for instance, built an effective and efficient school for Japanese. The army was persuaded to include the teaching of languages and area studies as one of the fields undertaken by the colleges as part of the Army Specialized Training Program which lasted for a year (Keefer 1988; Spolsky 1995a). After the war, the army developed its own language schools, both to teach English to foreign military personnel coming to the United States for training and to teach practical command of strategic foreign languages to US military personnel. Again, attempting to make up for the inadequacy of US foreign-language education, the Foreign Service and the intelligence agencies opened their own language schools.

Generally, it would appear that these programs failed to produce the number of graduates with the required level of proficiency to meet the needs of the agencies. More recently, other government agencies have recognized the cost of not having available adequately qualified speakers of various languages. The Federal Bureau of Investigation, for instance, has been severely handicapped in the wiretapping by not having agents fluent in Haitian creole or Jamaica Talk. The immigration courts spend large sums of money holding presumably illegal immigrants in custody until a suitable interpreter can be found for a court appearance. The terrorist attacks in September 2001 and the subsequent war in Afghanistan revealed again serious gaps in national language capacity, especially in languages like Arabic, Persian, Pashtu and Bengali (Brecht and Rivers 2000).

There were occasional governmental efforts to make up for the absence of the national foreign-language policy. In the burst of educational funding that followed the shock of Sputnik, programs in Russian were started with government funding in many colleges and some secondary schools. In the last few years, too, there have been efforts supported by the intelligence agencies to improve language teaching, especially at the advanced level. A contract has been signed to establish a university associated research center largely devoted to language. These examples of language management, not yet matching the Soviet language schools that produced fluent speakers of English and other languages for diplomatic and intelligence jobs, constitute language policy motivated by national security. Arguments have been presented of the value of developing a coalition of interest between all the language-teaching concerns, but they have so far failed to achieve consensus or critical political support.

It is possible to interpret this reluctance to get involved in language management as representing an underlying belief that this is something that government should not meddle with. It appears that negative programs – the attacks on bilingual education, the rejection of programs that recognized the existence of Afro-American vernacular English, the fear of Spanish spurring the various English-only campaigns, the long ignoring of the language of the deaf – and claims that it is only ignorance or stupidity or willfulness that prevents everyone speaking the approved variety of standard English, combine to firmly block any effort to develop a language policy that recognizes the diversity of US language practices.

During its thirty-four years of existence, bilingual education was in fact under regular attack. Part of the reason for this can be seen as defense of jobs and territory, for the promoters of bilingual education argued that only members of an ethnic community could teach or administer bilingual programs, and that ethnic communities should control the schools. Much of it was focused on confused goals and programs and on ambiguity of criteria for evaluation. Because the political decisions about the programs tended to restrict them to disadvantaged pupils and schools, the mere fact of developing a bilingual program was not enough to make up for years of neglect and the depressing context of poverty and crime. There were good programs, successful in standard as well as local terms (see, for instance, Rosier and Holm 1980 or Brisk 1998), but there were also enough failures of both kinds to provide for a steady stream of critical publication.

This criticism built up and culminated in the political campaign undertaken in 1998 by Ron Unz that led to the passage in a California referendum of Proposition 227, intended to eliminate bilingual education in the state. Similar votes against bilingual education succeeded in Arizona and Massachusetts. Crawford (2000) echoes Fishman (1971b) thirty years before in his criticism of the failure of educational professionals supporting bilingual education to realize that their work was politics and lobbying.

LANGUAGE IN CIVIL RIGHTS

What has perhaps blurred the view that has emerged so far in this chapter is a tendency to a linguicentric approach. We have been asking what happens to languages rather than what happens to the people who speak them. A somewhat more consistent view emerges if, instead of tracing the failure to provide formal support for schools taught in languages other than English, we ask about efforts made to deal with language-related impairment of civil and human rights. In both the United States and Europe, it has become accepted that there is a fundamental human and civil right for there to be no discrimination against an individual on the basis, among other things, of the language he or she speaks or does not speak. In its most rudimentary form, this led to the requirement that a person charged with a crime be told the details of the charge in a language that he or she speaks. At its most elaborate, in current European and United States practices, this entails the provision of government services in such a way that they are accessible to all, whether or not they speak or read the national language.

State provision of bilingual education is not a necessary conclusion to the acceptance of individual human or civil rights. In the case of the United States, bilingual education was recognized by the courts and by legislation as one method of dealing with the problem of non-English-speaking pupils, but it was interpreted by many of its practitioners as a method rather of preserving languages.

Defending English in the United States

In his analysis of French language policy, Ager (1999) argued convincingly that one of the dominant motivations for recent language-management activities had been a sense of insecurity, a belief that French was under attack both from within and from without. The enemies within are peripheral and stigmatized varieties and the laziness of speakers who let foreign words into the language. The principal enemy without is English, threatening and succeeding in replacing French as the language of wider communication in the world organizations and even in former francophone territories. But French resistance is official language policy, supported by Constitution, law, regulation, government and semi-government agencies.

Even in the United States, a movement has developed to defend the place of English and resist what is feared to be a shift to other languages in general or to Spanish in particular. English-only policies developed in the United States in special circumstances: in dealing with conquered peoples (Native Americans, Spanish in California and Puerto Rico, Hawaiians) and when there was a threat from linguistically identifiable immigrant groups (Germans in Pennsylvania and Wisconsin, for example). This was generalized in the early decades of the twentieth century, leading at first to an americanization movement, then to xenophobic English-only legislation in a number of states, and finally to a draconian law establishing immigration quotas. This had the effect of reducing the perceived threat of other-language-speaking minorities, at least until the 1960s, when action on behalf of the growing Spanish-speaking population led to federal support for bilingual education, presented originally as a method of teaching English to Spanish-speakers. It was two decades later that a movement emerged to correct what was perceived as a new threat to English.

US English Inc., founded in 1983 by US Senator Samuel Ichiye Hayakawa, claims to be the oldest of the organizations working to make English the official language of United States. In 1976, Hayakawa was elected US Senator from California, and served until 1983. During this period, he introduced an amendment to the Constitution to make English the official language, which was politely ignored. He founded US English after he left the Senate in order to continue this campaign. The philosophy of the organization is stated as follows: "US ENGLISH believes that the passage of English as the official language will help to expand opportunities for immigrants to learn and speak English, the single greatest empowering tool that immigrants must have to succeed."

Hayakawa's successor as head of the organization, which now claims 1.5 million members, was Mauro E. Mujica. It has been active in lobbying in Congress and in 1996 was successful in having the House of Representatives approve a Bill making English official; the Bill lapsed for want of Senate approval. In the meantime, however, it has managed to have similar laws adopted by over twenty states. These laws have not all stood up to court challenge. In March 2002, a superior court judge in Alaska held that the English-only initiative passed in 1998 violated the free-speech provision of the Alaska constitution. In the same month, a Bill was signed into law in Iowa making English official in that state. In April, the Oklahoma superior court ruled that a proposed statute to make English official was unconstitutional.

A second organization, English First, was founded in 1986 and claims to have 150,000 members. It lobbies in favor of English-only legislation and against Executive Order 13166 (see below p. 108) and various policies supporting bilingual education. A third organization, English for the Children, was formed in 1997 to work against bilingual education. Led by a Californian businessman, Ron Unz, it successfully lobbied in California in 1998 for Proposition 227 that banned bilingual education in the state. In the last two years, the organization has conducted similar campaigns, successfully in Arizona and in Colorado and most recently in Massachusetts. These three organizations see their task to be reversing what they see as a language policy that is encouraging shift from English to Spanish or other foreign languages.

The end of the Bilingual Education Act

Writing while the Bilingual Education Act was still alive, Marshall (1986) was aware of the growing threat to US cultural pluralism being posed by the supporters of the English Language Amendment. In a paper written before the Act expired, Garcia (2002) drew attention to the growth in numbers of such students, and made the prediction that in forty years, white majority students would in fact be a numerical minority in all public education. He pointed out that national funding of bilingual education under the 1994 re-authorization reached only 10 percent of US students with limited English proficiency. State programs continued to exist: a dozen states had mandated special educational programs for language-minority students, another dozen permitted such services. His major concern in the paper was how to obtain and pass on research knowledge that would contribute to these programs. His calm, scholarly approach was shared by many of the writers asked to comment on his article, but rejected abruptly by Crawford (2002b). Most research in bilingual education, Crawford (2002b: 93) complained, had been addressed to policy-makers in an attempt to help decide for or against existing policies. In spite of attempts to develop better models of education for linguistically diverse students, the whole issue was in fact now politicized. The bilingual movement, he felt, had failed to make an effective case. He ended pessimistically: bilingual education would come under increasing pressure, be marginalized, or turned into a "quick-exit remedial" program.

The end in fact came quietly. On January 8, 2002, Title VII of the Elementary and Secondary Education Act – also known as the Bilingual Education Act – expired. Congress took it peacefully, Crawford (2002c) reported in an "obituary." Conservative Republicans did not try to mandate English-only instruction and not a single member of the Hispanic caucus voted against the process. The English-teaching portion of the program was to be maintained in the No Child Left Behind Act, although a new paper by Crawford (2002d) has already analyzed some of the inadequacies of the new program.

The Bilingual Education Act was an intriguing manifestation of the complexity of US language policy. In some ways, it was a false dawn; in its name and in some aspects of its programming, it appeared to be offering not just a method for non-English-speakers to learn English, but also a program that was committed to the maintenance of minority languages, something far from the intention of those who instituted it. In practice, the programs developed were generally transitional, intended to provide a high-quality method of teaching English while continuing instruction in the student's home language, and the weight of research evidence – most recently, Thomas and Collier (2002) – supported this contention. But the profile of the program was too high: it was condemned not for what it actually did, but for its suggestion that it was an alternative to teaching English. While the United States may be ready to recognize the right of its citizens to continue to use their heritage languages in certain circumstances, it expects also that such citizens will acquire English. If the new programs for English-language learners are successful (and this admittedly is an optimistic view), the bilingual education program will not have interrupted US progress towards achieving language rights for its minority students.

LANGUAGE AS A CIVIL RIGHT, CONTINUED

The impact of Title VI of the Civil Rights Act continued in various spheres without regard to the Bilingual Education Act. The Office of Civil Rights was involved in regular activity to protect what it conceived as the language rights of citizens. A major development was when, on August 11, 2000, President Clinton signed Executive Order (EO) 13166, entitled "Improving access to services for persons with limited English proficiency." In 2000, just under 20 million US residents of the age of five would probably be classified in this way, about three-fifths of them being speakers of Spanish. The goal of the Order was "to improve access to federally conducted and federally assisted programs and activities for persons who, as a result of national origin, are limited in their English proficiency (LEP)," and so make sure that the programs did not discriminate on the basis of national origin in violation of Title VI of the Civil Rights Act of 1964. The order required every federal agency to prepare a plan to improve access, and every agency receiving federal financial assistance to develop appropriate guidelines. The Clinton Order was reaffirmed in October 2001 by the Bush Department of Justice, shortly after the failure of an attempt in the US House of Representatives earlier in the month to revoke the Order.

A campaign against the Order has been conducted largely by English First. Most of the objections deal with the cost of providing translation and translators, and many focus on the provision of hospital and medical services. Guidelines issued in October 2001 by the Department of Justice recognized the need of cost-effectiveness, and set out four "reasonableness" factors – the proportion of people involved, the frequency of contact with speakers of the particular language, the nature of the program and the resources available.

Some idea of the effect of the implementation of the Order can be gained from the preliminary report of the study conducted by the National Foreign Language Centre for the State of Maryland. Every county had clients with limited English proficiency; over 80 percent of state departments and over half of boards, commissions and independent agencies had clients with limited English proficiency. The most commonly encountered language was Spanish (about 60 percent), followed by Russian (24 percent) and Korean (22 percent); Vietnamese, Chinese and other Asian languages were also common. No more than 40 percent of public documents had a version available in any language besides English. A quarter of responding agencies have training and policies and procedures to overcome language barriers. Some areas and departments use minor children as interpreters.

Implemented even partially, the Executive Order could well be one of the major language-management decisions outside the education field. The fact that it is coming into force at exactly the same time that the Bilingual Education Act has been ended confirms the general argument presented in this chapter about the diversity and indeed ambivalence of US language policy. By the middle of 2002, most federal agencies had completed and published their plans for implementation.

The website of the Coordination and Review Section of the Civil Rights Division of the US Department of Justice, (http://www.usdoj.gov/crt/cor/13166.htm) provides details and links of the plans and guidance that have been developed under Executive Order 13166 for improving access to services for persons with limited English proficiency. The bureaucratic complexity is enormous, for the Order applies not just to federal agencies but also to all those organizations and agencies receiving financial aid through federal agencies.

By the middle of 2002, the agencies of the federal government responding to Executive Order 13166 had developed elaborate plans for their own agency and for the guidance of any agency receiving funds from the federal government to provide access to people who are not proficient in English.

Towards a comprehensive theory of language rights

Rodriguez (2001: 222) proposed a theory that could form the basis for "extending the accommodation of linguistic minorities to all spheres of civic life." She recognized the suspicion of bilingualism that has been common in American law, specifically in the acceptance of it as a reason for excluding jury members who could be expected to base their views on their understanding of the other-language testimony of a witness rather than on the official record of interpretation. She argued that existing US case law concerning language rights tended to be based narrowly on anti-discrimination law, underlying which was an assumption of the inferiority of languages other than English. In contrast to the prevailing view of the need for a lingua franca emphasizing unity and efficient communication, she presented a theory of "fluid civic identity" which accepted the multiple cultural and linguistic affiliations that a citizen might have. An assimilationist or integrationist policy was not suitable, she argued, for a nation with continuing waves of immigration. As the basis to dealing with this problem, she proposed the notion of accommodation, and suggested that the state needs to accommodate linguistic differences, just as it accommodates religious differences. In different spheres of life, this would need to be treated differently; in the workplace, for example, speakers of other languages should be protected against discrimination. In other spheres, the state should "take steps to preserve linguistic difference" (2001: 136).

This analysis by Rodriguez of the legal situation supports in general the picture that has emerged in this chapter. The courts generally recognize the need to avoid discrimination based on linguistic differences, but are not yet convinced that the maintenance of those differences is a state responsibility. Put somewhat differently, they generally agree that individuals and collectives have a right of access to the majority language and a right of access to civic services in spite of linguistic differences. But they do not agree that the state is obligated to maintain those differences.

We might perhaps extend the analogy of religion suggested by Rodriguez. It is a generally accepted human right to practice whatever religion one may choose, but the duty or obligation of religious practice devolves not on the state but on the individual. In the same way, the duty or obligation of maintaining a language might be considered to devolve on the individual.

LANGUAGE POLICY OR CIVIL RIGHTS: SUMMARY

Four principal factors have so far been presented as fundamental in determining the language policy of a nation: the sociolinguistic situation, the national ideology, the existence of English as a world language and notions of language rights. In its language practices, the United States has been and remains multilingual, with bilingualism and language shift the common fate of immigrant languages and multilingualism maintained by new immigration. The common language belief system started off pluralistic and multilingual, went through an anti-immigrant and isolationist monolingual phase starting in the late nineteenth century and continuing until the end of the Second World War, and is now in strong tension between pluralistic multilingualism on the one hand and resistance to Spanish monolingualism on the other. For the United States, as for other English-speaking nations, the third factor has the obvious effect of discouraging any effort to teach languages other than English. If everyone wants to learn it, why waste time on other languages? The rights issue is increasingly important. While language management was generally left to the states, whose policies reflected national beliefs, starting in 1962, the widespread implementation of Title VI of the Civil Rights Act, providing access to federally provided and funded services for persons with limited English proficiency, bolstered for a while by the Bilingual Education Act and theoretically continued in the English Language Learner programs of recent educational law, has been working to defend the language rights of those in the United States who do not speak English.

In sum, United States language policy continues to be complex and difficult to disentangle. Language practices, as long as immigration (legal and illegal) continues, will remain English dominant, with large pockets of multilingualism. Language beliefs, forming not a simple consistent ideology but rather the contradictory ideas expected in a democracy, hold that everybody should learn English, but also that all remain free to learn and use whatever other language they choose. Language management remains uncentralized, the exception being civil rights driven programs to assure access to education and federal services for all.

There is no question about the dominance of English. There are fears about the rapid increase in the numbers of speakers of other languages, fears that can be tapped locally by political pressures to bolster the English language. The failure to date of both the English Only movement and of what was misinterpreted as a bilingual education program aiming to replace English shows the continued balanced tension between beliefs. Educational language management (like judgments as to what constitutes obscene language) is constitutionally left to state and local decisions, but constrained by a rights-based requirement for teaching English to those who do not know it. The federal government (its defense and intelligence communities at least) has developed a strong policy aimed to build up national foreign-language capacity, but remains unwilling or unable to do the same in the educational system. Since 1964, the Civil Rights Act has been the main driving force to develop programs working against language discrimination. In the last year or two, this has grown into one of the most elaborate programs in the world for providing access to government services for those with limited proficiency in English.

Does this constitute a national language policy? It is true that US policy is not centrally directed and consistently aimed at a single purpose. In this respect, the United States is quite different from France and from many of the other countries discussed in this book. Like US economic policy or international policy, US language policy is under constant pressure from the differences of beliefs that have free rein in a democracy, but it is still able to respond, if clumsily, to continuing changes in the sociolinguistic situation.

8 Language rights

THE RIGHTS OF LINGUISTIC MINORITIES

With all its complexity, the language policy of the United States revealed an overarching monolingualism (the hegemony of a single national if not official language), with the large number of speakers of minority languages protected by language rights, or more precisely, by the application of civil rights to language, which emerged largely from the interpretation of courts, legislators and bureaucrats of constitutionally protected civil rights for minorities, as part of the understanding of the fourteenth Amendment and Title VI of the Civil Rights Act.

Many countries of the world have a similar "monolingual but . . ." policy. They may name in their constitution or in their laws a single national or official language, but then modify the intolerance by proclaiming protection for one or more minority languages. Even in France, there are occasional signs of attention to the rights of speakers of previously ignored regional languages. This chapter will trace the development and current state of minority language rights, a common factor in much contemporary discussion of language policy.

There are difficulties with the term "minority". The numerical implication of the term is not always appropriate, the relationship in fact generally being superordinate or subordinate status (Paulston 1998). Some ethnic minorities, Paulston pointed out, can be dominant (e.g. English-speakers in South Africa), and others (e.g. Christians in Lebanon) are not primarily linguistically different. The term must therefore be used with care. Two dimensions besides relative power seem important: whether the minority is legally recognized or not, and whether it is indigenous or immigrant.

Nor is the term language rights clear. Paulston (1997: 75) complained that three terms are used regularly in the literature without any attempt to differentiate or define them: language rights, linguistic rights and linguistic human rights. There is disagreement as to whether language rights are or should be distinct from or simply derived from other civil and human rights. There is also dispute over the distinctions to be made between the rights of an individual (the right, for instance, to choose which language to speak in private or inside one's own community) and the collective rights of a language community (the right to use and work to preserve its language). Finally, there is a difference of opinion as to where the responsibility for language maintenance resides – with the speakers of the language or with the nation state in which they live.

THE ORIGIN OF LINGUISTIC RIGHTS

In a working paper written for the UN Sub-Committee on the rights of minorities, Varennes (1997) noted that international treaties dealing with language are not new. He cited a 1516 treaty between France and the Helvetic state that gave benefits to Swiss who spoke only German, the 1815 Act of the Congress of Vienna which permitted the use of Polish in some parts of the Austro-Hungarian empire and an 1881 treaty protecting the Turkish language in Greece. Ruiz Vieytez (2001) added protection of some religious minorities as a result of the Congress of Westphalia in 1648 and the treaty of Oliva in 1660 which incorporated Roman Catholic communities in eastern Livonia into Sweden.

   The notion of linguistic minority had little meaning in the medieval period, when peasants spoke local dialects and members of the ruling classes were often intermarried and consequently plurilingual (Wright 2001). The Church, too, was international, in its use of Latin as lingua franca. Thus, the earliest examples are during the Renaissance, with the first stirrings of nationalism. Stable national borders started to develop in the sixteenth century, and slowly centrally governed nations started to raise the status of one language or variety, usually that of the region where the monarch lived, and so produce the likelihood of linguistic minorities. The Reformation had an important effect, with the development of national Churches and the permitting or encouragement of religious use of the national vernacular. There developed two opposing tendencies: one that treated every Christian language equally, and a second (illustrated by the Ordonnance de Villers-Cottêrets favoring French in 1539 and the Act of Union of England and Wales favoring English over Welsh in 1536) for a growing tendency to prefer one specific national language to all others.

   By the nineteenth century, following the French Revolution's proclamation of political and linguistic nationality (see p. 65 above), and confirmed by the German concept of nation as a cultural reality, belonging to a linguistic minority was commonly a cause for peripheralization, exclusion or, at best, forced assimilation. Compulsory education and universal military service became techniques for standardizing the national language. In spite of this tendency, and in opposition to it, legislation that provided support for certain kinds of linguistic diversity started to appear. But the principal argument for the language rights of powerless autochthonous groups was fairness: deriving from the belief in the civil or human rights of all individuals within a society, it led to anti-discrimination activity as a first step, and equal opportunity programs at a higher stage. The need to preserve linguistic diversity emerged as a rationale only later (Grin 1995: 34).

A second phase of international recognition of protection for minorities in treaties dealing with national minorities started with Serbian autonomy in the Treaty of Bucharest (1812), recognition of Polish populations in various clauses of treaties signed at the Congress of Vienna (1814) and continued with the treaty at the end of the Russo-Turkish war in 1829 and treaties signed in 1856 at Paris, 1878 at Berlin and 1881 at Constantinople (Ruiz Vieytez 2001). By the end of nineteenth century, there was ample precedent for arguing for the protection of ethnic and linguistic minorities. In the reorganization of some of the world that followed the end of the First World War, the rights of linguistic minorities played a role.

Language rights between the world wars

The peace treaties signed after the First World War with protection for selected minorities in defeated enemy countries or in new states carved out of defeated empires in Central and Eastern Europe and the Middle East, constituted, Ruiz Vieytez said, a third phase of development of language rights. The Treaty of Versailles and the League of Nations included provisions for rights for linguistic minorities in treaties imposed upon Austria, Hungary, Bulgarian and Turkey and in setting up new nations in Europe and the Middle East. Basic to them all was provision of equality for individual members of linguistic minorities; this included a means to preserve the special characteristics of minorities, including their language. Any state signing the treaties agreed that all its nationals, including members of minority groups, should be free to use any language in private, in business, in religion, in the press or any publications or at public meetings. The rights also included access to state organs. Appropriate interpreting and translation should be provided whenever necessary in court proceedings. In those towns and districts where there was a sufficient proportion of nationals with a mother tongue different from the official language, their children should be permitted to receive primary education through the medium of their mother tongue, provided at the same time that the learning of the official language could be made obligatory.

The various treaties setting up and recognizing nation states in the Balkans after the First World War called for equality for all racial, linguistic and religious minorities. This included a right for such minorities to establish their own institutions and their own mother-tongue education systems. However, Poulton (1998) observed, these paper provisions were often not implemented. In Greece, the government determined in 1925 that its Slav minorities were ethnically Greek and began a campaign of assimilation and population exchange. In Latvia, independent in 1918 and busily engaged in re-establishing the status of Latvian which had long been subordinated to German and Russian, there was only limited recognition of minority languages. Education, however, was offered in seven languages in some state elementary and secondary schools (Druviete 1998).

In the first half of the twentieth century, then, growing international recognition of limited language rights for minority populations was starting to appear in the legislation and constitutions of nation states. While largely limited to the territory of defeated enemy states, and not necessarily effective, these treaties and laws did provide important models for the legal expression of language rights.

One nation did establish its own policy of language rights for minorities. This was the Soviet Union, where there was recognition under Lenin of the right of "self-determination of all nations" as laid down in the 1896 International Socialist Congress of London (Lewis 1972: 67). Soviet language policy was designed to teach literacy and socialism in the fastest practical way, through the ethnic languages, with the consequent nationalism serving as a first step to desired socialist internationalism. Many national groups were told in 1917 that their languages, like other aspects of their national and cultural institutions, were "inviolable." Primary schools in the national languages were established in the 1920s, and during this ten-year phase, there was support for the language rights of minorities. Martin (2002) judged this the most ambitious affirmative action program that any state had so far tried to implement. It was, he says, collective and territorial rather than individual, and was implemented by setting up small ethnic administrative units. It was not a continuation of Czarist russification activities, because Russian children in the Ukraine were required to attend Ukrainian-language schools and in Turkestan and Kazakhstan, Russian settlers were expelled or subordinated. Russian bitterness against the affirmative action program emerged, and came to a head during the collectivization of agriculture in the 1930s and the grain crisis in December 1932. Stalin was angered at the resistance to collectivization in the Ukraine, which he associated with the nationalism encouraged by indigenization (*korenizatsiia*). Soon after, there were changes in policy: ethnic village Soviets were abolished, Russian-language teaching in schools was upgraded, ethnic units in the army were cut out and national republics were required to fit into the Soviet five-year plan. Martin was not convinced that this was russification (Russians were not given their own Communist party or capital city or Academy of Sciences); rather, he considered it sovietization, most conveniently expressed in Russian as the lingua franca.

The Leninist policy of indigenization started to be reversed in the 1930s under Stalin, but the Soviet Constitution kept its clauses on language rights. Some believe that Stalin's reversal of support for selected national ethnic languages was simply a continuation of Czarist russification, carried out more brutally and violently. Rannut (1995) described Stalin's policy in these terms, and showed how Estonia suffered through forced deportation of Estonians, organized immigration of non-Estonians, imposition of Russian language in many domains and the various other methods of enforcing language and ethnic policy available to a totalitarian state. At the same time, he did note that the Estonian Academy of Science continued in this period to carry out terminological development, providing some evidence of the continued constitutional principle of language equality. Ozolins (1996), too, was critical of Soviet policy, pointing out the bitter resentment that it produced among the minority languages and the way it swept under the surface the ethnic and national tensions that have re-emerged since the collapse of the totalitarian central power that held Soviet policy in place.

Other countries provided constitutional protection for minority languages during this period between the world wars: as Finland developed the status of Finnish, it continued to protect Swedish; Ireland developed Irish alongside English, Belgium worked out a compromise to protect French and Flemish and pre-Franco Spain recognized regional languages.

Linguistic rights in the second half of the twentieth century – international bodies

These steps taken in the first half of the twentieth century were developed and extended in the second half in a number of initiatives under the auspices of the United Nations and various regional organizations.

The United Nations Charter adopted in 1945 proclaimed respect for human rights and fundamental freedoms, equality and absence of discrimination. In 1948, the Universal Declaration of Human Rights (article 2/1) included language as one of the criteria that might not be used for discrimination. In 1957, International Labor Organization Convention no. 107 concerning the protection of indigenous and other tribal populations granted the children of such groups the right to basic education (reading and writing) in their mother tongue (or in the language most commonly used), "progressive transition" from the vernacular to the official language and measures to preserve the vernacular languages. The 1960 UNESCO Convention against Discrimination in Education allowed for the establishment of voluntarily separate educational systems offering education in accordance with the wishes of the pupils' parents, including the use of their own language, provided that this did not prevent members of the minorities learning the culture and language of the community as a whole.

The 1966 International Covenant on Civil and Political Rights included a number of specific language rights. Article 14 dealt with the administration of justice. Those charged with crimes were entitled to have the charge explained in a language they knew; any defendant in a court case was entitled to the free use of an interpreter. This provision of the Covenant, which came into force in 1976, appears to be echoed in a number of constitutions adopted about that time: those of Antigua and Barbuda (1981), Bahamas (1973), Barbados (1966), Belize (1981), Dominica (1978), Guyana (1980), Jamaica (1962), Nauru (1965–72), St. Kitts and Nevis (1983), St. Lucia (1978), St. Vincent and the Grenadines (1979), Solomons Islands (1978) and Tuvalu (1987). In most of these countries, it is the only language provision in the constitution, but in some it is accompanied by some language requirement for election to public office or naturalization. The provision also occurs in a number of constitutions adopted or revised in the 1990s.

An international covenant or convention is fundamentally a treaty between sovereign nation states. It needs to go through a number of stages. After preliminary discussion and lobbying (which may take many years) by proponents of the covenant, it is brought to a vote before an appropriate international body, with a date set (usually several years later) for it to come into force. As a treaty, it applies only to those member states that sign it (a preliminary step) and then ratify it. Thus, the fact that a convention passes the General Assembly of United Nations does not mean that all member states will automatically implement its provisions. We will look a little later at gaps between passage and implementation.

These concerns for language rights in the period after the Second World War were focused on individual rights rather than on the collective rights of linguistic minorities, as a result, Ruiz Vieytez (2001) explained, of aversion to the national and nationalistic feelings which had led to atrocities during the war and which resulted in the Holocaust. Whereas in 1920 new borders had been established, in 1945 populations were moved to provide for greater national homogeneity (the objection to what is now called ethnic cleansing developed only half a century later) and while concern for basic human rights and dignity was central, minority issues, with some exceptions, were considered less important.

Paulston (1997) noted the novelty of linguistic rights. While there were earlier references to language rights, the term linguistic rights starts to appear in book titles after 1979, and linguistic human rights in the 1990s. There are, she suggested, two main camps writing about the topic. One camp consists of (often) historians or lawyers who write descriptive or historical accounts. The other camp she labels as "exhortatory – at times quite wildly so," linguists and language-policy scholars advocating the use of collective linguistic rights to bring about some change that they personally support.

The efforts have not been without effect. Starting about 1990, an increasing number of international conventions and treaties have been asserting individual linguistic rights and the rights of linguistic minorities. In 1989, the International Labor Organization Convention no. 169 refined and clarified the rights of indigenous peoples. In the same year, the United Nations adopted the Convention on the Rights of the Child, which specifically dealt with "the linguistic needs of the child who belongs to a minority group or is indigenous." In 1990, the United Nations adopted an International Convention on the Protection of the Rights of all Migrant Workers and Members of their Families that included language rights. In 1992, the United Nations Commission on Human Rights adopted a Declaration on the Rights of Persons belonging to National or Ethnic, Religious and Linguistic Minorities, which included "whenever possible" state measures to enable minorities to learn or have instruction in their mother tongue. In 1993, a Draft Declaration on the Rights of Indigenous Peoples, which included the right to establish and control institutions providing education in the language of the indigenous people, was not adopted because of controversy over clauses concerning self-determination and land rights.

This last example should help remind us that linguistic rights are, to a large extent, not distinct from other human rights. Most linguistic rights, Varennes (2001) argues, are derivable from general individual human rights, namely the principles of non-discrimination and freedom of expression. These are straightforward enough when applied to the individual citizen. What adds complexity has been the recent extension of these rights to minority groups and, even more controversially, to the increasingly large migrant communities appearing in so many countries. The problem arises when one moves from the rights of an individual to use his or her own language to the requirement that the state both use and support the use of the minority language. Varennes believes that most rights of members of minorities to use their own languages in their private lives – in selecting names, in private conversations even in public areas, in private correspondence or business, in the establishment of private schools teaching in the language – are derived from individual human rights and are not special to minorities. Paulston (1997: 76) argued that the term "linguistic human rights," with its built-in tautology – how can linguistic not be human? – is basically an effort to reframe claims for language rights under the protection of accepted human rights. The leading proponents of this approach, she said, are Tove Skutnabb-Kangas and Robert Phillipson.

The rights associated with a fair trial mentioned earlier are probably the most basic of those requiring the state to make use of a minority language. It is now widely accepted also, as part of the European standards, and as expressed in two Council of Europe treaties – the Framework Convention on the Protection of National Minorities and the European Charter for Regional or Minority Languages – that public authorities have an obligation to provide other services in minority languages when justified by numbers and geographic concentration. A figure commonly used is 20 percent of the population of the district.

One of the more radical positions on minority rights is article 27 of the United Nations International Covenant on Civil and Political Rights, written in 1966 and in force where ratified ten years later. Skutnabb-Kangas (2002: 183) quoted it as follows:

> In those states in which ethnic, religious or linguistic minorities exist, persons belonging to such minorities shall not be denied the right, in community with other members of their group, to enjoy their own culture, to profess and practice their own religion, or to use their own language.

Originally, this was assumed not to apply to immigrants or other groups unless they had been recognized as minorities by the state, and only to provide protection against discrimination. In 1994, however, the United Nations Human Rights committee issued a General

Comment which reinterpreted article 27 as protecting all individuals in the state, including immigrants and refugees, as taking away from the state the possibility of deciding which minorities to recognize, and as imposing positive obligations on the state.

We have here, in this reinterpretation, a strong form of linguistic rights. Skutnabb-Kangas holds that the Hague recommendations specify positive obligations on the state: the provision of conditions in which parents can choose pre-school and kindergarten teaching in the child's language; conditions in which the primary curriculum can also be taught in the minority language, with the introduction of teaching in the state language by bilingual teachers; the continuation of some teaching in the minority language at the secondary level; and the provision of appropriate teacher training. It should be noted that even this strong statement is expressed somewhat weakly. States are not required to pay for these programs, but to "create conditions" in which they can exist. Revolutionary though the General Comment may seem, it does not go beyond the finding in 1923, by the US Supreme Court, that while the states could require the use of English as a medium of instruction in tax-supported schools, they could not do this for private schools.

The European Union and the European Community

The right to have a minority language used by public authorities where reasonable is now included in documents of the European Union (as part of the criteria for the admission of new states) and of the United Nations. At the same time, it remains cautiously limited: there must be sufficient speakers of the language, and it must not be too difficult for public officials to use the language. The European Court of Human Rights in 1967 held that while denial of education in a minority language could be discriminatory, the policy of regionalization being followed in Belgium was not unreasonable.

Nic Shuibhne (2001) believed that one should not expect much more from the European Union. The Union accepts limitations even as concerns the official languages of member states; neither Irish nor Letzeburgesch is afforded full rights. Some support for selected European minority languages is provided by the European Bureau for Lesser Used Languages, which has no official or working status. The European Parliament passed a number of non-binding resolutions in the 1980s calling for the protection of minority languages and has stressed the important role of minority languages in the field of culture. Implementation of these resolutions requires, Nic Shuibhne (2001) has pointed out, formally ratified Treaty provisions. These have tended to appear in the context of cultural programs which include references to the position of "Europe's small cultures and less widely-spoken languages." All of this constitutes European Union support for multilingualism, but not specific implementation of linguistic minority rights.

A number of legal cases in the European Court of Justice concern language matters. In 1985, the Court recognized the need to protect the linguistic rights and privileges of individuals in a German-speaking municipality in Belgium. A narrower ruling noted that Dutch, French and German were not in fact classified as minority languages in Belgium. A 1989 case concerning requirement for fluency in Irish for certain teaching positions in Ireland was also unclear because of the non-minority status of Irish. More recent decisions appear to confirm that language arrangements are a matter for internal language policy, providing that some language rights must be granted to nationals of another European Community member state. Nic Shuibhne (2001) concluded, "The extent to which the European Community can influence minority language rights protection within its Member States is a more problematic concept."

In the United States, as the last chapter showed, individual civil rights have been the basis for continuing efforts to improve access for non-speakers of English to government services. At the same time, US policy appears to be reluctant to provide specifically, bilingual education) to minorities. This tension can be traced also in the care with which the original members of the European Community selected and defined the languages that they recognized as minority or regional, their resistance to including recognition of migrant languages and the controversies over the application of the principle in the states selecting admission.

Some historically and perhaps ideologically monolingual states have been persuaded, or have agreed, to recognize in their constitution the linguistic rights of specific selected minority or indigenous groups. The existence of a constitutional provision or of a law does not guarantee implementation. Looking more closely, one quickly finds problems: the treatment of Russian speakers in some former Soviet republics, the treatment of Roma (I will use this term for gypsies) and the selection of recognized minorities in Europe, the degree of support for minority language programs everywhere, the reluctance to recognize immigrant languages. But the European conventions are an important first step, providing possible access for the minority group to legal or political remedies long denied them by national governments.

One important treaty doing this is the European Charter for Regional or Minority Languages, adopted by the Council of Europe in November

1992. The preamble to the Charter stresses a number of "ideals and principles." These include "the protection of the historical regional or minority languages of Europe," "the right to use regional or minority language in private and public life," "the value of interculturalism and multilingualism," provided, of course, that the protection and encouragement of these languages "should not be to the detriment of the official languages and the need to learn them."

The definition of regional or minority languages appeared precise but in fact left a great deal of room for maneuvering. They were to be languages traditionally used within a given territory of the state by nationals of that state, forming a group numerically smaller than the rest of the state's population, and different from the official language of a state. They did not include either dialects of the official language of the state or the languages of migrants. At the time of ratification, each member state was required to specify to which languages it would apply the Charter. Sweden, for example, which signed and ratified the Charter in 2000, declared that it applied to three regional or minority languages: Sami, Meänkieli (Tomedal Finnish) and Finnish. According to *Ethnologue*, the number of speakers of these varieties are respectively 6,000, 60–80,000, and 200,000. The Swedish declaration also lists two non-territorial languages, Romani Chib and Yiddish. *Ethnologue* estimates 25,000 speakers of Roma, but does not list Yiddish as spoken in Sweden. One significant variety listed in *Ethnologue* is noticeably missing from the recognized minority languages. It is Scanian (sometimes spelt Skanian), estimated by *Ethnologue* to have 1.5 million speakers. In 1995, a Scanian ethnic organization asked to be included in the European list of minority languages, but was told by the Swedish government committee responsible that their variety was a dialect and therefore excluded.

Under the Charter, languages may be either territorial (when the number of people living in the region justifies adopting relevant language policies) or non-territorial. As well as designating languages, member states are required by the Charter to make clear which provisions apply to which language. Part II provisions are more general, while part III details education at the various levels, judicial arrangements, administration and public services, media, cultural activities and facilities, economic and social life and transfrontier exchanges. Each state must select thirty-five items from part III, including three items concerning education and cultural activities and at least one from each of the other headings.

When one looks at the details provided by a number of the ratifying states, the possibilities of choice are clearly very large. Take education:

the state may decide to offer ("without prejudice to the teaching of
the official language(s) of the State") pre-school education in the language, or "a substantial part" of pre-school education, or to offer pre-
school education "at least to those pupils whose families so request
and whose number is considered sufficient." If the state has "no direct
competence" in pre-school education, it could offer to "favor and/or
encourage" one of these measures. The paragraphs in the Charter that
follow include the same provisions for primary, secondary, technical
and vocational, university and other higher education and adult and
continuing education.

The Charter thus does not present a single blueprint for dealing with
regional or minority languages, but allows individual states to develop
their own model as they see fit. In spite of this flexibility and continued
respect for national sovereignty, the signing and ratifying the Charter
by member states has been very slow. By August 2002, ten years after
the Charter was approved, only sixteen member states of the Council
of Europe (out of fourty-four) had ratified the Charter; another thirteen
had signed it but had not taken the final step of ratification. Liechtenstein was an early ratifier, happily declaring that the territory of
the principality had no regional or minority languages. France, which
signed in 1999, stated that when ratified (which has not yet happened)
the Charter would not affect the mandatory use of French by public-
law corporations and private individuals dealing with public services,
and that teaching of regional or minority languages would be optional
and would not remove pupils from the rights and obligations of all
others in public education. The Netherlands, ratifying the Charter in
1998, said that part III would apply only to Frisian in Friesland, while
part II general principles would apply to the Lower Saxon languages,
Yiddish, Limburgish and Romani. The United Kingdom, ratifying in
2001, declared it would apply part III to Welsh, Scottish Gaelic and
Irish, and part II to Scots and Ulster Scots. Among the more interesting countries who have not yet ratified, one notices Belgium, Estonia,
Georgia, Greece, Ireland, Italy, Latvia, Lithuania, Moldova, Poland, Portugal, Romania, Russia, Turkey and the Ukraine. The situation will no
doubt change with the expansion of the European Union, which is
requiring acceptance of the Charter as part of the conditions set for
new members. At the end of October 2002, the Ukrainian government
once again introduced a Bill to ratify the Treaty (a 1999 ratification
was ruled unconstitutional by the Constitutional Court), but there
was expected to be opposition still.

Recognizing the complexity of language practices in Europe, the
Council nurtured an ideological consensus for the principle of

multilingualism. It then carefully designed a system of language management that put the full onus on the independent member states to decide how much of the principle to apply to a selected group of their own languages. The slow pace of implementation shows that even this cautious approach is still challenging the nationalist ideology and traditional language policy of the member states. As Varennes (2001) complained, individuals have no way to appeal against the form or implementation of the Charter. He saw it therefore as weaker than the various international conventions based on human rights, and argued that only if linguistic minority rights are seen as derived from and part of general human rights will there be an opportunity for wider application.

The Organization for Security and Cooperation in Europe

There is another approach. The Organization for Security and Cooperation in Europe is primarily a security organization, and its interest in national and linguistic minorities comes from the perspective of conflict prevention (Holt and Packer 2001). All fifty-five participating states voluntarily agreed that human rights are of legitimate concern and are not exclusively their internal affair. The core of the activities of the organization are missions, assistance groups and field offices in individual countries with conflict, such as Albania, Bosnia and Herzegovina, Croatia, the Federal Republic of Yugoslavia, Kosovo, Estonia, Latvia, Belarus and at least a dozen other Eastern European places in 2001. Among its institutions are a Permanent Council and a Forum for Security Cooperation that meet weekly, annual summits or ministerial councils, an Office for Democratic Institutions and Human Rights, and a Court of Conciliation and Arbitration. In 1992, the Organization established a High Commissioner on National Minorities to seek "early resolution of ethnic tensions that might endanger peace, stability or friendly relations between OSCE participating States." Acting independently, with a budget floating about 1 percent of the total for OSCE, the High Commissioner has made recommendations to fourteen countries. In 1996, for example, the Commissioner corresponded with the government of Estonia on the teaching of Estonian, the use of language tests and the rights of non-citizens. In addition, the High Commissioner has issued four general recommendations, one concerning discrimination against Roma, the Hague recommendations on education rights of national minorities (1996), the Oslo recommendations on the linguistic rights of national minorities (1998) and the Lund recommendations on the effective participation of national minorities in public life. Each of these includes language.

The Hague recommendations regarding the Education Rights of National Minorities (High Commissioner on National Minorities 1996) were developed by a group of experts. They stated that members of national minorities should be able to develop their mother tongue to the fullest possible extent while at the same time acquiring the state language, asserted the right of minorities to establish their own private educational systems, called ideally for primary school children to be taught in the minority language, but if not, for teaching of the minority language and of the state language at this stage. In secondary school, some subjects should be taught in the minority language, preferably by bilingual teachers. There should be a gradual increase in the proportion of subjects taught in the state language. Whenever there is a demand, vocational and technical education and even tertiary programs should also be offered in the minority language. General programs should include teaching about minority cultures and offer the opportunity to learn the minority language. Members of the minority groups should be involved in developing curriculum.

The Oslo recommendations (High Commissioner on National Minorities 1998) deal with the right of minorities to use their own language in choosing names, in practicing religion, in setting up organizations, in the media and in private business enterprises. They recognize the right of access to administrative and public services in the minority language in regions where there are enough speakers. They support access in the language to independent national organizations like human rights commissions and ombudsmen, the right to use one's own language in the judicial process and the requirement for penal institutions to have staff able to address prisoners in their own language.

The implementation of the Oslo and Hague recommendations is up to the member states, but it is encouraged by the work of the High Commissioner. A report (High Commissioner on National Minorities 1999) admitted that these recommendations were not generally followed.

There have been, Holt and Packer reported, a number of specific cases in which language-related issues have been treated by the Organization and the High Commissioner. Basically, the linguistic rights of minority persons have turned out to be among the most common causes of dispute in a number of member states. This relates to the important role that language plays in collective cultural identity, especially in Europe. "Inadequate opportunities to learn or use one's own language in public or private" is seen as a threat to identity. Language policy also affects social integration and access to public goods.

There has been particular tension in the newly independent states of the former Soviet Union, as a consequence of the effort in many of these states to restore the titular state language to primacy. Some constitutions recognize minority languages: Georgia allows for the use of Abkhazian in the appropriate region; Tajikistan recognizes Tajik, Russian and Uzbek; and Uzbekistan and Ukraine have even more liberal approaches. The constitutional clauses and legislation are not always fully implemented. The High Commissioner was involved in Romania in 1996 with the fears of the Hungarian minority and was concerned with language laws in Slovakia and Kazakhstan. In basic documents and cautious interventions, the High Commissioner is working actively for the reduction of tension through the implementation of language rights in its member states.

What is intriguing to note is that while OSCE uses the rhetoric of human rights, its underlying motivation (and the justification for its existence) is to reduce tension in multilingual societies and to avoid conflict. The charge to the High Commissioner was to deal with national minority issues that might develop into conflict. The first High Commissioner found that language issues were often of great importance in many of the states within the area, and that minority status was regularly signaled by language. The implementation of language rights, he believed, would reduce the potential for conflict.

ADVOCATING LINGUISTIC HUMAN RIGHTS

The documents cited so far have all been under the authority of regional and international organizations, and have taken into account the need for acceptance by independent nation states. Just as any attempt to establish a national educational policy for the United States founders on the constitutional division of powers between the states and the federal government, so any effort to establish a single notion of language rights by European supra-national organizations or the United Nations is ultimately constrained by unwillingness or inability to force compliance by independent nations. Continued respect for national sovereignty serves as a serious check on the effort to impose restrictions on locally developed policies. Thus, in general, the language rights that have been accepted as suitable for international treaties and conventions are limited to protecting the rights of citizens to make their own choices about language use. Because of their acceptance of the sovereignty of nation states, they aim to mitigate but not prevent the pressures of pragmatic and nationalistic forces that are leading to shift to national languages. They are generally satisfied, it would seem, with territorially restricted transitional bilingualism.

This position must be frustrating to the advocates of absolute linguistic human rights, who base their argument on an imperative to maintain linguistic diversity. It is, of course, relatively easy for them to express their positions in published books and articles, and as Paulston (1997) remarked, many of the scholars writing in the field spend at least as much time on advocacy as they do on scholarly analysis, choosing what they label "critical and post-modern" approaches rather than "positivist structural" frameworks. But scholarly publication rarely leads to changes in public policy.

There is, however, a new framework available, the non-governmental organization, privately or publicly formed interest or activist groups, with complex and non-transparent membership or sponsorship. Just as in the field of economic and ecological policy, so in the field of language policy such groups, free from the constraints of political responsibility, are starting to provide initiatives in supporting the rights of selected minority groups and endangered languages. While perhaps they are stronger on rhetoric than implementation, they help set idealized goals for a better world.

The argument for the strongest form of language rights derives from belief in the critical importance of maintaining linguistic diversity. This argument, presented by linguists (language conservationists) rather than by civil libertarians or the spokesman for individual ethnic languages (who are usually more concerned to stress the individual value of their own language than the universal value of all), usually falls under five heads. Crystal (2000: 32ff.), for instance, presented five answers to the question: "Why should we care if the language dies?" The first answer was the widely accepted proposition that ecological diversity, in languages as well as in biosystems, is good. Damage to any element in an ecosystem can be harmful to other elements, and provided one accepts the analogy between language and living organisms, it is important to preserve every one. Of course, if one agrees that there is uncertainty about what aspect of biodiversity is to be preserved, and no clear evidence for the application of the principle to maintaining languages, then this argument falls down. Genetic diversity is at the base of evolution, and so linguistic diversity should be maintained, especially as it preserves the inherited knowledge of humankind. Crystal adds four related reasons: languages represent identity; they are repositories of history; they are individually "a unique encapsulation and interpretation of human existence" (p. 44) and together make up the sum of human knowledge; and, finally, they are interesting in themselves. Grin (1995: 34) himself preferred the argument for maintaining variety to the argument for fairness, because it avoids the "thorny model and political issues of legitimacy" of any single language and because it appears to offer benefit to all and not just linguistic minorities themselves.

One of the earliest attempts to develop acceptance of a strong version of linguistic human rights dates back to the establishment of the United Nations. There was an effort, Skutnabb-Kangas (2002) reported, in 1948, to widen the scope of the United Nations Convention by adding an extra article which included under genocide any prohibition of the use of the language of a minority group. The proposal was voted down. The Convention making genocide a crime was passed by the United Nations on December 1948, to come into effect in January 1951. Perusal of the reservations and objections to the Convention makes clear that the ratifying nations were far from unanimous in their acceptance of these definitions or of the proposed methods of implementing and enforcing the Convention. Nor do the actions of the world since the Convention came into force show any clear consensus on how to treat continuing cases of ethnic massacre. With all its difficulties over the Convention in its wider sense, it seems clear why the proposal to add "linguistic genocide" failed.

But efforts to obtain stronger statements continue. One was developed by a group of experts and approved and a meeting in Barcelona in 1966 attended by 220 people. The Universal Declaration of Linguistic Rights starts by noting the established tendency of most nations to discourage diversity, the damaging effect of globalization on language communities, and the "economist growth model" encouraged by transnational organizations and leading to social, economic and linguistic inequality. Any community, recognized or not, on its own territory or dispersed from it, that has a common language is a linguistic community, with full individual and collective rights. Nomads are also covered. So, too, are linguistic groups such as immigrants and refugees residing outside their original territory. The document recognizes collective linguistic rights to education, cultural services, media and access to government bodies and socioeconomic institutions. Assimilation should not be forced. All languages should have equal rights. The document calls for international funding for implementation, a system or enforcing rights and the creation of a council of languages within the United Nations and a World Commission on Linguistic Rights.

Another recent regional statement is the Declaration in African Languages and Literatures, accepted at a conference in Asmara, Eritrea, in January 2000. It represented a now common genre of resolutions, Blommaert (2001) claimed, presented at African meetings and workshops on language calling for strengthening local linguistic resources and fighting colonialism and its heritage. The Declaration says that African languages must speak for the continent and be recognized as the basis for future empowerment. Their diversity is an instrument of African unity. "All African children have the unalienable right to attend school and learn in their mother tongues." African languages must be used in science and technology and they are vital for democracy. Their gender bias must be overcome.

The enormous gap between idealized proposals like these and the much more pragmatic statements of rights in ratified international agreements and internal national policies, the latter still far removed from implemented policy, sets a major challenge. Without for a moment denigrating the value of respect for linguistic diversity, one wonders if the ultimate effect of a policy that attempted to apply these universal principles would not in fact simply be to enhance the development of the demand for monolingualism. Commenting on the problems of a language policy for Europe, Wright (2001) suspects that because of the great advantage bestowed on the speakers of any language selected as a lingua franca, an official decision is unlikely, leading to the probable unplanned acceptance of English. Full implementation of collective language rights often conflicts with individual linguistic rights: the preservation of a language often entails forcing individuals to learn or use it.

The derivation of the right to use one's own language, like the analogous right to maintain one's own religion, from civil or human rights is not difficult. But many of the advocates of linguistic rights go further, imposing on the state the obligation to maintain minority languages as part of its obligations to maintain linguistic diversity. Disagreeing with Nettle (1999), whose proposed unified theory of linguistic diversity showed it to result from individual human behavior motivated by economic considerations, they seem to argue that the loss of diversity is a correctable result of language management. But as John Trim (personal communication) remarks, the maintenance of a language by its speakers is as much a duty of the speakers as their right. While I may expect the state to recognize my right to practice a religion or speak a language, I do not expect the state to oblige me to carry out my religious duties or to continue to speak the language I happened to learn from my parents. Making it possible to speak a language of choice is a reasonable expectation of a state that respects civil and human rights. But so far, it is generally accepted that the responsibility to speak and so maintain the language falls on the individual speaker (and the collective speakers), not the state.

The decision of many African countries to continue to use colonial languages was based on the search for an ethnically neutral language (Blommaert 2001). Multilingualism was seen as favoring multiethnicity and so working against desired national unity; at the same time, selecting a single local language as national was feared as likely to produce a different kind of inequality. In Tanzania, a country with one of the better education systems in Africa, there is ongoing debate over the proposal to continue Swahili, already the medium of instruction in primary schools, as the medium for the secondary system. But only 0.5 percent of children who start school in Tanzania actually finish secondary education. There are, of course, large parts of Africa in which, because of war or extreme poverty, no education is provided at all. Might it not be better to work on improving the system as a whole rather than debating the medium of instruction?

Blommaert (2001) is attacking what I have called linguicentrism, the assumption that there is some simple manipulation of language policy that will solve serious social, political and economic problems. While he agrees with the goals of those who advocate linguistic human rights, he fears that concentrating on the goals prevents the needed analysis of actual social situations.

Summary on rights

Summing up, in the latter part of the twentieth century, language rights emerged as a major factor affecting national language policies. While the liberty, equality and fraternity of the French Revolution turned out to support the notion of one nation, one language (assuming that to be the way to achieve equality), the notions of individual rights developed by the American Revolution and expressed in the Fourteenth Amendment to the Constitution were recognized to include an individual's freedom to choose a language. In the United States, this has supported access to education and services for those who do not speak the dominant language, English. In Europe, too, international and European treaties have established a number of conventions and covenants supporting the language rights of selected minorities. Essentially, though limited in many ways by the need to obtain ratification by sovereign states, these treaties encouraged freedom of language choice in private and in commerce, the right of linguistic minorities to use and teach their own languages and the obligation of the state to teach its official language to all and to provide access to government services to speakers of other languages.

These notions of language rights continued to spread. Probably as a result of internal pressures, the traditional Latin American policy of completely rejecting indigenous languages was reversed in the 1990s. At much the same time, some of the newly independent states of the former Soviet Union found their efforts to ignore other languages while restoring their own national identity through raising the status of the titular languages blocked or questioned by language rights required for membership of the European Community.

The language rights described so far can generally be derived from principles established for civil or human rights. They apply to the rights of individuals to use their own language and teach it to their children. The approach to language rights that has developed especially in Western Europe and United States in the second half of the twentieth century has undoubtedly had a major effect on the shaping of language policies in a large part of the world today. Language rights have become by the end of the twentieth century a major force, alongside the pressure of the sociolinguistic situation, the drive for national identity and the challenge of the global language, in the development of the language policies of nations.

9 Monolingual polities under pressure

The theory developed so far claims that language policy for any in-dependent nation state will reveal the complex interplay of four in-terdependent but often conflicting factors: the actual sociolinguistic situation; a set of beliefs influenced by national or ethnic identity claims (with the number of Great Traditions critical); the recent pull of English as a global language; and the even more recent pressure for attention to the rights of linguistic minorities. This theoretical model needs to be tested against actual cases. We have already looked at two monolingual policies, and we continue.

The hypothesis for these policies, following Fishman (1971), is that nations which had a consensual single Great Tradition at the time of independence will tend to attempt to select the associated indigenous language as the national language. In the absence of an agreed Great Tradition, the tendency will be to continue with the metropolitan colonial language as national language.

POST-COLONIALISM 1 – MONOLINGUAL IN A LOCAL INDIGENOUS LANGUAGE

The transition from colonial status to independence provides an oppor-tunity for a country to decide or reconsider its language policy. The proclamation of national monolingualism, on the principle of "one nation, one state, one language," in a language other than that of the previous colonial power was (and remains) an obvious method of asserting real independence. A number of nations tried to do this.

Former French colonies choosing their own language

Algeria and the other North African Muslim polities that constitute the Maghreb share a common sociolinguistic history and a common Great Tradition with religious, cultural and linguistic components. After the Islamic conquest in the ninth century, Arabic was imposed over the indigenous languages, but the autochthonous Berber varieties survived underground. French conquest in the nineteenth century led to the imposition of French as the language of government and education. Independence in the 1960s was followed by expulsion of French colonists and Jews, accompanied by a language policy of arabization proclaimed in a constitutional clause establishing Arabic as the only official language. In all these Arabic-speaking countries, it is important to recall the existence of three significant varieties of Arabic: the Classical Arabic of the Qur'an and religious texts in a diglossic relationship (Ferguson 1959) with the local spoken varieties and dialects of Arabic, and the Modern Standard Arabic developing as a modified version of Classical Arabic for non-religious formal use and literacy.

Ferguson (1959) was the first to draw attention to diglossia, a situation as he defined it in which two distinct varieties of the same language divide up linguistic functions unevenly. The H variety (Classical Arabic in Arabic-speaking countries, French in Haiti, Standard German in Switzerland, *katharevousa* in Greece) is generally used for high status public and literate functions, while the L variety (the various regional varieties of Arabic, Haitian creole, Swiss German or *demotiki*) are the languages of the home and the neighborhood and normal social discourse. In an extension that is sometimes disputed, Fishman (1967) extended the term to cases where two unrelated languages similarly shared linguistic functions, such as Spanish and Guarani in Paraguay and Hebrew and Yiddish in the pre-nineteenth-century East European Jewish community. The language practices in diglossia are usually associated with clear beliefs in the superiority of the H language and most language management reflects this.

Arabization was not smooth. In 1950, Sirles (1999) noted, the French colonies in North Africa made up the largest single area of francophonie in the world. Even after colonial rule ended, French continued to be dominant in non-religious spheres of public life. The campaign of arabization began in the 1960s, teaching Modern Standard Arabic for literacy and developing spoken Arabic for formal domains. Of the three countries, Algeria, which had the strongest French influence, has, Sirles believes, been the most successful. Tunisia, with a nearly 100 percent Arabic-speaking population, and Morocco, with the smallest amount of French linguistic influence during the colonial period, both remain heavily francophone. It was political rather than linguistic factors that accounted for the degree of success, Sirles said: the make up of the elite, the ideological commitment of central government and the potential conflict between national development and traditional values. Most high-level bureaucrats of the newly independent countries had been educated in France or in francophone universities. There were significant differences in the length of French domination, too. France ruled Algeria for 132 years, Tunisia for 75 and Morocco for only 44 years. Morocco had a small European population; Algeria had received more than one million colonists from France or other European countries. In Morocco, there was little contact, but in Algeria and Tunisia, most Arabic-speakers were in close contact with French-speakers.

Since independence, Tunisia has continued to stress its ties to France and language issues have not been important. In Algeria, on the other hand, the seven-year-long war of independence resulted in intense nationalism and anticolonialism. Beginning in the 1960s, there was a strong commitment to complete arabization, the implementation of which was handicapped by the shortage of teachers trained in Modern Standard Arabic and a backlash from the 20 percent Berber speakers. Laws were passed requiring literacy in Modern Standard Arabic as a condition for government employment. In Morocco, government policy has zigzagged, with nominal support for arabization but a commitment to maintaining ties with France. The elite continued to send their children to francophone institutions. The tension created by this ambivalence, and the fact that millions of Moroccans have now migrated to coastal cities, strongholds of French language, suggests that arabization will be not be rapid (Djité 1992).

Moroccan language policy also involves the varieties of Berber identified with some 45 percent of the population, who firmly resisted both Islam and French rule (Sadiqi 1997). Berber language loyalty is reportedly strong, and Berber political parties want the language taught (Ennaji 1997).

Libya is different from the other three countries of the Maghreb first because it was an Italian rather than French colony and secondly because the degree of imposition of the colonizing language was much weaker. Nonetheless, its proclamation of arabization was equally strong. European colonization began in 1911 when Italy invaded Libya "to protect Italian interests." For the next twenty years, Italian colonial rule met strong local resistance. The language of instruction in schools was Italian, but few Muslims attended. After the Revolution in 1969 arabization began. Modern Standard Arabic was the medium of instruction at all educational levels including for humanities subjects at university, English was taught at primary school and used at universities in science and technology courses. About 10 percent of the 5 million population are foreign workers, a situation that Libya shares with other oil producers.

In the Levant, Syria is a former French protectorate that has proclaimed its independence by declaring Arabic its only official language. Speakers of Arabic make up some 90 percent of the population, but Kurdish, Armenian, Turkic and Syriac (Assyrian neo-Aramaic) are also spoken. French rule of Syria, which lasted until 1946, was oppressive, with the French language compulsory. While there continues evidence of allegiance to tribe, clan, ethnic group, or locality, a sense of patriotism, associated with desires to regain territory split off by the French and with an appeal to Arab nationalism and language, has developed. As in other parts of the region, the Kurds (about 10 percent) form an oppressed minority in Syria. There have been many forms of suppression: bans on the use of the Kurdish language, replacing Kurdish personal and place names with Arabic, bans on schooling and publication. The Syrian treatment of Kurdish, like the Maghreb treatment of Berber, makes clear that nationalistic demands for linguistic freedom are self-centered. When a previous linguistic minority gains power, it seldom shows tolerance or concern for other minorities.

There are former French colonies in Asia, too, which have tried to restore their national languages. Most of Cambodia's population of about 12 million is reported to speak the national language, Khmer, but there is a sizeable minority of several hundred thousand speakers of Vietnamese. From 1863 until 1953, Cambodia was under French colonial rule, and as in other French colonies, strong efforts were made to build French as the language of international communication and education (Clayton 1995). In the decade (1979–89) of Vietnamese occupation, Vietnamese and Russian were important (Clayton 1998). Economic development, Clayton (2002) notes, has increased the attraction of English, leaving a conflict between English and French as the language for advanced education and international communication.

Laos has a population of about 5,500,000, 3 million of whom are reported to be speakers of the official language, Lao: there are another eighty languages. When it was administered as part of French Indochina, a secular educational system was set up with French as the medium of instruction; it reached only a small elite. The Pathet Lao began to provide Lao language instruction in the schools under its control in the late 1950s, and by 1970, a third of the school-age population attended their schools. After 1975, the Laotian People's Democratic Republic established a ten-year plan for universal primary education, but economic problems have delayed implementation of this goal. French and English are auxiliary languages.

Madagascar, an island off the coast of Africa, was colonized by the French at the end of the nineteenth century. Most of the 15 million population speak varieties of Malagasy. During the colonial period, French had become the dominant language. In 1956, Madagascar became self-governing. After further fighting, the Republic ended in 1975, and Malagasy was declared the official language. The first Republic followed a policy of bilingualism in French and Malagasy, but French continued to dominate. In 1975, the Marxist-oriented military regime proclaimed an official policy of malagachization, and ceased to be a member of AIF (the agency for francophonie) (Metz 1994). However, Madagascar rejoined AIF in December 1989. Most of the leadership has been educated in French, and their children attended private French-language schools. Another 200,000 enrolled in French-medium Roman Catholic schools. The remaining 1,500,000 were in the public school system, with little chance of attaining the French-language fluency still needed for academic advancement. The constitutional assertion of Malagasy monolingualism is not carried into practice.

The pattern in these former French, mainly Arabic-speaking colonies has generally been an effort, not fully successful, to replace the colonial language with official Arabic. The effect of colonial rule is still stronger than the political ideology.

POST-COLONIALISM 2: FORMER COLONIES STAYING WITH THE COLONIAL LANGUAGE

Practically, in choosing a language policy, the newly independent colonies had three choices: they could, like the nations described in the previous section, reject the metropolitan language and proclaim a policy to establish their chosen national language as the sole official language; secondly, they could aim to keep the metropolitan language as an official language alongside their own (leading commonly to dyadic or triadic policies); or, thirdly, they could formally recognize the hegemony of the colonial language.

Cape Verde is an example of the third pattern, as it decided to keep the colonial language, Portuguese, as its only official language and as the language of instruction at all levels in the school system. About a third of the population speak any Portuguese: all, however, are speakers of the local creole, called variously Crioulu or Kaboverde. Cape Verde is the only country in West Africa with a monolingual policy (Bamgbose 2000).

A second African country maintaining the hegemony of the colonial language is Côte d'Ivoire. The Côte d'Ivoire retained French as its only official language for government and education in its 1966

Constitution, in spite of a brief effort in the late 1970s to include local languages. Immigrants from neighboring countries are about a third of the population. There are about seventy-five different languages, many mutually intelligible, so that most people can manage with a mother tongue, a regional language and one of the national lingua francas. As a result of urbanization and population movement, lingua francas such as Dyula are continuing to spread, but standard French is confined to elite functions such as administration and justice. Upward mobility is still constrained, as it was under French rule, by lack of competence in French. The choice appears to be whether to ask the elite 20 percent to learn another language of wider communication, or to expect 80 percent to become literate in French. There is continuing political turmoil.

Trying to lower the status of colonial languages, in the late 1970s, thirty-seven African countries promoted national languages in the curriculum to counter the former colonial language. Seven countries have as a result promoted local languages to official status: Ethiopia, Eritrea, Somalia, Tanzania, Burundi, Ruanda and the Republic of Central Africa. But many francophone countries still follow the recommendation of the 1944 Brazzaville conference that French be the exclusive language for all teaching in schools in French colonies in Africa. As a result, local languages were ignored in planning.

The main language of wider communication in Guinea-Bissau is Kiriol, spoken by more than half of the population (Hovens 2002). An indigenous language, Balata, is spoken by a quarter of the population. There are few native speakers of the official language, Portuguese, known by about 10 percent of the population. Experimental transitional bilingual education programs were begun in 1987 but stopped after ten years. In Niger, also with about twenty languages, about 70 percent of its population is able to speak Hausa and has a much more limited use of the official language, French. Experimental bilingual classes began as early as 1973. Here, too, there appears to be little if any political support for the use of the indigenous languages.

Two small European principalities, Liechtenstein and Andorra, have made compromises in their language choices. Although Liechtenstein has been independent since the beginning of the nineteenth century and most of the 30,000 population of the principality speak Swiss German, it maintains German as its official language. As there are no teacher training institutions in the country, most teachers are trained in Austria. Language practice is similar to that in the German areas of Switzerland: a diglossic relationship between formal use of High German and informal use of Swiss German.

In Andorra, on the other hand, with a population about 70,000 speaking Catalan and Spanish, Catalan is the only official language according to the 1993 Constitution. Andorrans are a minority in the country, and citizenship can only be obtained after twenty-five years' residence. While Catalan is the official language, education, compulsory up to the age of sixteen, is offered in schools built by the Andorran government but with teachers paid by Spain and France. About 50 percent of the children attend French primary schools, the rest Spanish or Catalan schools.

A final example of a country with monolingual policy after independence is Bangladesh. Under British rule, English-medium schools provided an elite education disconnected from the interests of the people of the whole. In Pakistan after independence, this policy was later modified, but the educational reforms did not in general affect East Pakistan. Friction developed between East and West Pakistan, separated by 1,000 miles. In East Pakistan, there was resistance to the proposal to make Urdu the sole national language. After its independence from Pakistan, Bangla became the sole national language and the language of communication of Bangladesh, most of whose population is reported to know it as a first or second language. Another thirty-eight languages are spoken in the country. English remains important, still a medium in some private institutions and taught in higher education.

MONOLINGUAL COUNTRIES WITH MARGINALIZED MINORITIES

Though constitutionally monolingual, a number of countries are practically multilingual as a result of significant but marginalized foreign minorities.

The Arab oil producers are a case in point. Small and lacking in oil reserves, Bahrain depends for its prosperity on petroleum processing and international banking. One third of its population of 650,000 is made up of foreigners. Thus, while Arabic is the official language, there are large minority groups, including nearly 50,000 speakers of Farsi, over 20,000 speakers of Philippine languages and 18,000 speakers of Urdu. Over half of the 2 million population of Kuwait were reported to be non-nationals, brought to work in the oil industry. In 1975, the literacy rate was just over 50 percent, but by 1990 had reached 70 percent. The majority of pupils in Kuwaiti schools in 1990 were non-national, as was a high proportion of the teachers. Many Kuwaiti males are educated overseas. During the Gulf War, more than half the population (nationals and foreigners) left the country, and while nationals were encouraged to return after the war, foreigners were not. The pre-1991, 400,000 Palestinian group of workers was reduced to under 30,000. Post-war policy is to keep the proportion of foreign workers to less than 50 percent of the total population, and to make sure that no single group is more than 10 percent.

Oman's population of 2,400,000 includes a high proportion of foreign workers, although there is currently a policy of indigenization in labor. Before 1970, there were only three primary schools in the sultanate, with places reserved for 900 boys selected by the sultan. Since then, the sultan has worked to develop general education and expand the school system.

Saudi Arabia has a population estimated in 2001 at 22.7 million, including 5.3 million non-nationals. Between 1985 and 1990, the foreign workforce grew from 3.5 million to 5.3 million, most from Arabic-speaking countries, but also Pakistan, India, the Philippines, Sri Lanka and the Republic of Korea (South Korea). Government policy was to reduce these numbers. There have been major investments in education, and a goal is to indigenize the secondary school teaching force, 40 percent of whom were foreigners at the end of the 1980s. The recent economic turndown threatens the success of these and other social programs. Many Saudi Arabians go to universities overseas. English is recognized as a valuable instrument for teaching non-Arab Muslims, and for providing access to modern technology and science for Muslims.

Portugal is a country with an ideologically monolingual national policy, like France. Recently, it has started to be forced, by its membership of the European Community, to recognize indigenous minorities. Most of Portuguese language policy activities in the last thirty years or so have been concerned with Portuguese language diffusion, although others have dealt with orthography, the use of Portuguese in trade names and one regional language. Starting in 1995, a number of laws confirmed treaties with former colonies or other Portuguese-speaking countries, and a Portuguese-speaking community was formally established in 1999 including the governments of Angola, Brazil, Cape Verde, Guinea-Bissau, Mozambique and São Tomé e Príncipe. There is one recognized regional minority language, Mirandese, with about 10,000 speakers living in small villages. In line with European Union language rights policies, laws were passed in 1999 recognizing Mirandese and authorizing public documents in the language. Mirandese is taught as an optional second language to a small number of pupils above the age of nine. It is not used, however, in courts, government and the mass media.

More like the oil-producing states than the countries of the Maghreb, the other Middle Eastern Islamic countries are largely monolingual in Arabic, with linguistic diversity maintained by dialectal variation and the diglossic patterning of standard and vernacular language. Egypt is marked by a distinction between the local vernacular Arabic (mainly Egyptian Arabic) and the standard Arabic based on Classical. Coptic, strong before the Islamic conquest, declined during the Ottoman period and was maintained only as a Church language. By the nineteenth century, most Egyptians spoke a local variety of Arabic. It was Egypt that took the lead in deciding to use the literary language rather than the spoken vernacular as the official language (Shraybom Shivtiel 1999). In the early twentieth century, the Ministry of Education tried to replace English with Arabic as the language of instruction in school, but foreign languages continued to be the main medium of instruction in the education system, with the exception of religious schools. In the early 1940s, foreign schools were instructed to add Arabic as a subject. The change finally came under 'Abd al-Nasser, who highlighted the close link between the Arabic language and pan-Arabic national unity. In this new ideological situation, colloquial Arabic lost recognition and literary Arabic was proclaimed as a language of communication for the elite at least. Foreign languages, especially English, remain important for economic reasons. English is compulsory as first or second foreign language in public schools. The national universities require English, and some use English as medium of instruction.

The defeat of Turkey in the First World War led to its partition and the granting of independence to many countries that had been part of its empire. One ethnic minority was not treated in this way; of all the ethnic groups recognized as deserving independence after the end of the war, the Kurds stand out as the one group who continued to form a minority in a number of countries such as: Turkey, Syria, Iran, Iraq and Armenia. In the various countries, Kurdish has developed differently, using the Latin alphabet in Syria, Cyrillic in the former Soviet Union and the modified Arab Persian script in Iraq. However, in Turkey, since the time of Kemal Atatürk and the 1923 Constitution, it has suffered serious oppression (Skutnabb-Kangas and Bucak 1995). The 1984 Constitution proclaimed in article 26 that "No language prohibited by law shall be used in the expression and dissemination of thought." The Constitution went on to say that "No language other than Turkish shall be taught as mother tongue to Turkish citizens at any institutions of training or education." Only the languages of foreign countries with which Turkey had treaties could be taught in schools. These provisions prohibited not just the teaching but also the use of Kurdish. This constitutional policy and its implementation have been cited as one of the main considerations in the decision of the European Community to delay Turkey's accession to membership. Only in late 2002, under pressure from this delay, has Turkey decided to grant some language rights to Kurdish.

CONSTITUTIONAL MONOLINGUALISM – CONCLUSION

The nation states described in this chapter are united in that they have their constitutions proclaim a single official or national language. Looking at each more closely, though, such a common characteristic disguises complexity in language policy. First, most of the countries have quite complex language repertoires, with indigenous or immigrant languages alongside the official language. In practice, various approaches have to be taken to deal with these languages and speakers, at local if not central levels. Proclaiming an official language suggests at the very least a requirement that the school system make it a priority to teach the official language to non-speakers. Second, the choice of a single language sets different language-management needs depending on the stage of cultivation. Nations that selected the colonial language had to build up a language education policy to handle the transition from the home language to the school medium; those that chose the local language needed to work on its cultivation and to teach it to speakers of other languages. Many polities that are constitutionally monolingual have already started to take measures to implement the rights of individuals and groups with other languages. At the same time, all of them face the need to cope with the growing importance of English as a global language. In the twenty-first century, monolingualism is no longer the simplest policy.

10 Monolingual polities with recognized linguistic minorities

MORE THAN MONOLINGUAL?

The countries listed in table 2 are similar to those in ch. 9 in that they name one language in their constitution, but are differentiated from them by constitutional recognition also of the rights of minorities.

In many cases, the constitutional proclamation of a single state or national or official language is followed by a qualifying statement to do with the linguistic rights of recognized minorities. Many of them take this extra qualification from some earlier constitution (in former Soviet republics, for instance). Others are influenced by the movement towards the recognition of rights of linguistic minorities.

A number of Latin American countries appear on this list: Brazil, Colombia, Ecuador, El Salvador, Guatemala, Nicaragua, Panama, Peru and Venezuela. In each case, the constitution proclaims Spanish (or, in the case of Brazil, Portuguese) as the official language, but adds, in more recent versions at least, recognition and protection for indigenous native languages and dialects. About 10 percent of the Latin American population (about 40 million people) is classifiable as indigenous, usually on the basis of language, self-perception and geographical concentration (World Bank 1993). These criteria are far from precise. Many different languages are involved: only Uruguay is monolingual, and other countries have from 7 to 200 indigenous languages. Indigenous people are in an inferior social and economic position and are commonly illiterate. Recently, there has been increasing recognition of the problem, and a number of changes have been made in language policy to deal with the issues.

Starting in 1992, Bolivia passed a series of laws dealing with the languages of Indian minorities, especially Guarani, Quechua and Aymara. There are thirty-seven languages in Bolivia. After Spanish, the two largest are Quechua (2.8 million) and Aymara (1.8 million). There is evidence of declining use. Government-sponsored programs for the education of indigenous children and adults are supplementing the work of

Table 2 *Monolingual countries with protection for minorities*

Country	State, national, official language	Other recognition	Year
Armenia	Armenian	National minorities rights	1995
Austria	German	Linguistic minorities	1929
Azerbaijan	Azerbaijan language	Other languages spoken	1995
Brazil	Portuguese	Indian native languages	1988
Bulgaria	Bulgarian	Alongside Bulgarian	1991
Burkina Faso	French	National languages	1997
Colombia	Spanish	Ethnic languages and dialects	1991
Costa Rica	Spanish	National languages of the native peoples	1999
Croatia	The Croatian language and the Latin script	Locally another language and Cyrillic alongside	1990
Ecuador	Spanish	All Ecuadorian	1998
El Salvador	Spanish	Autochthonous	1982
Eritrea	All Eritrean languages equal		1996
Estonia	Estonian	Minorities locally	1992
Ethiopia	Amharic federally	All locally	Draft 1994
Gabon	French working	National languages	1997
Georgia	Georgian	Abkhazian in Abkhazia; others protected	1991
Guatemala	Spanish	Vernaculars	1985
Hungary	Hungarian	National and ethnic minorities	1997
Indonesia	Bahasa Indonesia	Respected regional languages	1945–89
Iran	Persian	Regional and tribal languages and Arabic	1979–95
Iraq	Arabic	Kurdish regionally	1990
Kazakhstan	Kazak	Russian and others	1995
Kyrgysztan	Kyrgyz	Russian and others	1993
Latvia	Latvian	Ethnic minorities	1992–8
Macedonia	Macedonian	Others regionally alongside	1992
Malawi	All equal		1994
Mali	French	Other national languages	1991–2000

Table 2 (*cont.*)

Country	State, national, official language	Other recognition	Year
Malta	Maltese	English	1996
Mauritania	Arabic	Poular, Soninke and Wolof	1991
Moldova	Moldovan in Latin alphabet	Russian and others	1994
Mongolia	Mongolian	National minorities	1992
Mozambique	Portuguese	National languages	1990
Namibia	English	In private schools	1990
Nepal	Nepali in Devanagari script	Local mother tongues	1990
New Zealand	(English not mentioned) Māori Language Act	Minority	1990
Nicaragua	Spanish	Community languages	1987–95
Pakistan	(Urdu not mentioned)	Preservation permitted	1999
Panama	Spanish	Indigenous communities	1994
Peru	Spanish	Quechua, Aymara and indigenous	1993?
Philippines	Filipino and English	Regional	1987
Poland	Polish	National and ethnic minorities	1997
Romania	Romanian	National minorities	1991
Russia	All languages equal		1993
Serbia (Yugoslavia)	Serbian (ekavian and ijekavian dialects) in Cyrillic script	Latin script, national minorities locally	1992
Serbia (Serbia)	Serbo-Croatian and Cyrillic alphabet	Latin alphabet; national minorities regionally	1995
Serbia (Montenegro)	Serbian (iekavian); Cyrillic and Latin alphabets equal	National minorities locally	1992
Singapore	Malay, English, Mandarin, or Tamil		1965–1993

(cont.)

Table 2 (*cont.*)

Country	State, national, official language	Other recognition	Year
Slovakia	Slovak	National and ethnic minorities	1992
Slovenia	Slovene	Italian and Hungarian locally	1991–2000
Spain	Castilian	Autonomous communities	1978–1992
Tajikistan	Tajik	Russian and others	1994
Uganda	English	Any other	1995
Ukraine	Ukrainian	Russian and national minorities	1996
Uzbekistan	Uzbek	Respect for nationalities and peoples	1992
Venezuela	Spanish	Indigenous locally	1999

private and religious organizations (Plaza and Albo 1989). A decree in 2000 recognized thirty-four indigenous languages as official. A few programs are in operation, especially for Quechua (Hornberger and King 2001). Chile, the Constitution of which does not mention language, set up a commission in 1990 to consider education for indigenous linguistic minorities. Currently, rescue operations for endangered languages are reported to be underway. Colombia in 2000 required that teachers of the deaf be bilingual in Spanish and Colombian sign language. In 1999, Costa Rica amended its Constitution, proclaiming "that Spanish is the national language; nevertheless, the State will protect the continuation and development of national languages of the native peoples." This gave stronger backing to laws passed in the previous decade setting up protection for indigenous languages. Ecuador in 1999 set up a National Directorate of Bilingual Intercultural Education.

Issues concerning native peoples appear to be a source of considerable disagreement. A Commission for the Official Recognition of Indigenous Languages was established in Guatemala in 1997. Reports indicate the extreme poverty of indigenous peoples in Guatemala: nearly 90 percent are below the poverty line, and few have access to safe drinking water, sanitation or electricity. In 2000, Mexico established an agency whose purpose was to guarantee that bilingual intercultural education responds to the needs of Indian peoples. Policies are slow and contradictory, but there were signs of the growing influence of indigenous peoples. In 1980, Nicaragua authorized some teaching in the Miskita language on the Atlantic Coast, but more recent reports on indigenous peoples detail the taking of and deforestation of land and threats to environment as well as culture (Mueller 2002). In the mid-1980s, Peru established academies for Quechua and Aymara and set up a Directorate for Bilingual Education. Recently, local indigenous groups have protested that the main effect of these programs has been a shift to Spanish.

Language policy in Latin America is assimilationist, seeking "to impose the colonial languages on speakers of other languages, whether they be immigrant, slave, or indigenous peoples" (Hornberger 1999: 133). Spanish-speaking settlers in Latin America shared a puristic language ideology which initially considered anything indigenous to be impure. In actual practice, the situation is much more complex; apart from the two major languages, Spanish and Portuguese, there are pidgins and creoles, a wide range of immigrant languages (Italian in Argentina, German in Paraguay and Venezuela, Basque and Catalan in many countries, speakers of various Asian languages, and a not negligible number of speakers of Arabic). All this sits on a base of a highly diverse mixture of so far not fully classified indigenous Amerindian languages, spread in various density (substantial in Guatemala, Mexico, Paraguay, Bolivia, Ecuador and Peru but minimal in other countries). With the exception of Paraguay, any recognition of the rights of indigenous peoples to education in their own language appeared only in the 1980s, generally promoted by non-governmental agencies, but finally recognized by law or constitution. These programs are generally associated with other political efforts to improve the lot of the autochthonous peoples of Latin American.

While Spanish is the constitutionally official language of Costa Rica and must be learned by anyone wishing to be naturalized, a long series of laws dating back to 1976 provide some recognition for the half-dozen indigenous native languages. These were finally capped by the 1999 amendment to the Constitution providing that the state "will protect the continuation and development of national languages of the native peoples."

Most people in Honduras, a Central American country with a population about 6 million, are said to speak Spanish. *Ethnologue* reports that there are 13,000 speakers of an English-based creole. There are a number of legally protected Amerindian languages, the largest of which, Garifuna, has nearly 100,000 speakers.

Generalizing somewhat, the countries on table 2 are in practice multilingual in various degrees, but in ideology by-and-large monolingual.
Nonetheless, influenced by their multilingualism and by recognition
of the language rights of their minorities, they have proclaimed this
recognition in their constitution and many have established language
management activities to implement the recognition. The former
Soviet republics generally had their titular language recognized in the
Soviet-imposed constitution during the Leninist period. Because Soviet
policy was to work for the eventual replacement of nationalism, and
because of the mixtures of populations by which Stalin intended to
weaken the larger nationalities, the Soviet constitution also included
the rights of linguistic minorities.

After the breakup of the Soviet Union, the former republics modified their language policy in order to strengthen the place of the titular language vis-à-vis Russian and sometimes also the other minority
languages. Some of the constitutions recognize one or more specific
minority languages. Georgia, for example, singles out Abkhazian, a
Caucasian language spoken by about 100,000 of its 5 million population, as an official regional language. In Abkhazia, Russian- and
Georgian-medium schools were dominant until the end of the 1970s.
After this, Abkhazian went through revival, but since the Abkhazian–
Georgian war in 1992, the two populations have tried to separate
(Arutiunov 1998). In Yerevan, Armenia, half of the high schools used
Russian, although 90 percent of the population is Armenian. Since
independence in 1991, both Georgian and Armenian are becoming
dominant in their respective countries, transforming Russian into a
minority language. Mongolia, its alphabet changed to Cyrillic in 1941,
has 90 percent of its 2.7 million people using Mongol, which is the
standard and official language. There is a significant Kazakh minority, about 5 percent, and minority languages are constitutionally protected. Efforts to strengthen human rights include providing access to
government services for linguistic minorities and education in Kazakh
and other minority languages.

Two regions of the former Soviet Union are of particular interest
for the role that language policy is playing in the redefinition of new
national identities. The first are the predominantly Muslim states of
the Caucasus.

Of the 4.5 million inhabitants of Turkmenistan, about 3.4 million
are said to speak the state language, Turkmen. There are a score of
other languages with significant numbers of speakers, presumably
used to using Russian as a lingua franca. Since independence in
1991, tribal, clan and ethnic forces have since re-emerged (Landau and

Kellner-Heinkele 2001). So, too, has Islamic cultural practice, which exists alongside Russian Orthodox Christianity. Language had been used to create Turkmen identity. The country has been under the control of a strong national leader and is reported to be poor and corrupt, governed "in a Soviet-era authoritarian style." Under Soviet rule, Turkmen was forced to switch from its Arabic-based alphabet to a modified Latin alphabet in 1929, and to a Cyrillic script in 1940. After independence, the issue was raised again: there were few supporters of keeping Arabic, but growing support for the Latin script selected in 1993. There have been problems with the new alphabet. The Russian community complains about second-class status and inability to learn Turkmen and there has been steady emigration. The main language of instruction in schools is now Turkmen, but many schools still teach in Russian, Uzbek and Kazakh (Landau and Kellner-Heinkele 2001).

Kazakhstan has the largest absolute and proportional population of Russians of the Muslim states, living in areas that are contiguous to the Russian Federation and maintaining family ties with it. A Slavic movement succeeded in 1997 in gaining a new language law, permitting Russian to be used officially on a par with the state language, Kazakh. Kyrgyzstan also had a large but declining Russian minority, more than 20 percent of the 5 million population in 1989. While the Constitution mentions Russian, many Russians complain about discrimination and there is a high rate of emigration. Russian is referred to as "a language of inter-ethnic communication" in Tajikistan alongside Tajik, the state language, which became the state language in 1989, leading to a campaign by various members of the Russian community to defend the status of russophones. Many Russians have returned to the Russian Federation (Landau and Kellner-Heinkele 2001).

Azerbaijan was the first Muslim republic to declare its sovereignty, in September 1989. At that time, about 80 percent of the population of 7 million was Azeri: significant minorities were Russian, Armenian, Lezghin and Avar. The Russian minority in Azerbaijan report that they were well integrated, but there was sizeable migration at the time of the war with Armenia in the early 1990s. Declared the state language in the 1936 and 1978 Constitutions, Azeri was well established at the time of independence: in the 1989 Soviet census, 99 percent of Azeris claimed to speak it, and only a third claimed fluency in Russian. The 1995 Constitution mentions Azeri by name as the national language while guaranteeing continued use and development of the unnamed other languages of the republic (Landau and Kellner-Heinkele 2001): 115). After independence, Azeri was taught in Russian schools, which continued to exist.

In the Muslim states of Central Asia, apart from the generally difficult economic situation, a good deal of government activity is concerned with the re-establishment of national identity. As in most postcolonial situations, the challenge is to work out an appropriate redistribution of functions and status between the former colonial language, Russian, and the new titular language. The normal problems are exacerbated by a number of special factors. First is the potential impact of Islam, suppressed for sixty years under Communist rule, but offering not just an alternative cultural model but also a threat of radical fundamentalism. The second is the possibility of a common Turkic movement, particularly represented in a series of language conferences starting in the early 1990s and aiming at establishing a common alphabet. Third, as has been mentioned above, is the variation in proportion of minority-language speakers, whether Russian or other languages. With stronger economies, dealing with these problems might be much easier.

The three Baltic states, Estonia, Latvia and Lithuania, are similar in the legal and constitutional assertion of the official status of the national languages, but while the statement is not modified in the Lithuanian Constitution, in the Estonian and the Latvian the rights of ethnic and linguistic minorities are recognized. Because language policy has played and is continuing to play such an important part in the political life of the Baltic states, they provide further evidence of the nature and forces affecting its development. While they are often grouped together, their history, language situation and demographic patterns are sufficiently different to produce different policies.

Latvia remained largely monolingual through centuries of foreign rule (Druviete 1998). A nationalist movement developed by the end of the nineteenth century, and Latvian competed with German and Russian, but from the 1870s, only Russian was permitted in government, schools and courts. Latvia became independent in 1918, with Latvian as the primary language. In line with other nations established by treaty at the time, seven minority languages were recognized; many schools used minority languages as language of instruction. There were German and Russian universities, too. By the end of the 1930s, most citizens could speak Latvian. In 1939, 60,000 Germans left Latvia. In 1940, Latvia became part of the USSR and many Latvians were deported or emigrated, replaced by thousands of people from Russia, Ukraine and Belarus. During the Soviet period, language policy favored Russian, and by 1989, two-thirds of Latvians and most others claimed fluency in Russian. Even before independence, a start was made on re-establishing Latvian. A language law proclaimed Latvian the state language but maintained official functions for Russian. In 1991, the Republic of Latvia was established, and the language law strengthened. All residents have the right to master Latvian, but residents of other nationalities also have the right to be educated in their own language. The 1994 Law on Citizenship required knowledge of Latvian for naturalization (Druviete 1998).

By the 1980s, ethnic Estonians were only 62 percent of the total population in that country, ethnic Latvians were only 52 percent of the total population in Latvia, while in Lithuania, ethnic Lithuanians remained about 80 percent (Tsilevich 2001). Parallel but asymmetric bilingualism developed in all three countries, with education in both languages but Russian dominant in state government, transport, industry, military affairs and security. In 1989, just over 20 percent of ethnic Russians living in Latvia claimed proficiency in the Latvian language; by 1995, the figure had risen to over 50 percent. Language laws that declared Estonian, Lithuanian and Latvian as state languages were passed in 1989, but Russian remained an official language.

These language laws were tightened after independence, although they were delayed and modified as a result of external criticism by international organizations, including the OSCE High Commissioner on National Minorities. In general the laws or constitutions provided only the most general recognition of linguistic minorities. All three countries required that state legislatures use only the state language. In Estonia, other languages could be used internally. In Lithuania, minority languages could be used in areas with substantial numbers of speakers. In Latvia, however, municipalities might use only the state language. Election laws required that candidates have certificates of the highest level of competence in the state language. In certain professional fields, proficiency in the state language is required for employees: an attempt to extend this to the private sector failed because of opposition from OSCE and the European Commission. Many hundreds of thousands of people have had to take examinations to show their competence in the state language.

The main area of controversy remained education. Lithuania permits use of the mother tongue in "populous and compact communities of ethnic minorities," but Estonia requires at least 60 percent use of Estonian in secondary schools. In Latvia, the requirements for providing minority-language education are even tighter: it was planned to eliminate municipality-financed minority-language education by 2004. Underlying all these developments were citizenship policies based on the principle of "continuity;" only those who were citizens of Estonia and Latvia before 1940 and their direct descendants were automatically recognized as citizens after independence. The language policies were intended to support this policy, by protecting the state languages, asserting their symbolic role, breaking the link with the Russian period of domination and encouraging the "voluntary repatriation" of Slavs.

These policies came up against the pressures for linguistic and minority rights from supra-national organizations. With the proposal to expand membership of the European Union, a complex process began of negotiation with candidate members to adjust their laws and policies to suit those established for the union. Six of the ten current candidates are included in table 2: Bulgaria, Estonia, Hungary, Latvia, Lithuania and Poland. The other candidates are Cyprus, the Czech Republic, Malta and Romania. Human rights are, of course, a key feature of the required standards for accession, as are minority rights in general and the rights of linguistic minorities in particular.

Language-related issues were involved in the negotiations. All candidates were required to translate all European Union legislation and regulations into their national language; this involved setting up large teams of translators. Civil servants of various kinds (including border guards) were required to be trained in appropriate foreign languages.

Language rights played a central role in the negotiations with the three former Soviet Baltic nations, with the European Commission (2001a) requiring Estonia to be careful "not to infringe upon the language rights of the Russian-speaking population." The report on Latvia (European Commission 2001b) noted the importance of language training for the 40 percent of non-Latvians. In 2001, the first court case brought by an individual was taken to the Constitutional Court, concerned with the requirement to spell names and surnames in Latvian. Another case dealt with the requirement for elected officials to submit proof of Latvian language proficiency even after they had the appropriate language certificates to run as candidates.

The Baltic states, then, are deeply involved in the formulation and implementation of language policies that will enable them to reshape their nations after what they consider the serious damage of the period of Russian domination. While their activities in this area are being closely monitored and have been modified as a result of supra-national intervention, especially now that they are applying for membership of the European Union, the nature of the intervention makes very clear the limits that the European Community sets on its interpretation of language rights. It sees no fundamental problem with the goal of the three Baltic nations to switch from Russian-dominated bilingualism to national-language monolingualism, provided that the process avoids infringing the individual human rights of speakers of the minority languages, including Russian. Apart from a concern for Romany speakers that turns up regularly in European Community documents, there is no effort to determine which languages need protection, and no argument with policies that use regional or territorial considerations in deciding where to allow the minority languages. Nor is there any objection to a policy that will make sure that secondary and higher education is offered only in the state language, provided only that individuals from the minority groups are offered appropriate classes to learn that language. For all its rhetoric of European multilingualism, the European Community appears comfortable with the maintenance or even establishment of national monolingualism, provided only that appropriate officials have plurilingual proficiency in other European languages.

Language policy remains controversial in the Balkans, a region formerly part of the Ottoman empire and ethnically, linguistically and religiously highly complex. As a general rule, Ottoman rulers made little attempt to integrate and unify subject peoples. With the breakup of the empire at the end of the First World War, new ethnically based states were created, all required by the treaties that set them up to protect minorities, including recognition of their languages and mother-tongue education, but commonly these provisions were ignored. Nationalism and ethnic identity became key forces in language policy (O'Reilly 2001).

In the post-Second World War era, Greece denied virtually all minority rights, but there are dying communities of speakers of a number of languages: Albanian, a community between 50,000 and 100,000; Bulgarian, with 30,000, and Turkish. There are about 100,000 speakers of Turkish in Greece, in Western Thrace, who continue to use the language at home and in the community. Proficiency in Greek is increasing. As a result of agreements between Greece and Turkey, schools may teach in Turkish at the primary level. Another Slavic language is highly controversial, with a long-standing Greek government policy of discouraging the use of Macedonian and strong opposition to the use of the name Macedonia by the nation state of that name. The effect of government oppression has been rapid loss of the language. Finally, Wallachian, a Romance language, is reported as spoken by as many as 200,000 in a large number of villages, but after 1945, their schools and churches were closed. The Greek 1975 Constitution makes no mention of language, apart from a clause on the language of the Bible. There has, however, been considerable dispute over the correct form of standard Greek. Ferguson (1959) cited Greek as a paradigm example of diglossia, with its distinction between the higher *katharevousa* "puri-fying language" and the popular *demotic* "language of the people." In 1976, the Greek government acted to resolve the problem by abolishing *katharevousa*, but the result has been an intermixture of the varieties (*mikti* "mixed") leading to continued debates about the nature of pure Modern Greek (Kakava 1997).

Albania, while denying individual human rights, did allow some educational and cultural rights to minorities. The largest and most controversial minority group is Greek. Albanians constitute significant minorities in a number of states, including Greece and Italy. In Italy, there may be as many as 100,000 speakers, scattered over a wide area, but the Albanian language is not constitutionally recognized.

The Socialist Federal Republic of Yugoslavia, which existed from 1945 until 1991, was a meeting place of three distinct civilizations: Western European Catholic, Byzantine–Slavic Orthodox and Arabic–Turkish Islamic (Bugarski 2001). Yugoslavia under Tito recognized six nations of Yugoslavia: Serbs, Croats, Slovenes, Montenegrins, Macedonians and Muslims. Each of these had a national home in one of the republics. A second group called nationalities of Yugoslavia also had cultural and linguistic rights, but not republican status. The largest minority was the Albanians in Kosovo, followed by Hungarians, Roma, Italians, Bulgarians, Czechs, Ruthenians, Slovaks and Turks. A third classification was other nationalities and ethnic groups which included Austrians, Greeks, Jews, Germans, Poles, Russians, Ukrainians and others. All this was entrenched in the 1974 Yugoslavian Constitution.

Conflict between the groups was common. In Vojvodina, recognized with Kosovo as an autonomous province of the Republic of Serbia, Serbs were the majority but there were five official languages: Serbo-Croatian, Hungarian, Slovak, Romanian and Ruthenian. There were about 200 Hungarian elementary schools, a daily Hungarian newspaper and regular broadcasts in Hungarian on the provincial radio station. In Kosovo, however, ethnic Albanians were an overwhelming majority. While ethnic Albanians essentially ran the province, there was a movement calling for republican status. After the breakup, ethnic Albanians lost their autonomy.

The wars and ethnic cleansing that followed the breakup of Yugoslavia gave expression to these tensions. Language played a double role in the disintegration of Yugoslavia, first as an issue used by rising nationalism and secondly as an instrument for developing ethnic hatred. The attitude to Serbo-Croatian turns out to be a reflex of changing political situations: as O'Reilly (2001: 12) put it, "Both the creation and the eventual dismantling of Serbo-Croatian demonstrate the power of the one nation/one state/one language equation in the legitimization of the state."

Ethnic tension continues in the new states. In Vojvodina, Hungarians and other minority groups continue to fight for recognition, struggling with the pressures towards centralization and Serbian. In 1992, the education law was amended to require instruction in Serbian, with special conditions for using minority or world languages. In Kosovo, there was a continuing struggle between Serbs and Albanians. While the Constitution recognized minority rights, they were generally not implemented. The Albanians started underground parallel education after the new curriculum called for Serbian.

In Macedonia, Macedonians make up about two-thirds of the population, with Albanians constituting another 20 percent. The Albanian minority, too, wanted autonomy. In 1996, they established an underground university that the government did not recognize. There has continued to be serious tension. As a result of pressure from the European Community, the Constitution was amended in 2001. Albanian became an official language in areas where it is spoken by more than 20 percent of the population. Principles of decentralization have been agreed to.

In Macedonia, Romany has been used in schools for the first four grades since 1983. School materials are being developed, but one problem is the existence of three major dialects. About 80 percent of Macedonian Roma (variously estimated at between 60,000 and 200,000) are mother-tongue speakers of Romany.

Slovene became the official language of the independent state of Slovenia in 1991, at the end of a short war. Since the breakup of Yugoslavia, the use of Slovenian appears unchallenged. The 1991 Constitution expresses a direct link between Slovene nationality and the state (Tollefson 1997). At the same time, it protects the rights of the autochthonous Italian and Hungarian ethnic communities in regions where they live. In a number of schools in the Hungarian area, bilingual programs are offered. In the Italian region, schools are either Slovene or Italian. In 1993, the Council of Europe issued a report that considered that Slovenia provides a good model for protecting the human rights of linguistic minorities. Tollefson, however, found that Hungarians and Italians were not happy with policy implementation.

The status of Serbo-Croatian is a classic political and linguistic dilemma, with linguists regularly claiming that it is a single language, and governments and speakers regularly claiming the existence of two distinct languages. Croatian was standardized over a long period, from the sixteenth to the nineteenth century. Serbian

standardization started in the nineteenth century, and assumed that
Serbian was the "people's" language. The most obvious differences are
lexical. While unification was originally a Croatian campaign, it soon
became associated with Serbian domination. Serbian unification policy aimed to drop Croatian elements. With the breakaway of Croatia
and the continued changes in Croatian to differentiate the language,
the renaming of Serbo-Croatian as Serbian, even without changes in
the language, was obvious and inevitable (Ivić 2001). Similarly, the se-
cession of Bosnia-Herzegovina involved the recognition of Bosnian as
a new language. Since 1990, there is growing use of Cyrillic to write
Serbian. There continues to be debate over standardization and orthography. Pranjković (2001: 31) concluded that "ever since the mid-1800s,
the mutual relationship between the two standard varieties has been
inseparable from politics."

The breakup of Yugoslavia, then, was in part mobilized around language issues. Genocide and ethnic cleansing simplified a highly complex linguistic picture, and outside supra-national organizations are
now endeavoring to restore respect for language diversity. It is evident
that very serious social, political, religious and ethnic conflicts will
need to be brought under control before language policies can settle
down.

The Central European region, too, has serious problems with languages. The splitting of Czechoslovakia into the Czech Republic and
Slovakia had linguistic effects. The Czech Republic, established in
1993, restored a historical division that was blurred with the creation
of Czechoslovakia in 1918. Between the wars, efforts were made to
blend mutually intelligible Czech and Slovak. Vocal linguistic minorities remained: the Germans, the Poles and the Slovaks. After the Second World War, 2,500,000 Germans speakers were moved to Germany.
Czech and Slovak were both recognized and it was assumed that members of each group would use their own language wherever they lived.
Slovaks felt themselves not just different but unequal, leading to a
1993 decision to split along ethnolinguistic lines. Czech ethnics make
up 80 percent of the new Czech republic, which also includes Mora-
vians, Slovaks and a number of smaller groups. A third of those claiming Slovak ethnicity are probably Roma. The Poles were recognized
as an ethnic minority in Czechoslovakia. While a German minority
remains, it is not recognized. While the new government recognizes
individual rights, there is little consciousness of ethnic complexity and
no acceptance of variation (Nekvapil and Neustupný 1998).

In the new Slovak Republic, 86 percent of the population registered
as Slovak and 11 percent as Magyar (Votruba 1998). The Constitution

guarantees protection of the national minorities and ethnic groups. Slovak, Magyar, Czech and Ukrainian are recognized as established literary languages. Dispute continues between Slovak and Magyar groups concerning ethnic and linguistic rights. Slovak is the official language, but any linguistic minority making up 10 percent of the population of a town or village may use its own language in dealings with various levels of administration. The majority of schools teach in Slovak, but many use Magyar. The European Community has been monitoring human rights in Slovakia as the country is a candidate for accession, with problems being raised about the major disadvantages faced by the Roma minority. In June 2001 Slovakia ratified the European Charter of Regional and Minority Languages, to apply to the Bulgarian, Croatian, Czech, German, Polish, Roma, Ruthenian and Ukrainian languages in any municipality with over 20 percent of the minority. Acceptance of the Charter was in response to demands from the large Hungarian minority and accordance with the basic treaty with Hungary.

There are other countries with smaller but still significant minorities. While Bulgaria is assumed to be monolingual, Boneva (1998) noted that there were number of unrecognized minority languages. The most important is Turkish. The 1879 Constitution made Bulgarian the language of public schools, but Turkish private schools continued until the 1960s. A tenth of the population claim Turkish as their language, but they are assumed to be bilingual. There are about 200,000 Roma, and speakers of Macedonian, Armenian, Circassian, Tatar, Gagauz and other languages. Religion further complicates ethnic identity: some Turkish speakers are Christian and some Bulgarian speakers are Muslim.

Romanian language policy, too, long monolingual and assimilative, has recently started to come under external supra-national pressure. The region of Transylvania has been one of ethnic and political dispute ever since the Middle Ages (Jordan 1998). Ruled successively by Hungarians, Saxons, Ottomans, the Holy Roman empire and the Austro-Hungarian empire, Romania became independent in 1878 and took its present shape after the First World War. During this period, the Romanian nation state ignored the fact that a third of the population was not ethnic Romanians. Romanian was declared the only official language in the 1923 Constitution, and the Orthodox Church became the de facto state church. There was official discrimination against Jews and Roma. Under Communist rule, a first phase of ethnic cleansing was banishment of the large German minority; Jews and Roma were given some privileges that they lost again during the 1950s. All concessions to the Hungarian minority were cancelled in 1964, and minority rights virtually abolished. With demographic changes, the towns of Transylvania were romanized. Most Jews emigrated. In 1948, all schools were nationalized and the teaching of Romanian became compulsory. University entrance exams were given only in Romanian. The publication of Hungarian-language newspapers was curtailed, and television broadcasts in Hungarian and German was stopped in 1985 (Bachman 1989). Working against tolerance are three current issues: ethnic Romanian distrust of Hungarians; problems of dealing with an anomalous region in a centralized state; and the importance of nationalism in counteracting political, social and economic instability. But there are also forces supporting the position of the minorities, including the internal strength of the Hungarian ethnic political party. External support comes from Hungary and the European Union. It appears that the monolingual practices, ideology and language management that have been long established in Romania are starting to be challenged, in the case of the Hungarian minority in particular, both by ethnic political self-mobilization and by external national and supra-national intervention.

Deaf communities and sign languages

As Kaplan and Baldauf (1997: 79) observed, the deaf communities and sign languages are not usually topics considered in the context of language policy. The history of deaf education begins in late eighteenth-century France, and the first school for deaf students was established by Thomas Gallaudet in 1817, teaching at first French sign language (Gibson, Small and Mason 1997). A number of schools were opened in the USA, and as ASL (American sign language) developed, it was used and taught in them. Later in the century, however, the International Congress of Educators of the Deaf called for a change in policy and for oral language instruction for the deaf. Sign went underground, and only in the 1960s did schools for the deaf again recognize it as part of a total communication approach combining sign and oral language (Wilcox 1999). Recognition of sign languages as languages of instruction became more common in the 1980s, with ASL and LSQ (langue de signes québécois) recognized in Canada, Swedish sign language (to be taught alongside Swedish) in 1980 and Danish sign language about the same time. The Council of Europe has so far rejected proposals to treat sign languages as minority languages.

Claims are regularly made and occasionally met for granting appropriate language rights to the deaf (Lucas 2001). This has come to involve not just granting status, but also providing for various aspects of cultivation of sign languages: standardization, development of dictionaries and elaboration of terminology. One critical policy issue concerns education of deaf children, with a long controversy still continuing as to whether to teach them sign language or to provide them with other techniques (lip-reading, for example) for access to the local standard language. Since the 1970s, approaches favor combinations of the spoken to language and the sign language. However, in many parts of the world the use of sign languages as medium of instruction is quite recent. In institutions and countries where the rights of the deaf are starting to be recognized, provision is sometimes made for interpreters.

In 1987, the Tenth World Congress of the World Federation of the Deaf adopted a resolution calling for the recognition of the "distinct national sign languages of indigenous deaf populations" as their "natural language of right for direct communication." Application of this principle would be a major advance, but at the same time it leads to the development of standardized codes, often under the control of hearing people, that results in the loss of the various natural localized deaf community varieties (Branson and Miller 1998). In Australia, this has produced a single national sign language, called Auslan, to be learned and used by all non-aboriginal deaf, whatever their original language. Similarly, in South Africa, the twelve distinct communities with national sign languages are expected to acquire and use the single South African sign language that is being developed. In other words, they show that the same national pressure for homogeneity affects sign languages as well as spoken.

MONOLINGUAL POLITIES – CONCLUSIONS

While there may have been a time when it seemed simple for a nation state to announce its recognition of a single national and official language, analyzing actual cases reveals that countries monolingual in both practice and management are quite rare. Societal multilingualism and the pressures associated with internal or external belief that language is subject to the application of individual human and civil rights have forced most states to modify their language policy by recognizing, legally or constitutionally or in specific management practices, the existence of other languages and the rights of their speakers. Language rights are a salient issue in ideologically monolingual societies, for in the multilingual polities to be studied next, the competition between languages was sufficiently salient to force legal or constitutional acknowledgement of the need to partition linguistic space.

In the last two chapters, we have touched only incidentally on threats of globalization and the invasion of English. The cases studied have exemplified the force of the demand for a single language as the basis for national unity and identity on the one hand, and the counter-pressure provided partly by linguistic minorities, whether indigenous or imported, claiming competing identities (and associated languages) and partly by the growing acceptance (or imposition) of human rights as a countermeasure to the absolutism of nationalism. These nations, while multilingual in language practice and partly in language man-agement, might well have preferred to implement their monolingual ideologies. In the next chapter, studying nations whose constitution attempts to divide linguistic space between two or more languages, we will have a chance to see whether multilingualism is an acceptable kind of linguistic ideology and how it works in practice.

11 Partitioning language space - two, three, many

PARTITIONING LINGUISTIC SPACE – DYADIC AND TRIADIC POLITIES

The monolingual nation state exists ideologically if rarely in observable language practice. In multilingual nations, the significance of two or three or more major languages is recognized. However, there is no reason to suspect that it will be this linguistic fact rather than people's perception of it that will be the driving force of language policy. In this chapter, we deal with nation states that have recognized not just the existence but also the claims of more than one language and have attempted to satisfy these claims by partitioning their linguistic space and assigning a portion to each.

How might this be done? An initial problem is the sloppiness of the labels we have available. The word bilingual is used for both an individual and a society, and commonly assumed to carry the meaning of equality of proficiency or use. A bilingual individual in this sense is rare: plurilingual proficiency, as the Council of Europe experts more sagely named it, covers wide ranges of difference in the kinds and domains of language competence in two (or usually more) varieties of language. An Israeli may do physics in English, but prefer to talk about football in Hebrew. Most people probably continue to count in the language they first spoke and are more comfortable speaking of certain topics in one of their various languages. Plurilingual proficiency is better described or profiled than measured.

Similarly with nations and other social groups; it is unlikely ever to be the case that any two languages or varieties overlap completely in the spaces that they fill. The actual division may be demographic (with variation according to place of birth or residence, gender or age, level of education or occupation, social or economic status, religious or ethnic affiliation) or locality (a kind of variation which has given rise to dialect geography) or function/topic (the basis for Ferguson's proposal

161

of the concept of diglossia) or according to empirically determined domains, as Fishman proposed.

The management of partition is generally determined demographically (applying to a specific set of citizens, such as speakers of a particular language or members of a particular ethnic group) or by locality (applying in pre-selected regions or in villages or towns which reach a criterion level of percentage of speakers of a specific language) or by function (dealing with national or local government, in public or private business, in education or in the media). Each of these or some combination of them occurs.

On the evidence of what we have seen so far about interpretations of linguistic rights, we should not be surprised to find a preference for the simplest seeming solution, the region. The Belgian model solves most of its problems by determining that one area of the country should use Dutch, another French and the third German, leaving only one city, Brussels, to work out a more delicate language distribution. The same is largely true of Switzerland and India, with each canton in the former or state in the latter selecting its own preferred regional language. Ethnically diverse societies like Singapore accept that Chinese, Tamils and Malays will have social if not territorial spaces to use their own languages, while using English when together. Diglossic communities like Paraguay agree that Spanish and Guarani can be used for different functions, but also have some locality and class differentiation.

One inevitable result of any linguistic partitioning is the need for individuals capable of bridging any resulting communication gap. Societal multilingualism therefore puts some kind of premium on the plurilingual proficiency of some individuals. Ideally, many nations will endeavor to increase the membership of this brokering group, by requiring or encouraging the acquisition of the second (provided there are only two) language as part of normal education.

DYADIC AND TRIADIC POLITIES

Dyadic or triadic states are countries with two or three languages in active competition. In such cases, Lambert hypothesized that the principal issue in language policy would be the struggle between the two languages. A number of nation states formally and legally divide their sociolinguistic space by identifying two official (or national) languages in a constitution or language law; they are listed in table 3.

Looking over this list, a first distinction is between those countries where the bilingualism or multilingualism arose historically out of

Table 3 *Dyadic and triadic nation states*

Nation state	Languages
Afghanistan	Pashtu and Dari were official
Belarus	Belarussian and Russian are state languages
Belgium	Four regions are set up
Cameroon	French and English are official
Canada	English and French are official
Cook Islands	Māori and English are parliamentary languages
Cyprus	Greek and Turkish
Fiji	English, Fijian, Hindustani
Finland	Finnish and Swedish
Haiti	Creole and French official
Hong Kong	Chinese and English
Iraq	Arabic (Arabic and Kurdish regionally)
Ireland	Irish first and English second
Israel	Hebrew and Arabic (by law)
Kazakhstan	Kazakh and Russian
Kenya	English, Kiswahili
Malta	Maltese and English
New Zealand	English and Māori (law)
Niue	English and Niuean (parliamentary)
Paraguay	Guarani and Spanish
Philippines	Pilipino (English) also regional languages
Puerto Rico	Spanish (English?)
Rwanda	Kinyarwanda and French
Samoa	Samoan and English (parliamentary)
Seychelles	Creole, English, French
Singapore	Malay, English (Tamil, Mandarin)
Slovenia	Slovene and regionally Hungarian
South Africa (earlier)	English and Afrikaans
Sri Lanka	Sinhala and Tamil
Switzerland	German, French, Italian, Romansch regionally
Tajikistan	Tajik state language, Russian
Tanzania	English official, Swahili national?
Vanuatu	Bislama national, French and English official

the combination of two or more distinct speech communities into a single political unit (Belgium, Switzerland) or those where it may be explained by the introduction of another language by colonial powers (Samoa, Tanzania, Vanuatu). A third possibility, including some features of both, is where the colonial or imperial power was responsible for the settlement in the country by speakers of the second language (Fiji, Kazakhstan and New Zealand).

164   LANGUAGE POLICY

Belgium

The linguistic conflict between 6 million speakers of Flemish (Dutch) and 4 million speakers of French has been the focus of "heightened nationalist feeling" in Belgium for the past century and a half. Because of the successful revolt from Spanish rule of the northern Netherlands, Dutch developed there as a standard language. In the south, French was dominant; it became official in 1795 when the region was incorporated into the French Republic. French was the dominant public language in the new kingdom of Belgium (Howell 2000).

The Belgian Constitution recognizes French, Dutch and to a lesser extent, German as official. In fact, most Belgians speak unofficial varieties. There are three distinct Romance dialectal varieties (Walloon, Picard and Lorrain), and four Germanic (West Flemish, Brabantish, Limburgish and Luxemburgish) (Aunger 1993). The conflict between French and Dutch, then, which is the kind of status issue that Lambert predicted, has served to cover up the corpus issues of managing the gap between standard language and dialects.

Belgium has recognized three national languages, French, Flemish (renamed Dutch in 1932) and German, since its independence in 1830. In the 1870s, laws permitted official use of Flemish and it became the language of public affairs in Flanders in the 1920s. German was recognized as official in its region in 1925 (Aunger 1993). In 1932 Dutch became the language of instruction in Flanders and French in Wallonia, with German in some areas. Responsibility for schools has recently been transferred from two national Ministries of Education to three community councils.

The method of dealing with the tension between languages was the principle of territoriality, which McRae (1975) distinguished from the principle of personality, which means "the rules will depend on the linguistic status of the person or persons concerned." Territoriality applies in Belgium and in Switzerland; personality is the basis for Canadian federal legislation (Nelde, Labrie and Williams 1992). Regional unilingualism was a compromise between two alternative proposals: the status quo with French dominant or nationwide bilingualism.

Language conflict continued until at least 1992, when a majority finally agreed on federalism with the devolution of power to the regions (Covell 1993). Each language has separate institutions in many spheres and contact is decreasing. Only in Brussels is there continued contact between French- and Dutch-speakers (Murphy 1993). Nelde (1996) points out that there is no linguistic legislation prescribing plurilingualism.

The foreign-language teaching policy, which varies from region to region, does little to correct this. Only in Brussels is Dutch or French a compulsory language for students being educated in the other language.

Like most of northern Europe, Belgium, too, has a significant immigrant population, both legal and illegal, who add to potential language policy concerns. But as Lambert predicted, the essentially dyadic language situation in Belgium has for the last 150 years also been the principal focus of language policy conflicts. Belgian national identity has overweighed any desire by French- or Dutch-speakers to solve the problems by seceding and joining their French- or Dutch-speaking neighbors. The solution chosen to the language conflict has been separatism rather than multilingualism, leaving Brussels as a focus of contention.

Original multilingualism

Analysis of other cases of dyadic or triadic nation states finds similar complexity in practices and management, but a common belief that the key problem is a choice between the two or three significant languages. By original multilingualism, I mean other cases like Belgium where a national border enclosed two or more distinct ethnic or linguistic groups. Here, three countries are of special interest: Finland, with its long established and recognized Swedish minority; Switzerland, with its assumed bilingualism; and Sri Lanka, with its continued tension between speakers of two competing languages.

Finland, Vikor (2000: 117) noted, had no history of medieval independence but was slowly integrated into Swedish rule. Even before the Viking period, Swedes moved into the southwestern coastal region, and Finns expanded throughout the rest of the country. No effort was made by the ruling Swedes to replace Finnish, but Swedish remained the language of the elite and of the coastal areas. Under Russian rule, Swedish continued as the official standard language. A Finnish-language movement first appeared in the early 1800s and in 1863, Finnish was recognized as equal. By independence in 1917, Finnish had become the national standard language, with Swedish a minority language. The 1919 Constitution established strict equality. For the next twenty years, serious rivalry continued between supporters of the two languages, and only after the Second World War was official bilingualism generally accepted. In practice, Finnish is the language of 95 percent of the population, with Swedish used by 5 percent in southwestern coastal areas.

In addition to the two major groups, there are smaller linguistic minorities. The islands of Åland, part of Finland, were granted home rule and constitutionally recognized as monolingual Swedish. There is also an autochthonous minority, the Sami. Only a few thousand Sami live in Finland, but as a result of an organized struggle for ethnic and linguistic rights, the language received official status in the north Sami core area in Finland and Norway in 1992.

The borders of Switzerland by 1815 already included speakers of four main languages, German, French, Italian and Romansch, each in their own local areas. When the Swiss Confederation was established in 1848, maximum autonomy was given to the twenty-six cantons into which the country was divided. Seventeen of the cantons were German speaking, four French speaking, three French–German bilingual; one Italian speaking and one trilingual in Romansch, German and Italian. Currently, two-thirds of the population speak German as their first language, 20 percent speak French, over 6 percent Italian, and 0.5 percent Romansch. While it is commonly believed that the Swiss are plurilingual, in fact knowledge of a second national language is rapidly being overtaken by knowledge of English, and one canton (Zurich) recently started a national debate by proposing to give priority to the teaching of English in schools. Proficiency in English is associated with "remarkably high and statistically robust wage premiums which . . . range from 12% to 30%" (Grin 2001). German in Switzerland is one of the classic cases of diglossia recognized by Ferguson (1959).

Sri Lanka (formerly Ceylon) became a British crown colony in 1802, with English the official language, but only a tiny minority learned it (Fernando 1996). Until 1946, most education was in vernacular-medium primary schools. In 1956, the independent government made Sinhala the official language. Because of strong objections from the Tamil minority, in 1972 Tamil was recognized as a national language alongside Sinhala. In practice, English continued to be used by bureaucrats and professionals and remained the language of the law courts. Schools were separated ethnically and linguistically. In 1946, English became a second language for all; the English-medium stream in secondary schools was phased out by 1970. In 2001, the Ministry of Education proposed that selected schools in Colombo and Kandy would offer instruction to children from all three communities "in the medium of their choice," which in practice meant English for core subjects. The goal was integration, but some of the schools started the program without admitting children from the other community. Thus, while Sri Lanka assumed that it could manage with a single indigenous national language, and aimed to phase out the colonial language, the long conflict between the Sinhalese and the Tamils has led to different solutions being tried: first, the recognition of a separate Tamil school system, and most recently, the use of the old colonial language partly in order to attempt integration.

Postcolonial bilingualism (without extensive settlement)

As a general rule, the colonial sharing of the world among the major European powers in the eighteenth and nineteenth centuries introduced to the conquered territories a European language as language of government, power, education and commerce. Independence automatically allowed a new choice of official language. Some colonies chose a single language, either the former colonial language or the indigenous local language, but were constrained to recognize the languages not chosen. Other former colonies tried to resolve the problem by recognizing in their constitution both the indigenous and the former colonial language as equals. Again, closer analysis shows much complexity. First, the bilingualism asserted in the constitution is not necessarily consistent with the sociolinguistic pattern of the country. For example, Vanuatu, which declares itself triadic in policy, has at least eighty actively used languages, with an average of 2,500 speakers of each (Crowley 2000: 50).

The former British colony, Kiribati (once known as the Gilbert Islands), preserves the colonial language as official. Almost all of its population (about 60,000) are reported to speak Kiribati, and a third are said to be reasonably proficient in English. Most children attended mission schools conducted in Kiribati (Benton 1981: 130). Secondary education for an elite group is in English.

The two Samoas – independent Western Samoa and American Samoa – with all their differences, provide another example of postcolonial bilingualism. In the latter part of the nineteenth century, Samoa remained a semi-autonomous kingdom under a joint protectorate conducted by Great Britain, Germany and United States. In 1899, Germany took control of Western Samoa, leaving the smaller eastern islands to become United States possessions. After the First World War, New Zealand took over Western Samoa, continuing rule until independence in 1962. During the nineteenth century, conversion to Christianity had produced vernacular literacy, and elementary education was conducted in Samoan (Benton 1981: 87). Secondary education, whether in Samoa itself or in boarding schools in New Zealand, was in English. After independence, while the position of English continued to improve, Samoan remained strong in the school curriculum and in the villages.

The local language fared much less well in US Samoa, where public schools replacing the mission schools started teaching in English in 1903. In 1949, Samoan was recognized as an auxiliary language in schools, but only in the 1966 Constitution was the principle laid down of protecting the Samoan way of life and language (Benton 1981: 92). Many US Samoans have moved to the USA: by 1977, the local population was 34,000, with another 20,000 resident in the US. More recently, various efforts have been made to revive the teaching of Samoan in schools (Manase, Luaao and Fiamalua 1996).

With a population under 200,000, and at least eighty indigenous languages (none spoken by more than 6 percent of the population), Vanuatu, an independent republic spread over an 850-kilometer expanse of Pacific islands, sets a major challenge for language policy. It was governed under a joint Franco-British condominium until 1980. During this period, Bislama, an English-based pidgin developed as the lingua franca and was recognized in the 1980 Constitution as a national language and as an official language alongside English and French (Crowley 2000). Many local languages developed literacy thanks to missionaries, who avoided the use of Bislama until the 1960s; church services are still multilingual. A few English-medium and French-medium schools were set up. After independence, the systems were combined. Pre-school classes are conducted in Bislama or local languages and there are a few elite English- or French-medium secondary schools. Since independence, there has been a steady shift towards English-medium schools, in spite of the efforts of a francophile government. Language shift from the smaller vernaculars is slow, but there is no government support for languages other than English or French.

Tanzania is another nation that, while officially bilingual, has in fact 120 ethnic languages. Tanzania was under German rule from 1884 until 1919 and then under British. During the German period, Kiswahili was used for instruction and administration. Under the British, English became the language of government. Kiswahili was used in elementary education but English in secondary schools. Many missionaries preferred the local ethnic languages. When middle schools were opened in the 1950s, parents demanded they use English. Kiswahili was then restricted to the first two years (Yahya-Othman and Batibo 1996). The 1962 Constitution declared English and Swahili official languages. The role of the languages has remained the focus of debate. In 1967, Kiswahili was declared the medium of instruction in all primary education, and it was to become the medium for higher education. A 1982 recommendation that it replace English at the secondary level was rejected by the government. The comprehensive 1995 education plan reaffirmed the use of English in education, to be taught in primary school (Vavrus 2002). While most public life in Tanzania is now conducted in Kiswahili, English remains the medium of instruction in secondary and tertiary education. Major efforts continue to be expended on improving the teaching of English, which pupils believe is the way to escape from serious economic hardship.

The 1968 Malawi Congress Party Convention declared Chichewa and English official languages (Matiki 2001). In practice, policy implementation has favored English in all official domains of national life. During the British colonial period, Chichewa was used in the lower levels of primary education, and English in advanced instruction. It was assumed that the vernacular would grow in prestige after independence. At independence, three-quarters of the population understood Chichewa, while only 5 percent understood English. There have since 1994 been efforts to raise the status and use of other indigenous languages. English, however, is dominant in advanced education, national examinations and various government functions. The 1994 Constitution requires parliamentary candidates to be able to use English in debates. Government administration is mainly conducted in English. Newspapers are published in English with one of two pages in Chichewa. Enormous social engineering will be needed, Matiki believes, to change people's attitudes towards indigenous languages.

From a linguistic point of view, the fact that most people in Rwanda, with a population of nearly 7.5 million, speak the same language, Kinyarwanda, should make things simple. The language is national and official, although French, too, has official status and there are those who use Swahili and others who favor English. The murderous ethnic disputes over the last half century between the Hutu (about 84 percent of the population) and the Tutsi (about 15 percent), leading to the massacres in the early 1990s, had nothing to do with language.

The African countries using English as the language of secondary and advanced education and so preparing it to serve in the higher functions alongside indigenous lingua francas and local languages are clearly producing a new kind of diglossia. For Fasold (2002), the key point about diglossia is that the higher-status language of the two is not spoken natively within the community but acquired formally. On this basis, he includes Paraguay as a case of diglossia. Paraguay, since the classic study by Rubin (1968), has been considered a paradigmatic case of such dyadic functional division. With exceptions at the upper and lower socioeconomic extremes, most Paraguayans are reported to be bilingual in Spanish and Guarani, switching between the two according to social situation, interlocutor and topic. Exceptionally in

Latin America, an indigenous language has achieved a status equal to that of Spanish (Corvalan 1988). Among the influences leading to its special place was economic development: in the absence of the gold and silver mining which was important in the Andes, the economy was rural and based on cattle. Cheap labor was provided by native women, and the children of these women and their Spanish masters had a major effect in developing *mestizaje*. Paraguay never had a mass influx of Spanish immigrants, so the population was mixed. During the period of the Jesuit influence, up to 1767, Spanish was stressed, but there was also development of Guarani literacy, which was allowed to lapse after the expulsion of the Jesuits. The next hundred years constituted a period of isolation, with expansion of the Spanish language in education and in urban areas. Guarani emerged once again as the center of national mobilization during the War of the Triple Alliance (1865 to 1870) but it was suppressed again until the Chaco War in the early 1930s. Slowly, efforts were made to re-establish its formal recognition, and it was reintroduced into the curriculum in the 1970s. The National Constitution of 1967 recognized Spanish as the official language and Guarani as the national language. Language education policy assumes that Spanish will be developed for all skills, but Guarani only for listening and speaking. There are, however, recent efforts to encourage Guarani literacy. Since 1990, the teaching of both Spanish and Guarani has been mandatory at all levels. Gynan (2001) traced the complex political history of attitudes to Guarani, with the encouragement of the rural peasantry during Stroessner's thirty-five years of dictatorship, and the continued acceptance of national bilingualism since, influenced by statements of UNESCO and the Organization of American States on indigenous language rights.

Singapore is often presented as an example of successful implementation of language policy. Its partitioning of linguistic space recognizes both the complexity of its sociolinguistic situation and the need to carry out a number of specific language-management decisions. These include the assertion of national identity through Malay, the integration of three distinct ethnic groups by recognizing one language for each, the encouragement of all Chinese speakers to use Mandarin and the development of economic potential by creating English-based bilingualism for all. Singapore recognizes four official languages: Malay (the national language used for ceremonial occasions), Mandarin, Tamil and English. Home language use shows a different pattern. According to the 2002 census, in Chinese homes, about 45 percent use Mandarin, 30 percent use other Chinese dialects and 24 percent use English. In Malay homes, over 90 percent use Malay and 8 percent English.

In Indian homes, 43 percent use Tamil and 35 percent English (Wee 2002). English is the major language for government, trade and communication between the major ethnic groups. Since independence, government language policy has encouraged a high level of proficiency in English. Under colonial government, education was offered in the four languages, with English associated with elite education. The 1959 policy declared Malay the national language. In 1978, however, the Ministry of Education called for English-based bilingualism, intending both to strengthen the economic development of Singapore and to weaken the influence of the Chinese (Tickoo 1996). A 1980 policy increased the teaching of English at primary school and made it the medium of instruction in secondary and tertiary education. Subsequently, English-medium instruction was introduced at the primary level. Tickoo and others believe that this policy has been successful and contributed to the rapid economic development of Singapore. Recently, industrial competition from China and the consequent need to build better trade relations are providing pragmatic reasons to teach more Mandarin in schools.

Postcolonial plus settlement

Many countries include in their sociolinguistic make up a sizeable number of immigrants brought in during the colonial period. In some cases, they were European, adding weight to the claim for continuing use of the colonial language.

The new Constitution of South Africa recognizes eleven national languages, but does not prescribe the use of all of them under all circumstances. However, earlier, all discussion tended to focus on the rivalry between the two introduced numerically minority European official languages, Dutch (renamed Afrikaans) and English. When the British began to colonize South Africa in the early nineteenth century, they set out to replace Dutch by English. When the Union was set up in 1910, Dutch joined English as an equal official language, its rights protected in the constitution (Malherbe 1978: 176). African languages were marginalized. Between 1948 and 1976, the period of "grand apartheid," the dominance of English was slowly weakened. Some teaching of (but not in) African languages was also encouraged (McLean and McCormick 1996). Mother-tongue education for white speakers of English and Afrikaans and for the colored was the general policy: both languages were compulsory in the separate streams and schools. In black schools, mother-tongue (vernacular) instruction was the rule for the first eight years, with either English or Afrikaans as a compulsory second language. A later decision required black children to learn both official languages, but after the Soweto riots of 1976 the official insistence on Afrikaans was dropped. From 1976 to 1990, language planning as an apartheid project involved the codification and elaboration of African languages, but terminological development failed. After Soweto, English became the medium of instruction for most black pupils from the fifth year. The example of the Republic of South Africa as a dyadic country makes clear the importance of the notion of perception rather than reality: as long as Afrikaans and English were the two official languages, only they were perceived as salient. With the constitutional change, the new South Africa was recognized as a multilingual mosaic, and the policy developed was intended to make sense of this new recognition of previously existing diversity (see below).

The forcible movement of populations, whether for purposes of ethnic cleansing, finding new space to send emigrants or the provision of inexpensive labor has had a major effect on sociolinguistic situations and so on the development of language policy. Fiji is a prime example. The Fiji Islands, with its indigenous Melanesian population including an intermixture of Polynesian elements, became a British colony in the late nineteenth century. With the development of a labor-intensive sugar industry appearing hampered by Fijian unwillingness to work under the conditions proposed, the British solution was to bring large numbers of indentured workers from India. Recruitment misrepresented conditions and aimed to bring only uneducated workers and not potential community leaders. The program continued until 1919, when Indians were offered the possibility of returning to India. The majority, however, stayed on, but were prevented by law from purchasing farmland from the native Fijians. Indians were allowed to lease land for limited terms and moved also into commerce. By the 1980s, the two populations were more or less equally balanced, but following a military coup in 1987 and a new constitution, many Indians emigrated, leaving a situation where Melanesians make up 51 percent of the approximately 850,000 population and Indians are 44 percent. Under the British, English was the official language but Fijian and Hindi were recognized. Education, offered originally by missionaries and later by community organizations as well, provided primary schooling in the Fijian schools initially in the dialect of Fijian selected for the Bible translation, with transition to English. Schools for Indians run by the community and religious organizations also offered initial programs in standard Hindustani (not the mother tongue of many of the students) with transition to English. In 1969, the Fiji Education Commission recommended continuation of the transitional use of ethnic languages as an interim measure, to be replaced by English as the sole medium of instruction. The mother tongues were to be maintained as cultural languages (Benton 1981). Benton reported little support for bilingual education: apart from all its other obvious values, English offered a neutral lingua franca for the two communities regularly in conflict. While some sources report that English is currently the sole medium of instruction in the independently operated Melanesian and Indian schools, other reports say that the initial use of the community language continues.

MAKING SENSE OF MOSAIC MULTILINGUALISM

In Lambert's third category of nation states, he places countries with a complex mosaic of multilingualism. The challenge of a situation like this is obvious: the simple decision to recognize two or three languages and divide up their functions will not work in a country that includes a dozen or a hundred or several hundred languages. Lambert believed, then, that in these complex multilingual polities, the status of each language would be a continuing concern for language policy. The countries which, according to the sometimes generous count provided by *Ethnologue*, have a dozen or more significant languages, are listed in table 4.

India

The language policy of India has been extensively and deeply studied. It is obvious why. According to *Ethnologue*, India has 387 living languages. The Constitution that India adopted on independence from British rule in 1948 recognized eleven official languages: Assamese, Bengali, Gujarati, Hindi, Kannada, Kashmiri, Malayalam, Marathi, Oriya, Punjabi, Sanskrit, Sindhi, Tamil, Telugu and Urdu. English is recognized as associate official. Obviously, to attempt to make sense of language policy in such a large country, with all its political, cultural, religious and linguistic diversity, would take more than the few pages available in this chapter; several books at the very least would be needed to analyze the history and current status of even a handful of the languages involved. The purpose of this sketch, then, is to try to identify some of the major features that distinguish a mosaic multilingual from a dyadic or monolingual polity.

One might start with a seemingly simple question: how many languages are there? The first serious count was by Grierson, who in surveys in the 1880s listed 179 languages and 544 dialects (Pandit 1975). For comparison, in the 1961 census, 1,652 language names were reported, classified into about 200 languages (Srivastava 1988). The 1948

Table 4 *Countries with twelve or more languages according to* Ethnologue

Country	Number of languages	Constitutional recognition
Papua New Guinea	823	
Indonesia	726	Yes
Nigeria	505	
India	387	Yes (12)
Mexico	288	
Cameroon	279	
Congo, Democratic Republic	218	Yes (6)
China	201	Yes
Brazil	192	Yes
USA	176	
Sudan	174	
Philippines	169	Yes
Malaysia	139	
Tanzania	135	
Chad	132	
Nepal	120	Yes
Vanuatu	109	Yes
Burma	107	
Russia	100	Yes
Vietnam	93	
Peru	92	Yes
Canada	90	
Ethiopia	82	Yes
Laos	82	
Colombia	78	Yes
Côte d'Ivoire	77	
Thailand	75	
Ghana	70	
Iran	69	Yes
Pakistan	69	
Solomon Islands	69	Yes
Burkina-Faso	66	Yes
Congo, Republic	61	Yes (3)
Kenya	61	
Central African Republic	60	
Guatemala	54	Yes
Benin	51	Yes
Uganda	43	Yes
Togo	42	
Gabon	41	Yes
Zambia	41	
Mali	40	Yes
Venezuela	40	Yes

Table 4 (*cont.*)

Country	Number of languages	Constitutional recognition
Mozambique	39	
Bangladesh	38	Yes
New Caledonia	38	
Bolivia	37	
Senegal	36	Yes
Guinea	33	
Israel	33	
Italy	33	
France	29	
Namibia	29	Yes
South Africa	28	Yes (11)
Botswana	26	
Germany	25	
Bhutan	24	
Liberia	24	
Iraq	23	
Sierra Leone	23	
Ecuador	22	Yes
Singapore	21	Yes (4)
Guinea-Bissau	20	
Niger	20	
Paraguay	20	Yes
Zimbabwe	20	
Cambodia	19	
Micronesia	17	Yes
Netherlands	16	
Japan	15	
Malawi	15	Yes
Romania	15	
Suriname	15	
Syria	15	
Azerbaijan	14	
Panama	14	
Equatorial Guinea	13	
Greece	13	
Somalia	13	
Spain	13	Yes
Eritrea	12	Yes
Guyana	12	
Hungary	12	Yes
Mongolia	12	Yes
Switzerland	12	Yes (4)
United Kingdom	12	

Constitution recognized only eleven languages plus English as official. Hindi is the official language of five states and of two union territories. The other eleven states recognize each of the eleven major languages for various official purposes.

In practice, how does this multilingualism work? In India, language is often associated with conflict and even violence. Olson and Pearson (2001) studied twenty-seven events in which there were major conflicts about language that led to protest or violence. Violence, which occurred in twenty-two cases, followed proposals for policies which would discriminate against a specific language. Olson and Pearson concluded "language policy moves are now important in generating societal upheavals."

It may well be that this focusing on language conflict as a cause of violence is exaggerated. For example, Fishman (1989) did not find a clear association between the linguistic heterogeneity of a polity and reports of civil strife. Nor did Horowitz (2001), in his study of deadly riots, find a linguistic component in more than two recent Indian disturbances: in 1965, in protests in South India against proposals to make Hindi official (2001: 19), and in 1967, in riots protesting an attempt to make Urdu the second official language of Bihar (2001: 287). In his analysis of the many other deadly riots in India, he found the main associated factors not to be linguistic but religious, communal or generally ethnic.

Srivastava (1988) noted that two kinds of plurilingual proficiency are normal in India. One kind is elite plurilingualism, produced by education and usually consisting of English and one or more Indian languages. Much more widespread is folk plurilingualism, often a combination of a home or ethnic language with the dominant regional language. Depending on the local sociolinguistic repertoire, complex patterns of multilingualism and associated plurilingual competence may emerge. Left alone, communication in everyday life works almost as well in a multilingual as a monolingual society.

Multilingualism obviously produces pragmatic problems for central political control. While ancient and medieval governments could use interpreters and scribes to send occasional instructions to distant dependencies, modern active government is easiest when it can be conducted in a single language, providing translation services for as few others as possible. Simply from the point of view of efficiency, any government is forced to make some language-management decisions.

The establishment of educational systems in multiethnic and multilingual countries calls for hard decisions about language matters. Before the British conquered India, there were two competing educational systems: the Brahman, with its focus on Sanskrit and the sacred texts of Hinduism, and the Muslim, with its focus on the Qur'an. The schools that the British set up replaced both. In the nineteenth century, there was a serious debate in the East India Company and the British colonial government about language policy for the schools. Macaulay, whose Minute is often cited, took an extreme anglicist position. The goal of British education in India, he believed, should be to teach Western knowledge, and the best way to do this was in English, but to a carefully selected elite. The opposite, orientalist position agreed more or less to teach Western knowledge, but believed it should be done in the vernacular. This position was slowly accepted, but without replacing the regional English-medium schools.

During the nineteenth-century, opposition to British rule had linguistic components. In the United and Central Provinces, Hindustani was supported by government, but Hindustani written in Persian script and more or less identical with Urdu. With rising Hindu consciousness and the establishment of the Indian National Congress, a movement developed to promote Hindi written in the Devanagari script (Mehrotra 1993). Nationalists competed with English by cultivating their own language. Muslims did this by using Persian words in Urdu; Hindus cultivated Hindi by borrowing from Sanskrit. The two varieties slowly moved apart. Gandhi was unhappy at the elitist nature of Hindi language reform, hoping to develop an urban colloquial Hindi that could be written in either Devanagari or Persian script and unite Hindu and Muslim in independent India. The Hindi language reformers, however, supported the Sanskritist position.

All this provides some background to the complex language issues that faced newly independent India in 1948. The price of making Hindi official was the recognition of ten other official languages. If the issue had been merely winnowing down the mosaic of languages to manageable proportions, this could well have been the end of the matter. The largest language, Hindi, was selected as the national and official language that would ultimately guarantee Indian unity. Just as France, with the power of the French Revolution, could fight off the challenge of peripheral varieties like Basque, Breton and Occitan, so India with its independence could try to unify around a single language. Article 351 of the Constitution required the federal government "to promote the spread of the Hindi language, to develop it so that it may serve as a medium of expression for all the elements in the composite culture of India." Within fifteen years, Hindi was to replace English for all official purposes. As it turned out, the task was made difficult, if not impossible, by the fact that supporters of Hindi had to fight on two fronts: to establish Hindi as first among potential equals, and to take on English, a language that was soon to show its global strength. In 1963, recognizing reality, the Official Languages Act allowed the continuing use of English for official purposes.

English was in fact deeply entrenched by 1948. The main focus of national policy was on replacing English by Hindi, but a first necessary step was to replace English by the regional languages. Otherwise, as happened, restriction of the use of English was seen as divisive rather than unifying, promoting as it did Hindi over the regional languages.

Before independence, the compromise between the anglicist and orientalist policies had resulted in the development of three linguistic patterns in government schools. In the larger urban centers, there were elite English-medium schools. In towns, the British colonial compromise was in place: two-tier schools, with the vernacular used for primary education and English for secondary and advanced education. In rural areas, where only primary education was offered, it was in the vernacular (Khubchandani 1997).

After independence, India, like other newly independent states, was attracted by three competing views. The first was recognition of the importance of indigenous languages in official policy; the second was acceptance of the value of education in the mother tongue; and the third was the need to establish political unity by developing a national language. The first clearly implied rejection of the metropolitan colonial language, something that was widely accepted in theory but never implemented effectively. The second involved a decision on what to count as the mother tongue. Many Indian educators, Khubchandani reports, wanted to define as mother tongues only those languages which already had a developed written tradition. In India, however, the linguistic minorities managed to establish a more precise interpretation: mother tongue meant the home language of the child. To fulfill these conflicting goals, India developed the three language formula, which aimed at national unity through linguistic diversity. It accepted the home language as medium of instruction in primary and lower secondary school. Hindi was to be learned during these years and serve as the official medium and language of wider communication and national unity for all of India. English was to be kept for higher education and intellectual and international communication. In different parts of India, the three language formula was interpreted differently: some states included Sanskrit and others added a fourth regional language.

The planning and implementation of this policy proved extremely difficult. By the mid-1980s, no more than 67 of the 200 classified languages were actually being used in education. In higher education,

English continued virtually unchallenged. In fact, bilingual education appears to exist in India only because of continuing widespread multilingualism. Almost all rural schools use a vernacular as medium of instruction, while the more prestigious urban schools use English from the primary stage.

As a result, Dua (1996) believed that English spread more pervasively in India after independence than during the colonial period. Because of the pressure for modernization associated with westernization, there was little chance, Dua believes, to reform the educational system, so that English continued to be the medium of instruction in all systems except government schools using the regional languages. In recent years then, the place of English seems to be unquestioned, and Dua doubts if its spread can be stopped.

The case of India shows that it is too simple to say that polities with a complex linguistic mosaic are concerned mainly with the competition among the various languages. First, this competition is strongly influenced by the level of cultivation of the local languages, and in fact efforts at language cultivation become a significant part of language management. Beyond this, with the growing diffusion of English as a result not just of local pre-independence colonialism, but also of growing globalization, the existence of the mosaic turns out to provide further support for English as against the selection of a single national language.

Some other multilingual polities

Endowed with 500 languages, Indonesia, like India, had a major problem in language management if ever it was to establish national unity and efficient government. Indonesian is perhaps the only language in the region that has succeeded in establishing itself as the national language. In 1926, the Youth Congress discussed the language issue and at a Second Congress in 1928, Malay was selected as national language and renamed Indonesian. There was no objection from non-Malay speakers as the language was widely used as a lingua franca. Choosing Malay also meant rejecting Dutch, an easier task than rejecting English in other countries. In 1945, when Indonesia became independent, the Constitution named Bahasa Indonesia as the national language. In the next few years a language institute was established, renamed, reorganized and finally, in 1993, raised to the status of a ministry, responsible also for vernacular languages, for a common spelling system and for terminological innovation. The Constitution of 1989 stated that vernacular languages could be used as the elementary level. English is taught as the first foreign language, but not successfully. While it is widely assumed that Indonesian now serves as an interethnic language, the only empirical study to date (Goebel 2002) found it being used alternately with local languages.

China, with its enormous population, long and complex history, rich mosaic of peoples, languages and dialects, sets a major challenge not just for those who would develop a language policy but also for anyone who tries to discover and describe it. Language reform in China started in the nineteenth century. After the 1911 Revolution, the government set out to promote a national language, to develop a vernacular style of writing and to adopt an alphabet (Youguang 1986). In 1958, the People's Republic of China set three tasks for language reform: simplification of the characters, popularization of a common language (*Putonghua*), and revision of the Romanization (*Pinyin*). How many varieties of Chinese there are remains a disputed question. Youguang (1986: 7) lists eight regional dialects, dividing the largest, Mandarin, into four sub-regional dialects. Marshall (1990: 10) said there were fifty-six recognized nationalities, all but one with a differing language and many with national language committees. Hongkai (1992: 10) added that fifteen of the fifty-five minorities used more than two languages each.

The national spoken language was originally called Guanhua, "officials' language", usually translated Mandarin; it was later called Guoyu "state or national language" and since 1955, has been known as Putonghua, "general language." Since 1924, it has been accepted that the pronunciation used in Beijing, capital of China for 1000 years, should be the standard. In 1982, a clause was added to the Constitution stating that "the state is to popularize Putonghua that is current in the whole country." The success of the campaign to spread Putonghua is not known: the Institute for Applied Linguistics in Beijing is just carrying out a survey of language use throughout China that will ask about the areas and functions for which Putonghua is being used. The Institute has also prepared and administers a Putonghua proficiency test, which, of course, is oral.

The Chinese Constitution recognizes the equality of all the nationalities, and the right of every ethnic minority to develop its own language. Bilingualism is promoted in ethnic-minority areas; where possible, the ethnic language should be used as a school language of instruction, with teaching of the national language to begin in the last two years of primary school (Yaowen 1992: 37). There is, as might be expected, enormous variation in implementation. In the autonomous regions where there is a large ethnic community and in the undeveloped border and mountainous areas, only a small number of well-educated people are likely to know any Chinese. In more developed areas, the ethnic language remains dominant but a good proportion of adults are bilingual. Where there is a mixture of ethnic groups, bilingualism is more common. Some ethnic groups have adopted Chinese. Similarly, there are different patterns of bilingual education, some using the ethnic language until the end of secondary school and even at the tertiary level for some subjects, others switching to Chinese earlier; some where Chinese is well established by middle school alongside the ethnic language and others where the ethnic language is only used for two or three years. The development of bilingual education has depended, of course, on the existence of a writing system. White (1997) pointed out that there were some languages with a long history of literacy: Tibetan, Mongolian, Uygur, Kazakh and Korean. A few others have old systems. There are a number of alphabetic systems introduced by missionaries. Work is continuing on the development of new systems.

Multilingualism is a challenge in Africa, too. With over 270 languages and a history that included French colonial status for part of the country, Cameroon has adopted English and French as official languages. In 1972, the southern part of British Cameroons joined the French area to become the United Republic of Cameroon. English and French became, at least in theory, equal official languages. The indigenous languages, which had been taught in colonial days, were ignored after independence. Instead, the emphasis was on French–English bilingualism. Nonetheless, there have been a good number of efforts at mother-tongue education, which have been handicapped by the large number of vernaculars and by the lack of official status. Pidgin English is widely spoken but unrecognized. French remained the dominant official language: no language policy guarantees the rights of a minority (Chumbow and Bobda 1996).

Since 1990, there has been considerable debate over language policy in South Africa. Some argue that English should be the sole official language and others believe it should be co-official with Afrikaans and other languages. In spite of the fact that many speakers of Afrikaans belong to the "oppressed" group, the language is associated with apartheid. The new Constitution recognized eleven languages: "The official languages of the Republic are Sepedi, Sesotho, Setswana, siSwati, Tshivenda, Xitsonga, Afrikaans, English, isiNdebele, isiXhosa and isiZulu" (1996–7 Constitution). The Constitution called on the government to "elevate the status and advance the use" of these languages, to set up a Pan South African Language Board to work with these languages and with all others (Khoi, Nama and San languages), sign language and to "promote respect for all community languages (including German, Greek, Gujarati, Hindi, Portuguese, Tamil, Telugu and Urdu)" and also "Arabic, Hebrew, Sanskrit and other languages used for religious purposes in South Africa."

  Implementation of this policy is difficult, and in education, English has been gaining a stronger role (McLean and McCormick 1996). Kamwangamalu (2000) summed up by suggesting continued tension between two forces, on the one hand "an awareness of the necessity to revalorize the indigenous languages," and on the other, a strong tendency to accept English as a lingua franca. Occasionally, he conceded, the old rivalry between English and Afrikaans may reappear, but this is now a secondary issue. In South Africa, then, the pressure for recognition of indigenous languages (which led to a constitutional place for eleven of the twenty-eight South African languages) may be seen as supported by the actual language situation, by notions of language rights, and by concerns for ethnic identity. The principal counterforce is now the globalizing language, English, promoted in the twenty-first century from its nineteenth- and twentieth-century role as a colonial rival of Afrikaans.

  In much of Africa, as de Swaan (2001) noted, the newly independent nation states were unable and unwilling to resist the attraction of continuing to use the colonial metropolitan language or languages. Phillipson and Skutnabb-Kangas (1995: 335) put it bluntly: "the majority of Africans are governed in a language that they do not understand, but few African states have given serious attention to language policy." They recognize the economic, social and political problems (and, one may add a decade later, the staggering health problems) and argue that failures in language policy weaken the legitimacy of the state. While the Organization for African Unity adopted in 1976 a charter calling for teaching in national languages, there has been little implementation and African countries have essentially continued inherited colonial policies. Local languages continue to have low prestige and linguistic rights continue to be ignored. Most external educational aid has contributed to the widening of the gap between the educated elite, with their knowledge of the former colonial language, and the masses. Even in Tanzania, with its comparatively successful use of Swahili, a language to which many of the mother tongues are structurally related, in the primary school, English is used in secondary and higher education. In Zambia, English is the medium officially from the first grade. Essentially then, Phillipson and Skutnabb-Kangas claim, the problem of mosaic languages has not been tackled successfully, and the old reliance on the colonial language has continued. Even where the majority in such a country speak a single language, English is regularly promoted. In Botswana, for instance, where 90 percent of the 1.5 million population speak Setswana, it is not considered official, and English is used in education after early grades and in legal, administrative and other higher domains. However, the inadequacy of implementation means that in effect there is considerable language mixture. At the same time, the other minority languages are ignored (Nyati-Ramahobo 2000).

Namibia is another case of an African nation preferring English to the indigenous languages and to the widely spoken Afrikaans. It has a population of 1.8 million, speaking more than twenty-eight languages and dialects. Afrikaans was introduced at the end of the eighteenth century. German was the language of government during the German occupation from 1884 to 1915 and English during the South African occupation from 1915 to 1990 (Fourie 1997). The missionaries developed orthographies for some of the vernaculars. A commission in 1951 recommended developing Bantu languages to be used as medium of instruction in primary schools. A 1958 commission proposed to replace mission schools by community schools and the use of the mother tongue as medium of instruction. On the recommendation of a third commission, a Native Language Bureau was set up in 1963 to develop the indigenous languages so they could be used as medium of instruction. Indigenous languages started to be used at the primary level. There was, however, a low level of support for Black education. English and Afrikaans were the official languages; these two and German were national languages; and the indigenous languages were ethnic or tribal only. The 1990 Constitution promoted English to be the only official language, but provided that the indigenous Namibian languages and Afrikaans (considered national languages) could be used in primary education. After grade seven, English was to be the language of instruction. Efforts have been made to persuade people of the importance of indigenous languages, but the development of teachers and material for teaching in the vernaculars has been very slow, Fourie reported.

The underlying problem for language policy in the Philippines, Sibayan (1974) pointed out, was to deal with the need to learn English for access to the world's knowledge, to learn Pilipino for "participating in the ritual act of speaking to confirm or affirm and solidarity as one nation," and to preserve the large number of regional heritage languages. There are, he believed, about eighty such significant languages, although 86 percent of the population speak one of the eight major languages according to the 1960 census. Spoken as a first language by about a quarter of the population (but not the largest language in the 1960 census), Tagalog was selected to be national language in 1937, was first taught in schools in 1940, and was renamed Pilipino in 1959 to avoid regional associations. English had been used in schools ever since the United States took over government in 1900, replacing the Spanish dominant during the nearly 400 years of Spanish rule and still required in universities. In 1957, initial teaching in the vernaculars was instituted but it took ten years before materials were available in the eleven languages besides Tagalog. As late as the 1972 Constitutional Convention, there was strong opposition to the recognition of Pilipino and it was proposed in fact to treat English and Spanish as official languages "pending the adoption of the common national language." The 1987 Constitution set out a complex pattern of language recognition. Filipino (with an "F" rather than a "P") was declared the national language, to be enriched and used, as the government decided, as official language and medium of instruction. English, too, was to be used as an official language and as medium of instruction except where expressly provided by law. Regional languages could be used as auxiliary languages of instruction; Spanish and Arabic could be promoted voluntarily. A national language commission was to work on all this.

English, Sibayan and Gonzales (1996) believed, was an equalizer for the first quarter century or more of American rule, but started to decline once the national language became mandatory. By 1960, nearly 46 percent of the population was competent in the national language, and by 1990, 84 percent; as a result, the value of English as a lingua franca declined and its domains were reduced to school, the sciences and technology, the highest levels of business and international contact. The national language took over other domains, including mass communication and movies. In the meantime, Young (2002) reported, initial teaching in the vernacular continued to be a major problem. With all the effort put into developing control of the national language and providing access to English, vernacular teaching in the primary grades has continued to lag. The problem is compounded by experimental efforts to teach in a regional language, which is not necessarily the mother tongue of many of the students, who will still be expected to acquire the national language and English.

With a population of about 2 million, the kingdom of Bhutan, the only Buddhist country in the world, has twenty-four languages, according to *Ethnologue*. Most Bhutanese speak one or more of four major, mutually unintelligible languages. There is no constitution but the official national language is Dzongkha. Traditionally, most official and religious documents were written in *chhokey*, the classical Tibetan script, while a Bhutanese adaptive cursive script was developed for private correspondence. Through government education programs, Dzongkha was becoming widely understood throughout Bhutan by the 1970s. Until the 1950s, the only formal education available to Bhutanese students, except for a few private schools, was through Buddhist monasteries. In the 1950s, some private secular schools were established. By the late 1950s, there were twenty-nine government and thirty private primary schools, but only about 2,500 children were enrolled. Secondary education was available only in India. Eventually, the private schools were taken over by the government. A major education reform began in the 1960s, but by 1988, only a quarter of eligible children attended elementary school and tiny percentages at higher levels. Part of the government's effort to preserve traditional culture and to strengthen the contemporary sense of national identity has been its emphasis on Dzongkha-language study.

From these examples in so many different parts of the world, it is clear that maintaining multilingualism comes with a price.

MONOLINGUAL, DYADIC, MOSAIC: MORE SIMILAR OR MORE DIFFERENT?

Lambert's proposal to group countries and their language policies according to the degree of linguistic diversity has certainly proved a useful heuristic. At first glance, it is logical to assume that monolingual polities have no need to worry about the status of the national language. However, as we have seen, even a monolingual country usually comes to see its language as threatened from the outside. There are two obvious sources for such external intervention: the spread of English is a result of globalization on the one hand and the growing but still limited protection provided for minority languages by supranational policies for language rights. It is similarly logical to assume that dyadic and mosaic countries are mainly concerned with the status of the competing languages. Again, it turns out that level of cultivation becomes a very important topic, and resolution of status and function for local languages still leaves major policy issues unresolved. It is also becoming clear that by the end of the twentieth century, the diffusion of English as a global language has led to a major shift in the elements involved in national language policy. In spite of this lack of perfect fit, at the stage of seeking parsimony in a model, there are clear signs of congruence among language situations (patterns of language practices or ecology), beliefs and ideologies, and kinds of management and planning.

12   Resisting language shift

RESISTING LANGUAGE SHIFT

The theory of language policy that has been developed in this book proposes three principal components: language practices, language ideology or beliefs and language management or planning. Language practices develop and are influenced in large measure by the external social context, and include the necessity of choice among available variants on the basis of beliefs that assign values to the variants. Language management, then, becomes an attempt to modify the values or practices of someone else.

A not dissimilar model is suggested in the work of Pierre Bourdieu, with his notions of the linguistic habitus (Bourdieu 1981) and the linguistic marketplace (Bourdieu 1991); see also Gogolin (2001a; 2001b). The habitus is a "set of dispositions, which incline the manner of action and reaction of the individual." It generates both practices and attitudes, and is derived from the social background of the individual, leading to similarities in people from the same social class. Individuals function in a field or market, struggling generally to preserve or improve their positions. An individual's linguistic habitus governs language behavior as well as judgments about the value of languages and styles.

In ch. 7, we saw how changes in the demographic and economic systems could lead to changes in the values assigned to language varieties. As an individual moves from one level or field or market to another, or as globalization opens up and expands the scope of the relevant linguistic system, so one language rather than another becomes valuable. But this refers to one kind of value, what de Swaan (2001) labeled the Q-value. Bourdieu's model recognizes the existence of different sources of value or capital, as he labels them, such as economic, cultural and social, which add up to the symbolic capital or accumulated honor of a person. Perhaps the way to try to capture the process of choice underlying language behavior or practice is to assume a summary choice value, determining how the various values should be added up in a specific situation. Thus, while the Q-value helped account for the spread of English as part of globalization or the spread of French in French territory after the Revolution, other values supporting the maintenance of national or regional or local or sectoral or religious identity account for cases of resisting a language shift engendered by a high Q-value. Of these, in the case of nation states, the most common and influential value is national identity, but equally critical can also be ethnic or religious or sectoral identity.

In modern independent nations, there are, then, four significant forces – the language situation (ecology), the prevailing set of beliefs about language choice (ranging from nationalistic mobilization of a titular language for national identity to cultural and linguistic pluralism), the pull of globalization raising the value of English as a world language and finally, any internal or external pressure for language rights. Because of the amount of variation in each of these, the patterns of language policy that result are highly varied.

Within nation states, small groups of ethnic, religious and national minorities attempt to modify language policy. These groups have their own practices and beliefs. They can attempt to manage themselves and influence the language practices or beliefs of other members of their own group. This is a (perhaps even, the) critical aspect of the effectiveness of any policy they propose. But they can also seek to influence the larger political unit (the nation state) in which they exist, either in a call for political independence (with consequent authority over their own territory) or for more limited autonomy (either territorial or demographic) or in a campaign for defined language rights (perhaps independently but more often alongside other cultural or social or political rights).

The move to revive Hebrew in Palestine started as an effort in the 1890s to persuade other Jewish settlers to have their children learn the language, or to use it themselves at least in public; but by the time of the entry of the British Army into Jerusalem in 1918, a political campaign had started in England to have Hebrew recognized as an official language. The moves to reverse language shift from French to English in Quebec or from Spanish to Catalan or Basque in Spain were similarly political mobilizations of language claims meant to lead to political autonomy or independence together with economic equality. In these cases, and in the recent British devolution of limited home rule to Wales and Scotland, the compromise has been territorial autonomy, throwing the onus for changed language policy on to the newly established regional governments. India, too, hoped that the regional solution would not interfere with its goal of replacing English with Hindi as a national language. In the Netherlands, the Friesians appear to have been satisfied with purely linguistic autonomy. In the United States, the movement for equal recognition for Spanish is closely tied to a civil rights approach to social, political and economic equality, and is starting to show signs of major regional differentiation. These are all cases of reasonably large and salient minorities. Understandably, smaller minorities, especially those without dense settlement (such as the Roma scattered over so much of Europe) have been less successful in achieving external recognition and support.

The growing recognition of language rights, however, has, in recent decades, given smaller languages a better chance of getting attention. Of course, if nation states could be persuaded, either because of ideological acceptance of the values of linguistic diversity and related cultural pluralism, or by an acceptance of the strong version of linguistic rights, or even by a pragmatic realization of the cognitive value of individual bilingualism or the economic advantage of diverse language resources, to give even stronger support to minority languages, the chances of survival for endangered languages would be much better.

The study of the efforts of linguistic minorities to preserve their languages is another field initiated by the creative scholarship of Joshua Fishman. Just as his work pioneered research into language maintenance and the spread of English, so he too inaugurated the field that he calls reversing language shift. In the book with that title (Fishman 1991), and in a second volume he edited a decade later (Fishman 2001) in which he boldly invited other scholars to comment on his own work, Fishman set out a model which he called a graded intergenerational disruption scale, a description of the state of a language or variety in terms of its likelihood to be maintained. Usefully, the scale also suggests language-management activities that speakers of the language might undertake in order to resist further loss or to re-establish earlier strength. The scale has eight levels, starting at the lowest, most endangered. I briefly paraphrase Fishman's descriptions:

8 Only a few isolated older people still speak the language, which needs to be reconstructed and taught to adults.
7 There is a socially integrated group of speakers of the language, but they themselves are beyond child-bearing age. The management task is revitalization, re-establishing the practice of speaking the language to young children.
6 The language is still used by a good number of speakers, who live close enough to each other to use it and who share certain

institutions. Most important, they speak the language to their children. The language thus has what Stewart (1968) called vitality, and there is natural intergenerational transmission. Languages without this characteristic are generally assumed to be obsolescent or dying.

5 As well as oral vitality, the language has literacy functions within the home, the community and the schools supported by the community. There is not, however, external support for these activities. This level is implied by recognition of the right of a language community to conduct its own schools.

4 The language is used in pre-school and compulsory elementary school education, either in state-supported community schools or in state schools.

3 The language is used in the workplace outside the community or neighborhood in interaction with speakers of other languages.

2 The language is used by local government services and the mass media but not on higher levels.

1 There is some use of the language in higher levels of education, occupations, government and media, but there is not political independence for the speakers of the language.

In Fishman (2001), some writers raise questions about the exact nature of these descriptions. Do they really form a scale? Are they necessary stages in reversing language shift? How vital is natural intergenerational transmission? But they clearly give a very valuable heuristic for analyzing the language practices, beliefs and management of an endangered language.

What is an endangered language? In general use, it is one of the 6,000 or so identified languages of the world that is not expected to outlive the present century (Hale 1991; Krauss 1991). If one listens to the common rhetoric, there are some who seem to fear that even large languages are endangered. French policy, for instance, appears to be driven by a belief that English will shortly take over. Indeed, there are significant numbers of people in the United States who believe that English itself is at risk, and who support the English Only movement to prevent foreign languages taking over.

It is not altogether clear how to exclude such cases. Fishman's stage 1 would seem to provide a criterion when he adds, "the additional safety provided by political independence" (Fishman 1991: 107). However, the English Only movement might point out that even though the United States is politically independent, its failure to provide constitutional protection for the language means that English is still at risk. France, or any other nation state that feels itself threatened by English, might argue that political independence is not enough against the forces of globalization. Nor is it simple to determine how to deal with cases like Irish, constitutionally and institutionally recognized, but with its status threatened by lack of widespread use.

Rather than trying to resolve this quandary, I shall accept the list of cases that Fishman has chosen to analyze in his two books. Because of the wealth of detail given there, I will simply review the cases, adding occasional particulars, but mainly attempting to fit them to the model being used in this volume. The cases that Fishman studies are as follows – the number 1 refers to Fishman (1991), and the number 2 to Fishman (2001):

> Irish (1 and 2), Basque (1 and 2), Frisian (1 and 2), Navajo (1 and 2), Spanish in the USA (1, 2 – New York Puerto Ricans), Yiddish in America (1 and 2), Māori (1 and 2), aboriginal and immigrant languages in Australia (1 and 2), Hebrew in Israel (1 and 2), French in Québec (1 and 2), Catalan in Spain (1 and 2), Otomí (2), Quechua (2), Oko (2), Andamanese (2), Ainu (2).

In dealing with these cases, I will group them more or less according to the degree of political mobilization and success in obtaining political autonomy, including control of language management. This, it will be seen, is not necessarily the same as success in reversing language shift.

Independent or autonomous

Irish and Hebrew

Both Irish and Hebrew have been well described and discussed in the literature on language policy and planning. Fishman (1991: 122–3) summarizes the Irish case in a single long sentence:

> An unparalleled combination of culturally, economically, politically and demographically dislocating factors (occupation, warfare, transfer of populations, the establishment of a dominant English-speaking class in towns and urban areas which later developed into all-English cities [and into the country's only centers of commerce, industry, wealth and political power], repeated famines that destroyed indigenous and authentic rural life and its traditions, legal prohibitions against Irish, significant periods of *de facto* abandonment by most major Church authorities, the rise of an Anglo-Irish culture that is not only locally noteworthy but which has solid claims to worldwide attention, and, finally, the constant and still ongoing emigration to English-dominant countries both near and far), these have all contributed to an early, continual and still

ongoing erosion of Irish in spite of the various substantial efforts and repeated ingenuity on behalf of RLS for some 100 years (the first 30 under voluntary auspices and the last 70 under combined voluntary and state auspices).

Ó Riagáin (1997) explained the lack of success of a century of language management in Ireland by its failure to link closely with social and economic planning. There was no consistency in economic and language planning for the Gaeltacht, the western area of Ireland where the language continued to be spoken. Economic stagnation led to heavy emigration of Irish-speaking residents either to the United States or other English-speaking countries or to the more developed English-speaking urban areas of Ireland. Thus, while English speakers were being taught Irish in schools, no support was given to the areas where it was still spoken freely. In time, the policy was reversed and economic support was provided for the undeveloped Gaeltacht. The result, however, was a reverse flow of migration, bringing back English-speakers from the cities or from overseas. While this led to the improvement of socioeconomic conditions, it contributed to the continued erosion of Irish language use in the one area where maintenance should have been easiest.

Most scholarly treatments of the Irish case set out to explain the "failure" of Irish revival. Barbour (2000: 37) noted that "no other European language that is the first national language of a sovereign independent state is spoken as the first language by only a small minority of the population." Irish had to compete as a symbol for nationalist mobilization with other strong symbols: a territory, a popular national culture and national religion. Any linguistic nationalism had to contend with a common view that the language was a barrier to social and political progress. By the time Irish nationalism developed, the number of native speakers had already declined seriously.

Irish, then, is regularly presented as the classic case of the failure of language management. Either because of the strength of other pressures (as Fishman put it) or because of planning errors (as Ó Riagáin suggested) the shift to English was not reversed; indeed, as Ó Laoire (1996) believed, Irish linguistic identity for many people is well served by Irish varieties of English. In the Gaeltacht, evidence of diminishing use of Irish is leading to proposals to revise the boundaries (set in 1926 and last reviewed in 1956) after the next census. Another explanation offered by Coady and Ó Laoire (2002) is the fact that the major responsibility for Irish-language revival was from the beginning put on the school system. Irish schools continued to exist, but face, Coady and

Ó Laoire (2002) suggested, great difficulties because the children learning Irish in school found little support in the home or any outside community for the language. In the 1990s, in spite of this grassroots effort, the Department of Education appeared to have given up on the goal of a high-level of Irish–English bilingualism and biliteracy. Rather, many people seem on the whole to be satisfied with maintaining the symbolic importance by continuing to keep up knowledge if not use of the language.

The Irish case is regularly contrasted with that of Hebrew (Ó Laoire 1996; 1999). Just as the revival of Irish was associated with the Irish nationalist movement in the late nineteenth century, so the revival of Hebrew was a central feature of Jewish territorial nationalism at the same time. The outcome was, however, quite different: whereas the use of Irish continued to decline and the Irish Republic developed essentially into an English-dominant country, modern Hebrew emerged as a revitalized, revernacularized, restandardized, secularized and modernized language that is now the dominant language of Israel.

On Fishman's graded intergenerational disruption scale, Hebrew in the late nineteenth century was anomalous. There were no native speakers, so that stages 8, 7 and 6 simply did not apply. There was, however, a reasonably high-level of Hebrew literacy (stage 5). With minor exceptions, there was no use of the language outside the Jewish community, so that stages 4, 3, 2 and 1 did not apply either. The language had essentially been kept alive for religious and literary purposes. For nearly 2,000 years, the maintenance of Hebrew was the responsibility of community-supported educational systems, providing schooling up to the level of Hebrew literacy for all boys. The Jewish languages spoken as vernaculars included a strong component of borrowed Hebrew words.

Within fifty years of the start of the revival in the 1890s, Hebrew became the dominant official language of a modern state, vital in that it was passed on to children in the home, vernacularized in that it was used as the daily spoken language of all classes, standardized in that it had not just dictionaries and grammars and an academy but a school system ranging from kindergarten to postgraduate university levels, and modernized in that it could be used to talk about sport or physics or politics or any topic (Spolsky and Shohamy 1999). Such a major transformation in language practice is often seen as the result of successful language policy, contrasting with the inability of Irish language-management efforts to stem language shift. It offers thus a tempting example for all people concerned with reversing language shift or restoring the status of their own language. Fishman (1991: 291) usefully warned against such expectations. First, he stressed that the task adopted with Hebrew was not so much revival as revernacularization, taking a language with sanctity and literacy and starting its use in daily life. It was supported by a strong language and nationalist movement, not a miracle, but

> the rare and largely fortuitous co-occurrence of
> language-and-nationality ideology, disciplined collective will and
> sufficient societal dislocation from other competing influences to
> make possible a relatively *rapid and clean break with prior norms of
> verbal interaction.*

Spolsky and Shohamy (2001) stressed the differences from normal RLS situations. It makes little sense to speak of an attempt to reverse a shift that had taken place 2,000 years earlier, nor was the strictly secularized Zionist movement at the end of the nineteenth century trying to restore the religious-based Hebrew literacy teaching that was being weakened since the Enlightenment. Rather, it was a nationalist choice of language as focus of mobilization.

There was no single central language management organization. The ideological movement developed in Eastern Europe, but the process was undertaken in Ottoman Palestine, by Yiddish-speaking East European Jews who established small farming communities where, at the end of the nineteenth century, they requested schoolteachers to speak only Hebrew to the children (Nahir 1988, 1998). Ten years later, a second small wave of ideological Zionist socialists, the founders of the kibbutz movement, were committed to even greater changes in their way of life, not just switching to labor and farming, but also to a collective society in which most aspects of daily life became common and open. All public activities (and there were few private ones left) had to be conducted in the new language, Hebrew. The third critical event was the founding, in 1906, of Tel Aviv, the first Hebrew city, whose schools played a major role in spreading the language. A Hebrew teachers' organization, founded in 1893, refused to admit teachers who used any other language. In 1907, the Labor movement in Palestine voted to publish its official organ in Hebrew only. A bitter public debate in 1913 determined that as soon as practical, Hebrew should be the medium for tertiary-level education, including science and technology. Thus, when Palestine became a mandate under the British government, Hebrew was firmly established as the public language of the Jewish community and was being spoken by a growing number of native speakers. The British government was

persuaded shortly after it conquered Palestine from the Turks to recognize Hebrew as an official language alongside English and Arabic.

For the next twenty years, Palestine was under British rule, with
English as the main language of government and Arabic and Hebrew
recognized as languages for the majority and minority populations.
During this period, new immigrants joined the Jewish community and
came under ideological and practical pressure to learn Hebrew and
use it in public. Hebrew was the medium of instruction in all Jewish
schools (except the anti-Zionist ultra-orthodox schools and *yeshivas*),
and in the Hebrew University of Jerusalem and the Haifa Technion.
While newspapers continued to be published in other languages, the
principal Jewish newspapers were in Hebrew. By the 1930s, there were
an appreciable number of Hebrew native speakers.

The establishment of the state of Israel in 1948 on a portion of what
had been the territory of the British mandate did not lead to major changes in language policy. The new government dropped English
from the list of official languages. Jewish schools and universities continued to teach through the medium of Hebrew; government activities
were now mainly in Hebrew rather than English. The large number of
new immigrants who arrived without any knowledge of Hebrew were
encouraged to learn the language, and those with professional quali-
fications were given five-month full-time intensive Hebrew programs,
ulpanim, while being supported by the government. Immigrant children were immersed in the Hebrew of the school system.

Irish had thirty years before it gained official government support.
Hebrew had fifty, and during this time, managed to complete the un-
precedented task of language revival. It is important to clarify what
this means. The revived language is very different from the older varieties, not just in lexicon but also in phonology and grammar, highly
influenced by the various languages spoken by its revivers, by the
process of child language acquisition during the early years, and by
the effects of the many immigrant languages whose speakers became
Modern Hebrew-speakers.

One important decision about language management was taken
just before independence: each individual school should choose as its
medium of instruction the language of the majority of its pupils, Hebrew in the case of Jewish schools and Arabic in the Arab sector. Thus,
from the beginning, Israel provided instruction in its own language
at all levels up to the end of secondary school for its Arab minority.
In practice, there were problems in the implementation of this policy (Amara and Mar'i 2002). Paradoxically, the Israeli system is more
favorable to Arabic than the North African Arab countries that assume

the need to switch to French at the secondary level. But Israeli public life is dominantly in Hebrew; the nominal official status for Arabic is reflected in the use of the language in many public signs, but usually alongside similar use of unofficial English. The heavy migration of nearly a million immigrants from the former Soviet Union in the 1990s has been reflected in much wider use of Russian both on the streets and in signs.

With the exception of Arabic, one of the effects of the revival of Hebrew has been the endangerment of other languages. Jewish languages developed over the centuries in the diaspora as well as non-Jewish languages brought by immigrants from various countries are slowly disappearing. It is evidence, then, of the "success" of Hebrew revival that once revived, it functions effectively as a national language working towards the "one nation, one language" favored in most nation states.

Nonetheless, it would be oversimplified to consider Israel a strictly monolingual nation. First, language practices are obviously multilingual. Second, there is the role of Arabic, the language of the largest minority. Third, there is regular argument for linguistic as well as cultural pluralism, encouraged by continuing immigration of speakers of other languages. Fourth, there is the growing presence of English as a global language, reinforced by the existence of a significant number of English-speaking immigrants and by the close relationship of Israel with English-speaking communities abroad.

Apart, then, from the facts that Ireland and Israel start with the same letter and that their language revival efforts began about the same time, putting the two cases together produces more differences than similarities.

Catalan and Basque in Spain and French in Quebec

The next three cases share political context, being minority languages that have been a focus of mobilization for territorially defined ethnic groups later granted regional autonomy and thus able to act as government-supported majority groups.

The defeat of the French by the British established the dyadic nature of Canada. Quebec, dominantly French speaking, became bilingual because of migration, especially to the city of Montreal. By the 1940s, the two principal religious groups (Catholics and Protestants), guaranteed separate school systems by the 1867 Constitution, were able to maintain distinct French- and English-speaking communities. As the business world was largely controlled by English speakers, only French speakers were required to be bilingual. During the next fifteen years, economic conditions improved, but French speakers started to be conscious of English dominance. The decade from 1960 to 1970 was the period of the quiet revolution, marked by efforts to reform the provincial electoral system, nationalization of industry and development of French-language tertiary education. At the end of the period, many Quebec nationalists noted that immigrants were choosing education in English. In the 1970 election, Quebec nationalism showed its strength. After the 1973 election, Law 22 declared French to be the official language of Quebec and established a government agency to be responsible for promotion of the use of French in the workplace. Only children fluent in English were to be permitted to attend English-medium schools. After an election in which the language question was central, the successful Parti québécois adopted Law 101, the Charter of the French language. French became sole language of the National Assembly and the law courts. Only children whose father or mother had received English-medium elementary education in Quebec could go to English-speaking schools. Businesses were required to use only French for publicity.

There was anglophone opposition and a large number of younger well-educated anglophones left the province. In the 1980s, Quebec was forced by the federal Supreme Court to modify Law 101. By the beginning of the 1990s, it was clear that Law 101 had succeeded in moving immigrant children into the French educational system. On the other hand, English-language education in Quebec continued. There was more French in the workplace and French speakers did better economically. French had become the dominant spoken language, but English remained strong as a written language.

Fishman (1991: 316–18) pointed out that at the close of the century, supporters of French in Quebec still felt themselves under sufficient threat from English to be prepared to fight for Bill 101. Writing a decade later, Bourhis (2001: 133) echoed this view and while acknowledging the "remarkable gains" achieved for French by the language laws, noted that "many Francophones still feel threatened demographically as a minority in North America while Anglophones feel threatened as a declining minority in Québec."

The major difference between Quebec and Catalonia was probably that while the English-speaking immigrants in Quebec constituted a numerical minority but an economically and politically powerful group, the large number of Spanish-speaking immigrants who moved into Catalonia for economic reasons continued to be dominated economically and politically by the Catalans. By 1986, Fishman (1991: 319) reported, most of the population of Catalonia claimed to be able to speak Catalan. Catalan speakers formed the prestige group, as managers, shop owners and the wealthy.

Catalan had been well enough established as a modern language to be granted co-official status by the Second Spanish Republic, but under Franco, public use of the language was prohibited. When the region was granted autonomy in 1979, a program began of functional institutionalization of the language, re-establishment of literacy among Catalan speakers, and transformation of the passive skills of Spanish speakers to active use of Catalan. Catalan was declared compulsory in primary and secondary schools. The law of "linguistic normalization" adopted in 1983 granted Catalan equality with Spanish in all government domains, and set up a Directorate General of Language Policy that has been at the forefront of language management. Because Spanish speakers were constitutionally protected, the normalization campaign had to proceed cautiously and could not attempt the legal methods used in Quebec to weaken English. Strubell (2001) reported increases in the number of people claiming to speak and read Catalan. He was guarded, however, in his judgment, and assumed that there needed to be "a public discourse to relegitimize the language policy" if the language was to be fully restored.

Basque shares with Catalan the fact that it competes with Spanish and is supported by the government of a Spanish autonomous region. At the same time, its position is compromised by the continuing violence associated with strong Basque nationalism and separatism. Basque-speakers make up about a quarter of the Basque Autonomous Community, which includes three northern Spanish provinces. There are also Basque speakers in contiguous areas in the province of Navarre and in France. Historically, the Basque-language has seldom been developed for government, literary or scholarly purposes, but has remained the vernacular mainly associated with isolated rural areas, whose speakers have moved to Spanish with education and urbanization.

After the death of Franco, who dealt harshly with the Basques who resisted his rule, the central government quickly granted a Statute of Autonomy and the Basque government was formed in 1979. In 1982, the Basque government adopted a Basic Law on the Standardization of the Basque Language (Euskara), which called for the "normalization" of Basque alongside Spanish. Fishman (1991: 152) remarked that normalization was probably not the best term, for in fact what was proposed was to add to it functions that were still being filled by Spanish. Given the state of the Basque language, the task was considerable. Most traditional language use was oral, and there was limited popular support for Basque literacy. Natural intergenerational transmission of the language was mainly in the small towns and village. During the Franco period, Basque had been forbidden, so there was a shortage of Basque-speaking and Basque-literate teachers. By 1986, about 20 percent of school enrolment was in Basque-language immersion or semi-immersion schools, and increasing proportions in public bilingual schools. For most of these children, Spanish remained the dominant language.

Because of the Spanish Constitution, the Basque government has not been able to require knowledge of Basque for employment, but it increasingly encourages bilingualism. Place names now appear in Basque, Basque is increasingly used in government documents. Some of the newer universities are starting to teach courses in Basque. Summing up, Fishman (1991) believed that the language-management activities of the Basque government in the autonomous community were starting to offer hope for the survival of the language.

Writing a decade later, Azurmendi et al. (2001) added details about other regions to Fishman's earlier account. The Navarrese Autonomous Community adopted the Law of the Basque Language in 1986, setting up three separate language areas in one of which three-quarters of the population speak Basque and policy grants official status to both languages and encourages Basque-language maintenance. Overall, there had been an absolute increase in the number of those speaking the language. True, the number of Basque monolinguals had halved, but the number of active and passive bilinguals had gone up. Summing up, the authors noted increases in knowledge rather than use. There had not been significant increases in natural intergenerational transmission. Because of the significance of political power, areas other than the Basque Autonomous Community remained weak.

Heller (1999) suggested that linguistic minorities like those in Quebec and Catalonia, while forced to accept bilingualism, ideologically favor the notion of monolingual national states as proclaimed by the French Revolution and simply argue about who should control the state.

Politically active efforts to reverse language shift

The other cases included in Fishman (1991) might be characterized as having various levels of success or failure depending on the political power of ethnic minorities none of which has achieved political autonomy. They depend therefore not just on internal mobilization but also on persuading majority governments to recognize and provide support for their activities.

Frisian and Māori

Fishman (1991: 149) grouped Frisian with Basque, on the not unreasonable ground that both are indigenous minorities inside democratic Western European states, in relatively prosperous areas to which speakers of other languages had been attracted. Friesland is a province in the northeast of the Netherlands with a population about 600,000, just over half of whom claim Frisian as a mother tongue and three-quarters of whom claim to be able to speak it. While there is a provincial government, it has no political autonomy in cultural matters, unlike the case of Basque, which is why I prefer to look at Frisian alongside Māori.

Fishman (1991) explained the threats to the Frisian language: the high proportion of non-Frisian speaking immigrants, a growing rate of intermarriage between Frisian- and Dutch-speakers (well over 50 percent), with the children tending to speak Dutch rather than Frisian and the shift to Dutch as a result of Frisian-speakers moving from rural to urban communities. There were efforts at Frisian-language maintenance: theatre and other cultural activities, including literature which mainly reached the committed; some use in churches; a few programs for adult language learning; funding for some teaching of Frisian as a subject; some use in the work sphere; a few hours of radio; various efforts to have the language used in government; and virtually no use in tertiary education.

Writing a decade later, Gorter (2001) reported important developments. In 1985, the Provincial Council of Friesland adopted a report on language planning that called for Frisian and Dutch to be given equal status in public administration and legal matters in Friesland. After four years of negotiation between the central and the provincial governments, a covenant was negotiated offering a compromise, but this was blocked by a High Court ruling that Dutch had to remain the official language of all administration unless a law specifically decided otherwise. Frisian was recognized as an autochthonous minority language of the Netherlands under the European Charter for Minority or Regional Languages, which has resulted in funds for language-maintenance activities. An effort in the 1990s to modify the Constitution of the Netherlands declaring Dutch "the language of the Netherlands" did not gather the needed two-thirds majority, but an Act did pass making Dutch the official language of public administration, with some provision for the use of Frisian. Gorter reported stability in absolute numbers of speakers and in their abilities, but a decline in home language use and a growth in bilingualism. In schools, there had been little improvement, with the 1993 obligation to teach Frisian in the first stage of secondary education having little effect.

Māori was given a chapter to itself in Fishman (1991). In spite of all the differences, I put it together with Frisian because in both cases efforts to reverse language shift of an autochthonous language have been associated with political activity that has not led to separatism or autonomy.

There are, of course, major differences. Frisian might theoretically, because of the linguistic relationship to Dutch, have been treated as a dialect rather than as a minority language, just as Skanian was in Sweden, while Māori, a Polynesian language related to Samoan, Tongan and Hawaiian, is clearly different from the official English. Frisians are very similar to their neighbors, while Māoris are ethnically (in culture and appearance) distinct. In both cases, the central language policy questions are to what extent political and ethnic activities have influenced language management, and to what extent language management has influenced language practice and reversed language shift.

The changes in the fortune of the Māori language since the arrival of the Europeans can perhaps best be understood as the effort of two peoples to negotiate their relationships (Spolsky 2003). During the first years of contact, Māori were happy to learn English from missionaries in order to have access to attractive new ideas and objects and non-Māori learned Māori for communication. With the increase of English-speaking settlement after 1840, this relationship continued until the 1860s, when disputes over land led to war. After the war, the government took over the mission schools that had used Māori as a medium of instruction, and both government and many Māori leaders began a campaign to shift to English. This did not happen overnight, and only with the migration of Māori from the home communities to the cities in the first half of the twentieth century was there serious attrition in use and knowledge of the language (Benton 1991).

It was at this low point for the language, when remaining speakers of Māori were mainly over the age of forty and in only one or two communities were a few children still growing up speaking the language, that campaigning for Māori-language revival began. The Treaty of Waitangi Tribunal was persuaded that the Treaty also promised protection for the Māori language, and the Māori Language Act declared Māori an official language and established a Māori Language Commission.

Accompanying these legal steps was a growing program of teaching and learning Māori. First, starting in 1979, was the Te Aatarangi movement, which focused on adult education. Next, the Kohanga Reo movement, which began with grandparents speaking the language to young children, spread like wildfire; the two programs opened in 1980, had grown to 520 by 1988 and 819 by 1994. Varied as it was in success, Kohanga Reo became an important focus for language activism. Parents, most of whom did not speak Māori, demanded Māori bilingual classes in state schools and, when dissatisfied, established their own independent schools as part of the Kura Kaupapa Māori movement. By 1997, fifty-four such schools were recognized, including secondary programs, which are strictly Māori medium, with English restricted to a few hours a week as a subject. Bilingual and immersion classes were offered in regular state schools, too, so that by 1998 there were over 30,000 children in 472 different schools receiving some form of Māori-medium instruction.

Much of this development has taken place since Fishman (1991) wrote: at that time, the Kura Kaupapa Māori was still tiny and the regular school programs were minimal. Fishman was apprehensive that these programs were not changing home and community patterns of language use but simply producing children with passive knowledge. Writing in 1989, therefore, he expressed the fear that even these developments would not succeed in restoring the natural intergenerational transmission of the language.

Benton and Benton (2001) surveyed the next decade of activity. The 1996 census which showed that half of the people claiming to know Māori were now under the age of twenty-five, demonstrated the effect of the new educational programs, but few children appeared to be using the language in daily life. There had been little development of Māori literacy, apart from that associated directly with school use. There was also little evidence of the use of Māori in the workplace, except in the public sector, where there was increasing pressure to provide documents and access in Māori. Summing up, they remained "gloomy."

At the end of the 1990s, and so not covered by the Bentons, there were a number of important developments with regards to government policy. Starting in 1997, a series of working papers was written by a small language-planning group in the Ministry of Māori Affairs and submitted to Cabinet. As a result, the government agreed to five goals for Māori language policy: better opportunities to learn, higher proficiency in the language, more opportunities for use, language cultivation and modernization, and better attitudes to the language. During 1998, these goals were translated into guidelines for action by government and non-governmental bodies. In addition, there continued to be strong pressure for the provision of radio and television programs in Māori. While not yet producing the revitalization considered so basic to resisting language shift, the combination of educational and political efforts is having an important effect in regenerating the language and its status (Spolsky 2003).

US linguistic minorities: Spanish, Navajo and Yiddish

Fishman (1991) presents Navajo, Spanish and Yiddish as three examples of United States linguistic minorities. In fact, they were more than three cases, for secular and ultra-orthodox (Haredi) Yiddish are distinct cases and there are large differences in Spanish depending on country of origin and current region.

The 2000 US Census reported 35 million Hispanics or Ladinos, classified as 20 million Mexican, 3.5 million Puerto Rican, 1.2 million Cuban and 10 million others. Spanish speakers made up 10 percent of the US population (over the age of five), with larger proportions in New Mexico, Texas, California, Arizona, Florida, Nevada, New York and New Jersey. Spanish is the major non-English language in the United States. Fishman (1991), however, made clear that its speakers cannot be considered a single ethnocultural entity. Mexican Americans, centered in the southwest, range from an upper class dating back to Spanish colonial days through rural and urbanized older and more recent legal and illegal middle and lower class. Puerto Ricans mainly settled in the urban concentration from Boston to Washington are generally poor and recent immigrants. Cubans living in southern Florida include a solid and prosperous middle class. The other groups, from the Caribbean, Central America or South America are, like the Puerto Ricans, recent and poor immigrants. Most (the Cubans are an exception) suffer from prejudice against "people of color."

While there has been an increase in the number of speakers of Spanish, there has been a matching increase in the number who know English well. Without continued immigration, the number of Spanish speakers would start to diminish dramatically. Most Hispanic adults are fluent speakers of the language, but the proficiency of children diminishes according to generation in the United States or in cities. There have been few community-engendered efforts to develop Spanish literacy. The main educational efforts at language maintenance have depended on the civil rights instigated programs associated with bilingual education. Fishman (1991) concluded that the maintenance of Spanish in the USA depended on the continuation of immigration.

Studying Puerto Ricans a decade later, Garcia, Morin and Rivera (2001) observed that in spite of considerable shift to English, the group had not achieved social and cultural integration but remained marked as a minority group suffering continued discrimination. In school programs in New York, many of the non-Spanish-speaking students in dual-language programs are in fact second and third generation Puerto Ricans. While these programs provided an opportunity to make up for language loss, the attitude of the Puerto Rican community appears not to be strongly supportive.

Spanish is not just the largest minority language in United States, but also a representative of those languages like French and German that were already spoken here before independence, and that were subsequently enlarged by immigration. The second US language selected by Fishman (1991) to study reversing language shift activities was Navajo, representing autochthonous or indigenous languages and also marked by having the largest number of speakers of any of the Native American languages. Because of its numbers, and because of its concentration on a large and relatively isolated reservation in the southwest United States, it should be expected prima facie to have the best chance of indigenous languages at maintenance, but by the end of the 1980s half the Navajo nation were no longer Navajo speaking.

The 1990 United States census counted about 220,000 Navajos, 150,000 of them living on the reservation. While knowledge of English among Navajos was quite limited before the Second World War, by the mid-1970s most were bilingual, and about 10 percent already monolingual in English. It was still the case that a good proportion of children coming to school were dominantly Navajo speakers, but increasing numbers were starting to arrive with experience in English and with limited proficiency in Navajo (Spolsky 1975).

Navajo literacy was supported only by some churches and by a few Navajo-controlled bilingual schools. Schools were divided among three authorities. Boarding schools were controlled by the Federal Bureau of Indian Affairs. Public schools were under local control, under the authority of one of the four state boards of education (Arizona, New Mexico, Colorado and Utah). The third group were independent schools, established by contract with the federal government and controlled by local parents. The tribal council of the Navajo nation had no direct control over education. From the beginnings, the schools on the Navajo reservation had strong English policies, with little if any tolerance for the use of Navajo (McCarty 1998). In the 1970s, some schools offered transitional bilingual education with the support of Title VII programs, and a handful of contract schools had more serious Navajo-immersion programs in place.

Lee and McLaughlin (2001) apologized for appearing "pessimistic, perhaps even fatalistic" about the shift from Navajo to English. In 1992, a half of the Navajo children in Head Start programs were English speakers. The following year, less than a third of Navajo kindergartners were considered fluent in Navajo. Only a handful of schools were still offering Navajo-medium classes, and the Navajo-subject classes that still existed in other schools were being driven out by pressure to meet state examination requirements. Where once the Navajo tribal council was a preserve of pure Navajo, meetings now took place in a mixture of the two languages, with English dominating in committee meetings.

Even in the independent schools where the place of Navajo seemed strongest twenty years ago, the amount and quality of Navajo teaching has declined. While recent studies (McCarty 2002; Spolsky 2002b) agree that it should still be possible to reverse the shift to English, there are no signs of strong mobilization to this end.

In both these cases, then, reverse language shifting activities have turned out to have very limited effect. Neither Spanish-speakers nor Navajo-speakers appear to have had either the motivation or the power to put into place language management that might guarantee the future of the languages. However, it is clear that the political influence of Spanish-speakers is starting to be recognized in United States. For example, candidates for public office have recently been reported giving major speeches in Spanish, and the most obvious reason that the Republican government did not reverse Executive Order 13166 was concern for the votes of linguistic minorities in the swing states of California, Arizona, Florida and Texas. The political power is there, but not yet mobilized for language maintenance.

The third US language selected in Fishman (1991) was Yiddish, representing post-independence immigrants. Like many other immigrant languages (for example, Dutch or Swedish), it can expect no significant reinforcement from new immigrants. It is, however, in an even more precarious position, as a result of the Nazi annihilation of the vast majority of Yiddish-speakers who constituted the East European ethnocultural base of the language and of the Soviet repression of the language from the 1930s until the end of the 1980s (1991: 193). There are two distinct Yiddish-speaking communities in the USA. The first consists of mainly foreign-born immigrants and their children, most of whom now use English. Within this group, a small group of secular proponents of Yiddish work to preserve the language and its culture. Less self-conscious but more successful in language maintenance are 150,000 or so ultra-orthodox (Haredi) Jews, especially members of Hasidic groups who keep the language active in the home, school and community as a method of maintaining their self-chosen separateness.

Almost all Yiddish speakers in America, including the Hasidim, also know and use English. Among the secularists, the rich literature in Yiddish developed especially in the nineteenth century is considered important, and there are efforts to preserve and teach it. For the Haredi Yiddish speakers, it is sacred literacy in Hebrew that is important, and those programs that teach Yiddish literacy to girls are particularly careful to avoid secular literature. Education for Hasidic children is provided in separate schools for boys and girls conducted by each sector following its own language policy. For boys, this generally means spending most of the day studying traditional religious Hebrew and Aramaic texts with the class conducted in Yiddish, and spending a few late hours of the day studying secular subjects in English. For girls, who are not expected to study the same religious texts, there is greater time given to English secular study and also allocated to the formal teaching of Yiddish. The two Yiddish communities (Fishman 1991: 215) are completely separated in ideology and lifestyle.

Fishman (2001) wrote his own follow up. In spite of continued attrition, the next decade had shown continued activities in support of secular Yiddish, with cultural and literary events and debates demonstrating the continued ideological support for the language by a small but influential group, accompanied by a willingness of a few younger people to continue to learn (and even, more rarely, to use) the language. In contrast, there had been continued growth in the number of Haredi speakers of Yiddish, estimated now at close to 300,000 in United States. With the effect of intermarriage on the demographics of other Jewish groups, the ultra-orthodox were likely to continue to grow in prominence and importance. There was also starting to develop Yiddish literacy both in religious books and in community newspapers. Of all groups studied, Fishman (2001: 98) believed that the "triumph" of ultra-orthodox Yiddish was evidence of the possibility of the effectiveness of reverse language shifting activities for threatened languages.

Essentially then, these three cases confirm some of the principles laid down in Fishman (1966). Number of speakers alone will not guarantee language maintenance, although continued emigration of speakers will make up for the normal attrition of minority languages. Physical isolation can help, but in the modern world, its effects are diminishing. Ideological commitment that is linguicentric keeps the issue of language maintenance salient, but cannot stop language shift. Unless language becomes a central issue in ethnic or religious mobilization and succeeds in gaining political power, language movements are unlikely to be successful. Only an ideologically supported, preferably religious, separatist movement that involves not just language but also a community willing to cut itself off from many of the features of modern life, can also hope to build the kind of separation that will maintain a minority language distinct and safe from the concurrent use of the language dominant in the outside society.

Australia

Of the cases selected in Fishman (1991), almost all were languages, although they were minority languages within a specific country. One chapter changed the focus by looking at two distinct groups in a single country. This was Australia, and the variegated activities on behalf of aboriginal languages on the one hand and the languages of post-Second World War immigrants on the other. Justifying the decision to look at these two together was the unusual coalition of language interests (including ethnic communities, foreign language teachers, English and literacy teachers and linguists) which successfully lobbied for the 1987 Australian national policy on languages (Lo Bianco 1987), reflecting a transformation in the Australian demographic pattern so that by 1990 one Australian out of twelve spoke a language other than English at home.

The tragic story of European destruction of the indigenous Aboriginal peoples of Australia during the first 150 years of contact is well known, the numbers reduced from about 250,000 to about 80,000. While there has been improvement in conditions and treatment over the past fifty years, Fishman (1991: 254) found that "Aboriginal life is still marked by some of the highest rates of alcoholism, illness, discriminatory arrest and detention, unemployment, suicide and other indices of personal and social dislocation to be found anywhere in the world." There were probably about 270 distinct Aboriginal languages at the time of contact, but 80 percent are either extinct by now or have fewer than 100 speakers remaining. Only 18 languages have more than 500 remaining speakers. For most languages, then, the main activity appears to be recording and analyzing whatever evidence can be collected from the last few remaining speakers. Intergenerational communities remain, but generally, because of resettlement policies and the poverty of the conditions under which the Aboriginals live, reverse language shifting activities are virtually excluded. A small number of communities, settlements outside the country towns and urban centers where Aboriginals generally live, are starting to provide more supportive environment for 3 or 4 percent of the Aboriginal population. There are a handful of community-based adult literacy programs. There are also a few independent Aboriginal schools that stress culture, but not necessarily language, and a few schools that teach the vernacular.

There are also some radio stations broadcasting Aboriginal languages. Fishman (1991: 277) concluded that "a few, fortunate (i.e. governmentally benignly neglected) Aboriginal languages" might survive because they still had intergenerational mother-tongue transmission. But essentially, the once rich linguistic diversity of the autochthonous inhabitants of Australia was rapidly becoming a graveyard of dead and dying languages.

Looking at the post-Second World War immigrant languages in Australia, including Italian, German, Croatian, Greek, Macedonian, Chinese, Vietnamese, Russian and Hebrew, Fishman (1991) found little effect of reverse language shifting management apart from a slight slowing down of the normal rate of immigrant language loss. Generally immigrants were settled in urban areas, and while there were some concentrations of population when the first generation arrived, this effect was rapidly eroded with social mobility. Language maintenance therefore could not depend on neighborhood interaction, but rather on less frequent visits to ethnic stores, schools, clubs, churches, family and friends. There were, however, large numbers of community-supported ethnic schools, meeting after school hours or on weekends. In the 1980s, there were over 65,000 students attending 1,200 such schools and studying fifty-one different languages. There had been government funding to support the schools, but it was unclear that they had developed a level of literacy that could function other than as an identifying mark. In addition, there were about fifty community-sponsored all-day schools, commonly under religious auspices, that included in their curriculum teaching of community languages: Italian, German, Polish, Spanish, Portuguese and Vietnamese in Catholic schools, Greek in Orthodox schools and Hebrew and Yiddish in Jewish schools. As a result of various government policies, the teaching of some foreign and community languages had increased. There were radio and television programs in community languages, but their impact appeared limited. Fishman (1991: 277) summed up Australian policy in support of the maintenance of recent immigrant languages to be "positive but ineffective."

In the follow-up volume, Aboriginal and immigrant languages are treated separately. In welcoming this decision, Lo Bianco and Rhydwen (2001) noted that there remained sufficient variation in the hundreds of different settings for Aboriginal languages to make it difficult to generalize. They remarked that the speakers of these languages lived in complex multilingual and multidialectal communities, with a linguistic ecology quite unlike mainstream Western society. This raised problems with applying Fishman's model. About 20 languages still had strong vitality, intergenerational transmission and were the primary language of the community, 50–60 were threatened with no intergenerational transmission and 170–180 had no fluent speakers or even semi-speakers left. Attrition was rapid, and the number of healthy languages would be halved in another generation. In the last decade, there had been a number of public inquiries but none of their reports had led to a consistent or workable policy.

While most of the languages appeared to be beyond saving, there continued to be a large number of maintenance and revival initiatives. In Northeast Arnhem Land, about 6,000 people spoke Yolngu Matha, a group of dialects. While the language appeared strong, in many areas Yolngu children were now speaking Dhuwaya, a *koiné* based on Gumaji which was used for Bible translation and school bilingual programs. In other areas too, lingua francas were beginning to replace clan languages. Sometimes, schools teach Aboriginal languages that are not local to the region. The languages, too, were changing: the varieties of Warlpiri and Tiwi spoken by children showed signs of English influence. Two creoles, Kriol across North Australia and Torres Strait creole, were widely used in school programs and as lingua francas. In at least four cases, language revival efforts had been modestly successful. Summing up the current situation in Australia, Lo Bianco and Rhydwen (2001: 418) remarked that these and other initiatives to strengthen Aboriginal languages ran up against current ideologies of global competitiveness and "economic rationalism."

Looking at Australia's immigrant languages, Clyne (2001: 364–5) found that the 1986 and 1996 censuses confirmed an increasing rate of shift to English for all groups. There were some signs of intergenerational maintenance, but generally, as Fishman predicted, social mobility and lower concentration of population were breaking community–family–neighborhood links. Ethnic-community schools continued, but provided only two or three hours of language instruction a week. Religious private schools continued to support community languages. Foreign language teaching in state schools did not encourage maintenance: in fact, state education examination boards had developed methods to discount the home-language knowledge of immigrant pupils so that they should not gain an advantage over others studying the language. Radio broadcasts in immigrant languages continued and had increased. However, there had been changes in policy. The 1987 national policy included support for the maintenance and development of community languages. A subsequent policy essentially relegated support of community languages to individual states, each of which were to support their own priorities. In 1994, a new policy moved emphasis to Japanese, Indonesian, Mandarin and Korean, believed to be economically valuable. Summing up, Clyne (2001: 388) concluded that "reversing language shift is not something that has occurred widely or successfully in Australia, although opportunities for language maintenance and delaying language shift are quite plentiful."

Languages at severe risk

To the dozen languages studied in the first volume, Fishman (2001) added five: Otomí in Central Mexico, Quechua in South America, Oko in Nigeria, Andamanese in the islands in the Bay of Bengal and Ainu in Japan. These provide a sketch of activities to reverse language shift that are less well known than the others studied, and give some idea of what is happening with languages at greater risk.

First, it might be appropriate to attempt to define a language at risk. Of course, if we accept the position of the English Only movement in the United States, no language is not at risk. Otherwise, following Nettle (1999), any geographically isolated language spoken by a community that is able to sustain itself economically (not at ecological risk) with a minimum of 150 speakers is likely to be safe in the short term. The 600 languages (about one-tenth of those existing today) with fewer than 150 speakers are presumably the most endangered. The median number of speakers for the languages of the world is calculated by Nettle at 5,000. Assuming that 10,000 speakers are enough for safety in the medium term, 60 percent of all languages will be lost in this period. Assuming what Nettle considers a more realistic number, 100,000 speakers, over 80 percent will die out. Setting the safety level at one million speakers, 95 percent of all languages will be lost, which includes every language indigenous to North America, Central America, Australia, Papua New Guinea, the Pacific and almost all of those indigenous to South America.

Quechua helps test these estimates. In three countries, Quechua is reported to have over one million speakers: 4.4 million in Peru, 2.2 million in Ecuador, 1.6 million in Bolivia. In addition, there are 120,000 speakers in Argentina, 4,000 in Argentina and a few hundred in Brazil (Hornberger and King 2001). From a numerical point of view, then, Quechua seems safe. The social and political treatment of the speakers of Quechua by the Spanish conquerors and settlers had led to a lowered status for the language and produced a gradual shift towards Spanish. As in much of South America, the indigenous people had gradually been castilianized. When Ecuador, Peru and Bolivia gained their independence from Spain at the beginning of the nineteenth century, they continued to recognize Spanish as the dominant language and ignored or oppressed autochthonous languages and cultures. In recent years, there has been an increase in indigenous political movements that have influenced governments to take some steps to support language maintenance efforts. In Peru, the percentage of Quechua monolinguals declined from 31 percent in 1940 to 11 percent in 1982, and the percentage of Spanish monolinguals rose from 50 percent in 1940 to over 70 percent in 1982. The loss has been gradual, with domains being taken over by Spanish one at a time, but steady. Of course, the pattern varies from country to country and region to region, and there is considerable diversity in the language itself (*Ethnologue* recognizes forty-seven different Quechua languages).

Hornberger and King (2001) traced the various efforts at reversing language shift. There were projects that attempt to cultivate the language by collecting examples of "pure" Quechua; there were groups which attempted to persuade young people to use the language; there were efforts to slow down the tendency of many to speak Spanish rather than Quechua at home; a number of institutions were working to develop Quechua literacy; a few state schools or schools under community control were trying to maintain the language and culture; Quechua is occasionally used in work spheres outside traditional communities; some government services (some health clinics in Peru) offer access in Quechua; and the language is taught as an academic subject in universities locally and internationally. There is support for the movement among non-Quechua groups, and programs that cut across national borders. Hornberger and King, however, concluded that the odds for long-term survival are unfavorable.

Otomí, a language of Central Mexico, has suffered severe attrition over the past century, with reduced numbers and territory (Lastra 2001: 147). The 1990 census recorded 280,000 speakers, monolingual and bilingual, compare to 300,000 in the 1980 census. Lastra believed that schooling in Spanish was the main cause of language shift; there had also been demographic changes, with relocation of villagers, inmigration of Spanish speakers and outmigration to urban areas. In general, the poor economic position of the Otomí reduced any chances for reversing language activity. In many areas, the language is virtually extinct. Traditional Mexican language policy discriminated against indigenous languages, and while since 1964 there has been nominal support for transitional bilingual education, the emphasis is on transition. A small group founded an academy in 1986 with the purpose of reversing language shift: it teaches literacy to adults, sponsors song contests and advises a handful of bilingual schools.

Oko is one of the 500 or so languages of Nigeria. The village where it is spoken shares its language with another village 3 kilometers away and is marked by strong efforts at local language and culture preservation (Adegbija 2001: 288). Other languages spoken by the villages include Ebira (a group with which there is intermarriage), Yoruba (the language of pastors and therefore used in church) and English (used in official contexts, in a local Anglican church and by young people to exclude their parents). In the village, Oko is still spoken by all ages, but it is probable that people who have emigrated to urban centers no longer speak it. Literacy in Oko is rare and while official policy requires the use of mother tongues in public education, there are very few schools in Nigeria that follow this policy. The language is not used in the work sphere outside the community, and of all Nigerian languages, only Hausa, Yoruba and Igbo are likely to have any official use even at the lowest levels of government. These three languages are the only ones taught as subjects in higher education. Summing up, Adegbija concluded that while the language was still spoken in the village, it was probably already dead among those from the village who had moved to urban centers.

When in 1858 the British government of India founded a penal colony in the Great Andaman Islands, the native population constituted ten different ethnic groups speaking a number of related dialects (Annamalai and Gnanasundaram 2001: 310). The population was largely wiped out by killing and disease and had dropped to twenty-three by 1951. In 1971, a score of speakers surviving, from five different ethnic groups and mixed with others, were moved to Strait Island in South Andaman. By 1998, the population had risen to sixty-five. The current language spoken by the Andamanese appears to be a mixture of various extinct varieties. There are now seven families on the island, with a chief selected by the community. Incest and marriage rules have been relaxed. Houses have been built and the government also provides clothes and canoes. A high level of demoralization is reported. All Andamanese are now bilingual in Hindi; a few know Bengali and Burmese. People over the age of forty continue to have a good grasp of Andamanese. Children appear to develop dominance in Hindi, but to keep up Andamanese. The school taught in English until 1996 and in Hindi since then, with initial use of Andamanese. There is no literacy in Andamanese outside the school. The community as a whole appears to support language maintenance, but intergenerational transmission is weakening.

While it was long proclaimed that Japan has no racial or linguistic minorities, the recent acceptance of cultural pluralism has led to a renewed interest in Ainu, signaled in a court decision in 1997 holding that the Japanese Constitution makes the government responsible for protecting minority cultural rights and that this applies to the Ainu (Maher 2001). Japanese policy until the middle of the nineteenth century opposed Ainu assimilation, but later the traditional communities were broken up, and by the end of the century all were required to have education in Japanese. Public activism picked up in the mid-1980s, when the government recognized the Ainu as a minority under the United Nations International Covenant on Civil and Political Rights in 1991. In 1997, the hundred-year-old law requiring Japanese education was abolished and the Ainu Culture Promotion Law passed. How many fluent speakers remain is unclear, perhaps thirty, all in their eighties. The Ainu population is estimated at between 25,000 and 50,000; there may be many more. The new law promotes culture, including some programs for teaching language in language centers, but not in public or private schools. Many of those learning Ainu are in fact Japanese and not ethnic Ainu.

This added group of languages involved in reversing language shift makes clear the complexity and richness that one would expect in the great diversity of language situations. Language management plays quite different roles in the various cases. With Quechua, centuries of colonial oppression have produced socioeconomic situations that seem to make it quite unlikely that weak governmental recognition of minimal language rights will correct loss. Similarly, recognition of cultural pluralism by the Mexican government appears too little and too late to save Otomi. The use of Oko in the earliest grades of the school may help a little, but growing migration to the city suggests that the language will not last very long. The Andamanese case shows that forced resettlement in an isolated community might help preserve identity for a short time, but the basic socioeconomic and cultural distress being suffered by the people makes it hard to interpret this positively. While Ainu is close to extinct, a combination of ethnic mobilization around the language with government recognition of cultural pluralism does hold out some hope of a cultural revival of the language, but the teaching has not yet moved into the schools.

There are many other small programs in various parts of the world. Two small Native American communities show the potential. The Pueblo villages in New Mexico have a long tradition of maintaining identity, but they, too, in recent years have suffered serious language loss. The language spoken in Acoma Pueblo is a variety of Keres. The community has 3,000 enrolled members living on the reservation, and another 2,000 who have moved to town looking for work (Sims 2001).

Schooling in English began at the beginning of the twentieth century. By the 1980s an increasing proportion of children were entering school with English as the first language and with parents who now spoke in English at home. In 1997, a survey showed that many speakers in their thirties and forties had limited proficiency. Two short immersion camps for school-age youth led to increased enthusiasm and plans to continue a community-based approach.

The Pueblo de Cochiti, a New Mexico community of about 1,000 people, also speaks a dialect of Keres. By 1993, only people over the age of thirty-five were still fluent speakers (Pecos and Blum-Martinez 2001). There was, however, strong motivation for reviving the language, considered a key factor in religious life. In 1995, a start was made by teaching the language to adults in the tribal offices. The first effort at teaching children was a six-week summer program in 1996. On the basis of its success, plans were being developed to introduce language teaching into Head Start and pre-school programs, to continue classes for adults, and to offer afternoon activities in the language for school-age children.

How can one best represent all the other languages? For the last few years, the Endangered Language Fund (http://www.ling. yale.edu/~elf/grants2002.html) has been making small grants to support projects. In 2002, there were fifty applications, twelve of which they were able to fund. The sample is clearly biased by the fact that each of the applicants was a linguist capable of developing proposals, but they help round out the picture of efforts to resist language loss.

Five grants are to projects in South America. The youngest fluent speaker of Kawki, a Jaqui language of Peru with perhaps 2,000 speakers, is teaching about forty children in Cachuy. The grant will purchase materials used in the classes. Zapara is spoken in the rainforest province of Pastaza in eastern Ecuador. There are currently three fluent speakers. The project will develop materials to reintroduce Zapara into the curriculum of schools in five communities. The last remaining Iquito community is San Antonio in the Amazon basin of Peru; it has about 150 speakers. Recently, the community has decided to start a language revitalization project. The project will train the speakers themselves as linguists. Kuruaya, a language of the Munduruku family of Tupi stock, has only five elderly speakers remaining, who no longer use Kuruaya in their daily lives. The project will collect wordlists and texts. Tsafiki (Colorado) is spoken by about 2,000 Tsachila living on seven communes situated at the western base of the Andes in Ecuador. While children are still learning the language, the Tsachila are under strong pressure from the dominant Spanish culture. The project will support work on a dictionary.

Another four are projects in North America. The songs used in Muskogee Creek Indian churches will be collected. The more complicated, meaningful songs are being lost to simpler, repetitive tunes that are easier to learn. Tahltan is a critically endangered Athapaskan language spoken by fewer than one hundred adults in British Columbia. Tahltan-language animal stories and forms of address will be collected. The Splatsin are one of the seventeen tribes that make up the Secwepemc (Shuswap) nation in British Columbia. Sixteen remaining speakers are fluent in the eastern dialect of this Salishan language, and there are four nearly fluent learners of the language who have been mentored by the elders. The project will develop a wordlist. The San Juan Paiute tribe, the easternmost of ten Southern Paiute tribes, is located in Arizona and Utah, with about 30 of the 300 tribal members still fluent speakers; only one child (a four-year-old) is learning it. The tribe set up a language revitalization program that will include short immersion camps. It will videotape traditional narratives.

The other projects are in Europe, Siberia and Papua New Guinea. Faetar, a variant of Francoprovencal, is a language spoken by perhaps 700 people in two small, mountain-top villages in southern Italy: Faeto and Celle St. Vito. The project will develop an orthography to allow Faetar to gain a foothold in the schools. When Yupik Eskimo was introduced into the school curriculum of Siberia in the 1930s, all the children still spoke it as their mother tongue and the task was literacy teaching. After sixty years of demographic, social and economic pressure, formal education and residential schooling, the situation has changed drastically. Now, school-age children speak mainly Russian and learn their ethnic language at school as a second language from teachers who are not themselves fluent. The language situation is somewhat better on the US side of the Bering Strait, where most children on St. Lawrence Island still speak the language. In the changed political situation, it is now possible for Yupiks to visit their relatives on the other side. The common language is Yupik, though the Russians speak it haltingly if at all. The promotion of Yupik to the status of an international language contributes to its prestige and has spurred Siberian Yupiks to learn it. The project will use material collected over years of field work to develop a practical conversation book. Wutung is a small coastal village in the far northwest of Papua New Guinea, on the border with Indonesia. Sandaun Province is an area of great linguistic diversity, with approximately 110 languages. None of these languages has yet been described in detail. Texts will be collected to be made into books to be printed in Australia and sent back for use in the school and by the general community.

Essentially in each of these cases, it is the force of non-linguistic factors – demographic, socioeconomic, political – that is driving language shift, and it is at the moment hard to see how efforts at language management will do more than delay eventual language loss.

New support for activities like these has now been promised with the donation of £20 million to the School of Oriental and African Studies in London to establish programs for endangered languages. The emphases of the programs are the scholarly preservation of dying languages. One program offers an MA in language documentation and description and a Ph.D. in field linguistics. A second will provide funds for field studies and language documentation. The third will establish at SOAS an endangered language archive. The implication of these programs is that for those concerned with the preservation of language diversity, it is enough to preserve in the archives details of the grammar and lexicon and examples of the language. No doubt some of these activities will encourage remaining speakers of the languages to recognize their value, but the focus is on the language and not on the speakers.

Is reversing language shift linguicentric?

Fishman's theory of reversing language shift has made a major contribution to the understanding of language management intended to aid in the maintenance of endangered languages. Among the questions that still need to be answered is its tendency to treat all language policy issues as a dyadic choice, presented regularly in the form of the struggle between a weak David and a threatening Goliath (Lambert 2002).

A second question is whether the theory puts too much emphasis on language and language management, and so distracts attention from the social and economic factors which are likely to be the major sources of changes in language practices and ideologies involved in language shift. Usually, these critical factors are presented as background, but when appropriately foregrounded, they turn out to suggest the relative weakness of language management activities in reversing language shift.

Crystal (2000: 130) recognized this when he listed the six factors which he considered to be "postulates for a theory of language revitalization." They were increased prestige in the dominant community for speakers of the language, an increase in wealth for speakers of the language relative to the dominant community, increased "legitimate power in the eyes of the dominant community" for speakers of the language, "a strong presence" in the educational system for speakers of the language, a writing system for the language and access to electronic technology. Only one of these, the availability of a writing system, is usually considered a language-management activity; the others deal with social, economic, political and technological factors.

Thus, there is an argument for considering reverse language shifting activity only one part of the successful mobilization of a minority community to maintain its identity while adapting to life in the modern world.

There remains the question of responsibility. Those who argue that there is a moral responsibility on the world and its governments to maintain linguistic diversity, by analogy with the movement to maintain biodiversity, have no difficulty in arguing for stronger agreements on linguistic rights. To date, their arguments have not convinced nation states or the bodies they have formed. While there are honorable exceptions, it would seem that linguists as a profession are satisfied with recording languages before they die. That seems to leave the responsibility where it must ultimately reside, with speakers of the language. Whatever blame may reasonably be attached to language policies and social, economic, religious and political forces, it seems that the loss of linguistic diversity results less from linguistic genocide than from linguistic suicide.

13 Conclusions

THE MODEL – COMPONENTS

Language policy is about choice. It may be the choice of a specific sound, or expression, or of a specific variety of language. It may be the choice regularly made by an individual, or a socially defined group of individuals, or a body with authority over a defined group of individuals. It may be discovered in the linguistic behavior (language practices) of the individual or group. It may also be discovered in the ideology or beliefs about language of the individual or group. Finally, it may be made explicit in the formal language management or planning decisions of an authorized body.

At the most basic level, individual speakers and groups of speakers demonstrate a belief that some of these choices are bad or undesirable and that others are good or valuable. Growing up and becoming socialized, children are generally expected to learn how to differentiate between good and bad language. Their mentors and caretakers regularly take on the responsibility of assisting, first by encouraging the use of language that can be widely understood, and second by encouraging the use of language that is judged favorably. The beliefs that some variety of language is better than others and that it is possible to influence speakers to select the better variety are fundamental to language management.

However, language practices, beliefs and management are not necessarily congruent. Each may reveal a different language policy. The way people speak, the way they think they should speak, and the way they think other people should speak may regularly differ. Looking at the language policy of established nations, one commonly finds major disparities between the language policy laid down in the constitution and the actual practices in the society. Within social groups, it is also common to find conflicting beliefs about the value of various language choices. One is therefore faced regularly with the question of which the real language policy is. In many nations, one is hard pressed to choose between the complex multilingual ecology of language use and a simple ideological monolingualism of constitutionally stated language-management decisions.

The most realistic answer resides in language practices; look at what people do and not at what they think they should do or at what someone else wants them to do. Language management remains a dream until it is implemented, and its potential for implementation depends in large measure on its congruity with the practices and ideology of the community.

In looking at the language policy of a state or other unit, it is appropriate to start off with an effort to capture the complex language situation. This involves analyzing the existence and nature of the named and unnamed varieties used in it, and their demographic, territorial and functional distribution in the unit. An ecological approach requires going beyond the linguistic to the relevant social, political, ethnic, religious, economic and cultural make up of the unit and the way that each of these factors interacts constructively with the linguistic. From this first analysis, there will be evidence of the communicative value of each of the varieties. A second step involves attempting to identify the relevant beliefs about the potential values, symbolic as well as pragmatic, of the varieties. With this background, one can search for the specific language-management and language-planning decisions that have been made and ask if they have in fact had any effect on language beliefs or on language practices.

THE MODEL – CONTEXTS

Looking at language policy ecologically has two different implications. First, it implies considering all the varieties of language that make up the sociolinguistic repertoire of the community being studied, and not just the named varieties that are considered official or that represent specific ethnic groups. The failure to recognize that the language spoken by most Belgians is neither French nor Dutch, but a dialect of either can lead to a serious misunderstanding of the nature of the gap between school and home languages. The sociolinguistic repertoire then will include various linguistic items, variables and varieties, but cross-linked with the appropriate non-linguistic factors with which they co-exist: demography, location, topic, function. The second implication is to realize that language policy exists in the wider social, political, economic, cultural, religious and ideological context that makes up human society.

Without taking these contextual factors into account, any description of language policy will be severely restricted.

THE MODEL – FORCES

In analyzing the various cases in this volume, we have found four main forces that co-exist with the various kinds of language policy. Forces may be too strong a word, with its implication of causality. Rather, they may be better thought of as conditions that co-occur with policies. The first of these was the sociolinguistic situation: the number and kinds of languages, the number and kinds of speakers of each, the communicative value of each language both inside and outside the community being studied. Here, a critical factor turned out to be not so much the factual situation as common perception of the situation. Thus, a community will be found to ignore a number of language varieties that are marginalized or that are used by marginalized members of the community. Many putatively monolingual communities turn out on closer analysis to be multilingual in practice.

The second condition had to do with the working of national or ethnic or other identity within the community. In modern nation states, the symbolic value of what is felt to be the national language is a critical force working to try and direct language management. Schools are expected to teach the national language, citizens are expected to use it in public life. Counteracting this unifying force can be the identity values associated with languages used by ethnic or religious sub-groups within the nation, many of which might aim to have their language recognized alongside or instead of the national language. Once empowered, a former minority (whether numerical or in terms of influence) regularly asserts the primacy of its own language.

If we follow the analysis by Bobbitt (2002), it may well be that the concentration on national concerns in language policy is about to become outdated or reduced. Bobbitt, basing his analysis on the development of warfare, proposes a series of stages in the development of constitutional states. The Thirty Years' war led to the development of the kingly state, superseded by the beginning of the eighteenth-century by the territorial state, in which the monarch became, the "first servant of the State." The French Revolution and Napoleon produce a move to the state nation, transformed to the nation state, in which the national identity which underlies so much of the language policy that we have been studying achieved its importance. There was conflict between democratic, fascist and communist views of the nation state, but all

seemed to have agreed on the contribution that language choice had
to make to national identity. With the defeat of fascism and, half a
century later, the collapse of communism, history did not in fact end,
but the nation state was transformed into what Bobbitt labels the market state. One version, the Washington model, is no longer concerned
about nationalism. A second, the Tokyo model, continues to nurture
national identity and cultural exclusivity. A third, the Berlin model,
attempts to maintain the welfare aspects of the nation state, but now
has to face up to the challenges of globalization and immigration.
Bobbitt recognizes also the changes of the post-September 11 world,
noting the threat of the virtual, non-territorial market state terrorist
reality. Challengeable as Bobbitt's model might be in its particulars, it
raises intriguing questions about the changing relevance of national
interests in language policy.

The third force or condition had to do with changes that have taken
place in the world in the last few decades as a result of globalization,
and the consequent tidal wave of English that is moving into almost
every sociolinguistic repertoire. Associated with it is the instrumental
value of gaining access to an economically advantageous network by
developing proficiency in the language of widest communication. In
the last few decades, this force has multiplied in effect and narrowed
in language choice, so that currently most societies feeling the effects
of globalization are also moving rapidly to acquire greater proficiency
in the global language, English.

This has various effects on national language policies. In some, it
becomes the target for language management aimed to fight its influence. In others, it becomes a natural goal for language acquisition
planning and the potential replacement for less well-cultivated indigenous languages. Even when it does not affect language management,
it affects language practices.

The fourth condition has to do with the gradually increasing recognition that language choice is an important component of human
and civil rights. Slowly, there are signs of the weakening of national
autonomy. The ratification of international covenants or the influence of supra-national organizations, respectful though they remain of
national sovereignty and territorial limits, have led to a growing value
for linguistic pluralism and an acceptance of the need to recognize
the rights of individuals and groups to continue to use their own
languages. As a result, more and more nations include in their constitution or in their laws and regulations affecting language provisions
recognizing a limited set of rights for the speakers of languages other
than the national language. The limitation is generally territorial; a

language is recognized as deserving of rights when a significant proportion of the population living in a defined region speaks it. It may be demographic; rights are much more likely to be granted to indigenous groups than to immigrants, and even less likely to people marginalized as foreign workers. There can be a functional limitation; states are more likely to accept responsibility for providing access to state services for speakers of other languages than they are to provide educational services in the language. At most, a state may permit a minority-language community to provide its own education, usually on the condition that it teaches the national language alongside the minority one.

A final dimension to this complex interplay of forces is the growing recognition that human and civil rights require attention to the problems of those who do not have control of the dominant language of a society. It is widely accepted that this involves teaching the dominant language to all citizens, providing access to minimal public services in minority languages and permitting linguistic minorities to work for language maintenance. There are those who argue that the maintenance of linguistic diversity is just as much the responsibility of states as is the maintenance of biodiversity, while others hold that everyone should be free to choose which language to speak and so free to choose not to speak their minority language.

With the complexity of factors concerned, and with the certainty that they will pull in different directions, it is not surprising that a simple theory of language policy has not yet achieved consensus.

There are other factors that occur regularly, but they can generally be subsumed under one of these four headings. For example, a language policy motivated by the search for economic advantage will generally fit under the first condition, as will the desire for access to specific written resources. A language policy motivated by fear will probably be part either of the second or the third, depending on whether it is fear of an internal or external group.

THE MODEL – PREDICTION

The challenge in developing a theoretical model is to attempt to predict cases that have yet to be studied. Can one suggest some hypotheses? Essentially, the generalizations in Fishman (1971) look hard to beat. A nation with a consensual Great Tradition and an associated cultivated language will be most likely to have a monolingual language policy. A nation with competing Great Traditions and associated cultivated languages will endeavor to work out a territorial or demographic compromise if it is practical to do so. A nation without established great traditions and cultivated indigenous languages will generally continue to use its colonial language, or attempt to build the role of an international language, especially English. Without a strong ideological urge to maintain identity even at the cost of social and economic isolation, most small weak languages will not have the power to encourage their speakers not to shift to the nearest available stronger language.

In all of this, the potential success of language management will depend on its congruity with the language situation, the consensual ideology or language beliefs, the degree to which English has already penetrated the sociolinguistic repertoire and its consistency with a minimal degree of recognition of language rights.

WILL THE REAL LANGUAGE POLICY STAND UP?

The implication of this analysis is that the real language policy of a community is more likely to be found in its practices that its management. Unless the management is consistent with the language practices and beliefs, and with the other contextual forces that are in play, the explicit policy written in the constitution and laws is likely to have no more effect on how people speak than the activities of generations of schoolteachers vainly urging the choice of correct language.

There is another complication that needs to be taken into account; several parties in the community may each have their own conflicting policy. There are cases, like the United States, with differences between federal and state policies, and with strong interest groups working to develop their own desired policies. For this reason, it makes sense to look generally at the policy revealed in the language practices of the society.

The existence of language management suggests that the putative language manager has recognized some inconsistency between the desired state of affairs and the actual. In most states there is likely to be continuing tension over language choices, and constant pressure on the part of some people to modify the practices of others. If language management is to do more than simply record either the present situation or some idealized but unrealizable state of affairs, it must represent some ideologically and practically achievable modification of current language practices. This brings us to the next major question.

CAN LANGUAGE POLICY SUCCEED?

Students of language policy fall naturally into two main groups: the optimists who believe management is possible and the pessimists who assume that language is out of control. The record seems to favor the pessimists, for there are comparatively few cases where language management has produced its intended results. There are striking failures, such as the fact that reversing language shift activities, unless managed by a combination of government power and ideological strength, generally failed to prevent continued attrition.

Consider some cases. The two centuries of determined French language policy have had important effects, but they have not managed to destroy the languages of the periphery, or to replace the indigenous languages of the former colonies, or to fight off the growing threat of English. A century of politically backed and governmental efforts to revitalize Irish has succeeded only in increasing knowledge but not use of the language. Rigorous (indeed brutal) Soviet language policy succeeded in spreading literacy and weakening many indigenous languages, but the collapse of the Soviet Union has left space for reinvigorated claims for many of these languages to establish their own dominance. While revernacularization and revitalization of Hebrew have achieved their initial goals, the revived language is quite different in character and the cost in terms of loss of other languages has been high. In many former colonies, the efforts to establish indigenous languages for official use have turned out to be increasingly problematic. In states with large-scale immigration, failures to adopt language policy to recognize the new sociolinguistic situation have led to major social problems.

The record is not good, although it can be argued that the failures of language policy are no worse than the failures of economic policy. But the goal of this book has not been to advocate language policy, but attempt to understand what it is and how it might be influenced. It has tried to identify the structure and nature of policy, and to explore the interactions between its various components. The knowledge developed will not show how to manage language, but help understand what is involved in such management.

References

Adegbija, Efurosibina, 2001, Saving threatened languages in Africa: a case study of Oko, in Fishman (ed.), pp. 284–308.

Ager, Dennis E., 1996, *Language policy in Britain and France: the processes of policy*. London and New York: Cassell.

   1999, *Identity, insecurity and image: France and language*. Clevedon, England, Philadelphia and Adelaide: Multilingual Matters Ltd.

   2001, *Motivation in language planning and language policy*. Clevedon, England and Buffalo, USA: Multilingual Matters Ltd.

   2003, *Ideology and image: Britain and language*. Clevedon, England: Multilingual Matters Ltd.

Aikhenvald, Alexandra Y., 2001, Language awareness and correct speech among the Tariana of Northwest Amazonia. *Anthropological Linguistics* 43 (4), 411–30.

Alexandre, Pierre, 1963, Les problèmes linguistiques africains vus de Paris, in Spencer (ed.), pp. 53–69.

Amara, Muhammad Hasan, and Mar'i, Abd Al-Rahman, 2002, *Language education policy: the Arab minority in Israel*. Dordrecht, Netherlands: Kluwer Academic Publishing.

Annamalai, E., 1989, The linguistic and social dimensions of purism, in Björn Jernudd and Michael J. Shapiro (eds.), *The politics of language purism* (pp. 225–31). Berlin and New York: Mouton de Gruyter.

Annamalai, E., and Gnanasundaram, V., 2001, Andamanese: biological challenge for language reversal, in Fishman (ed.), pp. 309–22.

Armstrong, Robert G., 1968, Language policies and language practices in West Africa, in Fishman, Ferguson and Das Gupta (eds.), pp. 227–36.

Arutiunov, Sergei, 1998, Linguistic minorities in the Caucasus, in Paulston and Peckman (eds.), pp. 98–115.

Aunger, Edmund A., 1993, Regional, national and official languages in Belgium. *International Journal of the Sociology of Language* 104, 31–48.

Azurmendi, Maria-Josi, Bachoc, Erramun, and Zabaleta, Francisca, 2001, Reversing language shift: the case of Basque, in Fishman (ed.), pp. 234–59.

Bachman, Ronald D. (ed.), 1989, *Romania: a country study*. Washington, DC: Federal Research Division Library of Congress.

Bamgbose, Ayo, 2000, Language planning in West Africa. *International Journal of the Sociology of Language 141*, 101–18.

Barbour, Stephen, 2000, Britain and Ireland: the varying significance of language for nationalism, in Barbour and Carmichael (eds.), pp. 18–43.

Barbour, Stephen and Carmichael, Cathie (eds.), 2000, *Language and nationalism in Europe*. Oxford: Oxford University Press.

Bartsch, Renate, 1987, *Norms of language: theoretical and practical aspects*. London and New York: Longman.

Benton, Richard A., 1981, *The flight of the Amokura: Oceanic languages and formal education in the Pacific*. Wellington: New Zealand Council for Educational Research.

Benton, Richard A., and Benton, Nena, 2001, RLS in Aotearoa/New Zealand 1989–1999, in Fishman (ed.), pp. 422–49.

Berry, Jack, 1958, The making of alphabets, in Eva Siversten (ed.), *Proceedings of the VIII International Congress of Linguistics* (pp. 752–64). Oslo: Oslo University Press.

Bilingual Education, United States Senate, 90th Congress, First Sess. 681 (1967).

Bilingual Education Programs, House of Representatives, 90th Congress, First Sess. 584 (1967).

Blommaert, Jan, 2001, The Asmara Declaration as a sociolinguistic problem: reflections on scholarship and linguistic rights. *Journal of Sociolinguistics 5* (1), 131–42.

Bloomfield, Leonard, 1935, *Language*. London: George Allen and Unwin.

Bobbitt, Philip, 2002, *The shield of Achilles: war, peace, and the course of history*. London: Allen Lane, the Penguin Press.

Boneva, Bonka, 1998, Ethnicity and the nation: the Bulgarian dilemma, in Paulston and Peckman (eds.), pp. 80–97.

Bourdieu, Pierre, 1981, Structures, strategies, and habitus, in C. C. Lemert (ed.), *French sociology, rupture, and renewal since 1968*. New York: Columbia University Press.

1991, *Language and symbolic power*. Cambridge, UK: Polity Press.

2001, Uniting to better dominate. *Items and Issues 2* (3–4), 1–6.

Bourhis, Richard Y., 2001, Reversing language shift in Quebec, in Fishman (ed.), pp. 101–41.

Branson, Jan, and Miller, Don, 1998, Nationalism and the linguistic rights of deaf communities: linguistic imperialism and the recognition and development of sign languages. *Journal of Sociolinguistics 2* (1), 3–34.

Brecht, Richard D., and Rivers, William P., 2000, *Language and national security in the 21st century: the role of the Title VI/Fulbright-Hays in supporting national language capacity*. Dubuque, IA: Kendall-Hunt.

Breitborde, Larry B., 1983, Levels of analysis in sociolinguistic explanation: bilingual code switching, social relations and domain theory. *International Journal of the Sociology of Language 39*, 5–43.

Breton, Roland, 1991, The handicaps of language planning in Africa, in David F. Marshall (ed.), *Language planning* (vol. III of *Focusschrift in honor of Joshua A. Fishman on the occasion of his 65th birthday*, pp. 153–74). Amsterdam and Philadelphia: John Benjamins.

Brisk, Maria Estela, 1998, *Bilingual education: from compensatory to quality schooling*. Mahwah, NJ: Lawrence Erlbaum.

Brosnahan, L. H., 1963, Some historical cases of language imposition, in Spencer (ed.), pp. 7–24.

Bugarski, Ranko, 2001, Language, nationalism, and war in Yugoslavia. *International Journal of the Sociology of Language* 151, 69–87.

Cabantous, Alain, 2002, *Blasphemy: impious speech in the West from the 17th to the 19th century*. New York: Columbia University Press.

Caxton, William, 1490, *Here fynyssheth the boke yf Eneydos, compyled by Vyrgyle, whiche hathe be translated oute of latyne in to frenshe, And oute of frenshe reduced in to Englysshe by me Wyllm Caxton*. Westminster: William Caxton.

Cebollero, Pedro Angel, 1945, *A school language policy for Puerto Rico*. San Juan de Puerto Rico: Impr. Baldrich.

Cenoz, Jasone, 1998, Multilingual education in the Basque country, in Jasone Cenoz and Fred Genesee (eds.), *Beyond bilingualism: multilingualism and multilingual education* (pp. 175–91). Clevedon, England: Multilingual Matters Ltd.

Chaudenson, Robert, 1993, Research, politics, and ideology: the case of the Comité International des Etudes Créoles. *International Journal of the Sociology of Language* 102, 15–25.

Chomsky, Noam, and Halle, Morris, 1968, *The sound pattern of English*. New York: Harper and Row.

Chumbow, Beban Sammy, and Bobda, Augustin Simo, 1996, The life-cycle of post-imperial English in Cameroon, in Fishman, Rubal-Lopez and Conrad (eds.), pp. 401–30.

2000, French in West Africa: a sociolinguistic perspective. *International Journal of the Sociology of Language* 141, 39–60.

Clayton, Thomas, 1995, Restruction or resistance? Educational development in French colonial Cambodia. *Educational Policy Analysis Archives* 3 (19), 1–12.

1998, Building the new Cambodia: educational destruction and construction under the Khmer Rouge. *History of Education Quarterly* 18, 145–57.

2002, Language choice in a nation under transition: the struggle between English and French in Cambodia. *Language Policy* 1 (1), 3–25.

Clyne, Michael, 2001, Can the shift from immigrant languages be reversed in Australia? In Fishman (ed.), pp. 364–90.

Coady, Maria, and Ó Laoire, Muiris, 2002, Mismatches in language policy and practice in education: the case of Gaelscoileanna in the Republic of Ireland. *Language Policy* 1 (2).

Conrad, Andrew W., 1996, The international role of English: the state of the discussion, in Fishman, Rubal-Lopez and Conrad (eds.), pp. 13–36.

Cooper, Robert L., 1984, The avoidance of androcentric generics. *International Journal of the Sociology of Language 50*, 5–20.

1989, *Language planning and social change*. Cambridge: Cambridge University Press.

1991, Dreams of scripts: writing systems as gift of God, in Cooper and Spolsky (eds.), pp. 219–26.

Cooper, Robert L. (ed.), 1982, *Language spread: studies in diffusion and social change*. Bloomington, IN: Indiana University Press.

Cooper, Robert L., and Carpenter, S., 1976, Language in the market, in M. L. Bender, J. D. Bowen, R. L. Cooper and C. A. Ferguson (eds.), *Language in Ethiopia*. London: Oxford University Press.

Cooper, Robert L., and Spolsky, Bernard (eds.), 1991, *The influence of language on culture and thought: essays in honor of Joshua A. Fishman's sixty-fifth birthday*. Berlin: Mouton de Gruyter.

Corvalan, Graziella, 1988, Bilingualism in Paraguay, in Paulston (ed.), pp. 356–77.

Coulmas, Florian, 1990, Language adaptation in Meiji Japan, in Brian Weinstein (ed.), *Language policy and political development* (pp. 69–86). Norwood, NJ: Ablex.

1991, The future of Chinese characters, in Cooper and Spolsky (eds.), pp. 227–43.

2003, *Writing system: an introduction to their linguistic analysis*. Cambridge: Cambridge University Press.

Covell, Maureen, 1993, Political conflict and constitutional engineering in Belgium. *International Journal of the Sociology of Language 104*, 65–86.

Cowan, J. Milton, and Graves, Mortimer, 1944, A statement on intensive language instruction. *Hispania 27*, 65–6.

Crawford, James, 2000a, *At war with diversity: US language policy in an age of anxiety*. Clevedon, England: Multilingual Matters Ltd.

2002b, Comment. *International Journal of the Sociology of Language 155/156*, 93–9.

2002c, Obituary: The Bilingual Education Act: 1968–2002, at http://ourworld.compuserve.com/homepages/JWCrawford/T7obit.htm.

2002d, Section G: Programs for English language learners, in *ESEA Implementation Guide* (pp. G1–G6). Small Axe Educational Communications.

Crowley, Tony, 2000, The language situation in Vanuatu. *Current Issues in Language Planning 1* (1), 47–132.

Crystal, David, 2000, *Language death*. Cambridge: Cambridge University Press.

de Swaan, Abram, 1999, *The language constellation of the European Union*. Paper presented at the International status and use of national languages in Europe: contributions to a European language policy, Brussels.

2001, *Words of the world: the global language system*. Cambridge, UK and Malden, MA: Polity Press and Blackwell.

Dittmar, Norbert, Spolsky, Bernard, and Walters, Joel, 2002, *Convergence and divergence in second language acquisition and use: an examination of immigrant identities in Germany and Israel* (Final scientific report No. Contract No. G-0500–157.04/96 GIF). Ramat-Gan and Berlin: Bar-Ilan University and Free University.

Djité, Paulin G., 1992, The arabization of Algeria: linguistic and sociopolitical motivations. *International Journal of the Sociology of Language 98*, 15–28.

Dornyei, Zoltan, and Csizer, Kate, 2002, Some dynamics of language attitudes and motivation: results of a longitudinal nationwide study. *Applied Linguistics 23* (4), 421–62.

Druviete, Ina, 1998, Republic of Latvia, in Paulston and Peckman (eds.), pp. 160–83.

Dua, Hans Raj, 1996, The spread of English in India: politics of language conflict and language power, in Fishman, Rubal-Lopez and Conrad (eds.), pp. 557–88.

Dunayer, Joan, 2001, *Animal equality: language and liberation*. Derwood, MD: Ryce.

Eisenstadt, S. N., 2000, The resurgence of religious movements in processes of globalisation – beyond end of history or clash of civilisations. *MOST Journal of Multicultural Studies 2* (1).

Ennaji, Moha, 1997, The sociology of Berber: change and continuity. *International Journal of the Sociology of Language 123*, 23–40.

European Commission, 2001a, *2001 Regular report on Estonia's progress towards accession* (No. SEC (2001) 1747). Brussels: Commission of the European Communities.

2001b, *2001 Regular report on Latvia's progress towards accession* (No. SEC (2001) 1749). Brussels: Commission of the European Communities.

Eurydice, 2000, *The position of foreign language in European education systems 1999/2000*, from http://www.eurydice.org/Documents/langues.

Evans, Stephen, 2002, Macaulay's Minute revisited: colonial language policy in nineteenth-century India. *Journal of Multilingual and Multicultural Development 23* (4), 260–81.

Fasold, Ralph W., 2002, The importance of community. *International Journal of the Sociology of Language 157*, 85–92.

Ferguson, Charles A., 1959, Diglossia. *Word 15*, 325–40.

1968, St. Stefan of Perm and applied linguistics, in Fishman, Ferguson and Das Gupta (eds.), pp. 253–65.

1977, Sociolinguistic settings of language planning, in Rubin, Jernudd, Das Gupta, Fishman and Ferguson (eds.), pp. 9–29.

1982, Religious factors in language spread, in Cooper (ed.), pp. 95–106.

Fernando, Chitra, 1996, The post-imperial status of English in Sri Lanka 1940–1990: from first to second language, in Fishman, Rubal-Lopez and Conrad (eds.), pp. 485–512.

Fishman, Joshua A., 1967, Bilingualism with and without diglossia; diglossia with and without bilingualism. *Journal of Social Issues 23* (2), 29–38.

1969, National languages and languages of wider communication in the developing nations. *Anthropological Linguistics 11*, 111–35.

1971a, National languages and languages of wider communication in the developing nations, in W. H. Whiteley (ed.), *Language use and social change: problems of multilingualism with special reference to Eastern Africa* (pp. 27–56). London: Oxford University Press for the International African Institute.

1971b, The politics of bilingual education, in James E. Alatis (ed.), *Report of the Twenty-first Annual Georgetown Round Table Meeting of Languages and Linguistics* (pp. 47–58). Washington, DC: Georgetown University Press.

1972, Domains and the relationship between micro- and macrosociolinguistics, in John J. Gumperz and Dell Hymes (eds.), *Directions in sociolinguistics* (pp. 435–53). New York: Holt Rinehart and Winston.

1977, Comparative study of language planning: Introducing a survey, in Rubin, Jernudd, Das Gupta, Fishman and Ferguson (eds.), pp. 31–9.

1983, Modeling rationales in corpus planning: Modernity and tradition in images of the Good, in Juan Cobarrubias and Joshua A. Fishman (eds.), *Progress in language planning: international perspectives* (pp. 107–18). The Hague: Mouton.

1989, Cross-polity perspective on the importance of linguistic heterogeneity as a "contributory factor" in civil strife, in Joshua A. Fishman (ed.), *Language and ethnicity in minority sociolinguistic perspective* (pp. 605–26). Clevedon, England: Multilingual Matters Ltd.

1991, *Reversing language shift: theoretical and empirical foundations of assistance to threatened languages.* Clevedon, England: Multilingual Matters Ltd.

1995, On the limits of ethnolinguistic democracy, in Phillipson, Rannut and Skutnabb-Kangas (eds.), pp. 49–62.

1996, Summary and interpretation: post-imperial English 1940–1990, in Fishman, Rubal-Lopez and Conrad (eds.), pp. 623–42.

Fishman, Joshua A. (ed.), 1966, *Language loyalty in the United States: the maintenance and perpetuation of non-English mother tongues by American ethnic and religious groups.* The Hague: Mouton.

1977, *Advances in the creation and revision of writing systems.* The Hague and Paris: Mouton.

2001, *Can threatened languages be saved? Reversing language shift, Revisited: A 21st century perspective.* Clevedon, England: Multilingual Matters Ltd.

Fishman, Joshua A., Cooper, Robert L., and Conrad, A. W., 1977, *The spread of English: the sociology of English as an additional language.* Rowley, MA: Newbury House.

Fishman, Joshua A., Cooper, Robert L., and Ma, Roxana, 1971, *Bilingualism in the barrio.* Bloomington, IN: Research Center for the Language Sciences, Indiana University.

Fishman, Joshua A., Ferguson, Charles A., and Das Gupta, Jyotirinda, 1968, *Language problems of developing nations.* New York: Wiley.

Fishman, Joshua A., Rubal-Lopez, Alma, and Conrad, Andrew W. (eds.), 1996, *Post-imperial English*. Berlin: Mouton de Gruyter.

Fishman, Joshua A., Solano, Frank R., and McConnell, Grant D., 1991, A methodological check on three cross-polity studies of linguistic homogeneity/heterogeneity, in Mary E. McGroarty and Christian J. Faltis (eds.), *Languages in school and society: policy and pedagogy* (pp. 21–30). Berlin and New York: Mouton de Gruyter.

Fourie, David J., 1997, Educational language policy and the indigenous languages of Namibia. *International Journal of the Sociology of Language* 125, 29–42.

Galtung, Johan, 1980, *The true world: a transnational perspective*. New York: Free Press.

Garcia, Eugene E., 2002, Bilingualism and schooling in the United States. *International Journal of the Sociology of Language* 155/156, 1–92.

Garcia, Ofelia, Morin, Jose Luis, and Rivera, Klaudia M., 2001, How threatened is the Spanish of New York Puerto Ricans? Language shift with vaiven, in Fishman (ed.), pp. 44–73.

Garvin, Paul, 1973, Some comments on language planning, in Joan Rubin and Roger Shuy (eds.), *Language planning: current issues and research* (pp. 24–73). Washington, DC: Georgetown University Press.

Geerts, G., Van den Broeck, J., and Verdoodt, Albert F., 1977, Successes and failures in Dutch spelling reform, in Fishman (ed.), pp. 179–245.

Gibson, Heather, Small, Anita, and Mason, David, 1997, Deaf bilingual bicultural education, in Jim Cummins and David Corson (eds.), *Encyclopedia of Language and Education* (vol. 5, *Bilingual Education*, pp. 231–42). Dordrecht: Kluwer Academic Publishers.

Glinert, Lewis, 1995, Inside the language planner's head: tactical responses to new immigrants. *Journal of Multilingual and Multicultural Development* 16 (5), 351–71.

Goebel, Zane, 2002, Code choice in interethnic interactions in two urban neighbourhoods of Central Java, Indonesia. *International Journal of the Sociology of Language* 158, 69–87.

Gogolin, I., 2001a, Linguistic habitus, in Raj Mesthrie (ed.), *Concise encyclopedia of sociolinguistics* (pp. 650–2). Amsterdam: Elsevier.

2001b, The linguistic marketplace, in Raj Mesthrie (ed.), *Concise encyclopedia of sociolinguistics* (pp. 612–13). Amsterdam: Elsevier.

Gorter, Durk, 2001, A Frisian update of reversing language shift, in Fishman (ed.), pp. 215–34.

Greenwood, J. D., 1994, *Realism, identity, and emotion: reclaiming social psychology*. London: Sage.

Grenoble, Lenore A., 2003, *Soviet language policy*. Dordrecht: Kluwer Academic Publishers.

Grimes, Barbara A. (ed.), 2000, *Ethnologue: languages of the world* (14th ed.). Dallas, TX: SIL International.

Grin, Francois, 1995, Combining immigrant and autochthonous language rights: a territorial approach to multilingualism, in Phillipson, Rannut and Skutnabb-Kangas (eds.), pp. 31–49.

2001, English an economic value: facts and fallacies. *World Englishes 20* (1), 65–78.

Groeneboer, Kees, 1998, *Gateway to the West: the Dutch language in colonial Indonesia 1600-1850: A history of language policy* (Myra Scholz, trans.). Amsterdam: Amsterdam University Press.

Gynan, Shaw N., 2001, Language planning and policy in Paraguay. *Current Issues in Language Planning 2* (1), 1–52.

Hale, Ken, 1991, On endangered languages and the safeguarding of diversity. *Language 68* (1) 1–3.

Hall, Robert A., 1950, *Leave your language alone!* Ithaca, NY: Cornell University Press.

Harris, Judith Rich, 1995, Where is the child's environment? A group socialization theory of development. *Psychological Review 102*, 458–89.

Harshav, Benjamin, 1993, *Language in time of revolution*. Berkeley, CA: University of California Press.

Haugen, Einar, 1966a, *Language conflict and language planning: the case of Modern Norwegian*, Cambridge, MA: Harvard University Press.

1966b, Linguistics and language planning, in William Bright (ed.), *Sociolinguistics* (pp. 50–71). The Hague: Mouton.

1971, The ecology of language. *The Linguistic Reporter Supplement 25*, 19–26.

1987, *Blessings of Babel: bilingualism and language planning: problems and pleasures*. Berlin, New York and Amsterdam: Mouton de Gruyter.

Heller, Monica, 1999, Alternative ideologies of *la francophonie. Journal of Sociolinguistics 3* (3), 336–59.

Hennoste, Tiit, Keevallik, Leelo, and Pajusalu, Karl, 1999, Estonian sociolinguistics: introduction. *International Journal of the Sociology of Language 139*, 1–16.

Hernandez-Chavez, Eduardo, 1995, Language policy in the United States: a history of cultural genocide, in Phillipson, Rannut and Skutnabb-Kangas (eds.), pp. 135–40.

High Commissioner on National Minorities, 1996, *The Hague Recommendations on the Education Rights of National Minorities*. The Hague: Organization for Security and Cooperation in Europe.

1998, *Oslo Recommendations on Linguistic Rights of National Minorities*. The Hague: Organization for Security and Cooperation in Europe.

1999, *Report on the Linguistic Rights of Persons Belonging to National Minorities in the OSCE Area*. The Hague: Organization for Security and Cooperation in Europe.

Hoffman, Charlotte, 1998, Luxembourg and the European Schools, in Jasone Cenoz and Fred Genesee (eds.), *Beyond bilingualism: multilingualism and multilingual education* (pp. 143–74). Clevedon, England: Multilingual Matters Ltd.

Holm, Wayne, 1972, *Some aspects of Navajo orthography*. Unpublished Ph.D. dissertation, University of New Mexico, Albuquerque, NM.

Holt, Sally, and Packer, John, 2001, OSCE developments and linguistic minorities. *MOST Journal of Multicultural Studies 3* (2).

Hongkai, Sun, 1992, Language recognition and nationality. *International Journal of the Sociology of Language 97*, 9–22.

Hongxu, Huang, and Guisen, Tian, 1990, A sociolinguistic view of linguistic taboo in Chinese. *International Journal of the Sociology of Language 81*, 63–86.

Hornberger, Nancy H., 1999, Language education policy – Latin America, in Bernard Spolsky (ed.), *Concise encyclopedia of educational linguistics* (pp. 133–9). Amsterdam and New York: Elsevier.

Hornberger, Nancy H., and King, Kendall A., 2001, Reversing language shift in South America, in Fishman (ed.), pp. 166–94.

Horowitz, Donald L., 2001, *The deadly ethnic riot*. Berkeley, CA: University of California Press.

Hovens, Mart, 2002, Bilingual education in West Africa: does it work? *International Journal of Bilingual Education and Bilingualism 5* (5), 249–66.

Howell, Robert B., 2000, The Low Countries: a study in sharply contrasting nationalism, in Barbour and Carmichael (eds.), pp. 130–50.

Hunter, Melvin, 1991, Racist relics: an ugly blight on our botanical nomenclature. *The Scientist 5* (23).

Hymes, Dell, 1967, Models of the interaction of language and social setting. *Journal of Social Issues 23* (2), 8–38.

1974, *Foundations in sociolinguistics: an ethnographic approach*. Philadelphia, PA: University of Pennsylvania Press.

Ivić, Pavle, 2001, Language planning in Serbia today. *International Journal of the Sociology of Language 151*, 7–17.

Jackendoff, Ray, 1983, *Semantics and cognition*. Cambridge, MA: MIT Press.

Jernudd, Björn, 1995, Personal names and human rights, in Phillipson, Rannut and Skutnabb-Kangas (eds.), pp. 121–34.

Jernudd, Björn, and Thuan, Elizabeth, 1983, Control of language through correction in speaking. *International Journal of the Sociology of Language 44*, 71–97.

Jones, John Paul, 2001, *Constitution Finder*, from http://confinder.richmond.edu.

Jones, Mari C., 1998a, Death of a language, birth of an identity: Brittany and the Bretons. *Language Problems and Language Planning 22* (2), 129–42.

1998b, *language obsolescence and revitalization: linguistic change in two sociolinguistically contrasting Welsh communities*. Oxford: Clarendon Press.

Jordan, Peter, 1998, Romania, in Paulston and Peckman (eds.), pp. 160–83.

Judge, Anne, 2000, France: "One state, one nation, one language"? In Barbour and Carmichael (eds.), pp. 44–84.

Kakava, Christina, 1997, Sociolinguistics and Modern Greek: past, current, and future directions. *International Journal of the Sociology of Language 126*, 5–32.

Kamwangamalu, Nkonko M., 2000, The new South Africa, language, and ethnicity: a prognosis. *International Journal of the Sociology of Language* 144, 137–8.

Kaplan, Robert B., and Baldauf, Richard B., 1997, *Language planning from practice to theory*. Clevedon, England: Multilingual Matters Ltd.

Keefer, Louis E., 1988, *Scholars in foxholes: the story of the Army Specialized Training Program in World War II*. Jefferson, NC: McFarland.

Kermode, Frank (2002). Zounds. *London Review of Books* 24, 19–20.

Khubchandani, Lachman M., 1997, Language policy and education in the Indian subcontinent, in Ruth Wodak and David Corson (eds.), *Encyclopedia of language and education* (vol. 1: *Language policy and political issues in education*, pp. 179–87). Dordrecht: Kluwer Academic Publishers.

2003, Defining mother tongue in plurilingual contexts.

Kloss, Heinz, 1966, German-American language maintenance efforts, in Fishman (ed.), pp. 206–52.

1969, *Research possibilities on group bilingualism: a report*. Quebec: International Center for Research on Bilingualism.

1977, *The American bilingual tradition*. Rowley, MA: Newbury House Publishers.

Kratz, E. E., 2001, Islam in Southeast Asia, in Sawyer and Simpson (eds.), pp. 65–6.

Krauss, Michael, 1991, The world's languages in crisis. *Language* 68 (1), 4–10.

Kroskrity, Paul V., 1998, Arizona Tewa Kiva speech as a manifestation of a dominant language ideology, in Bambi B. Schieffelin, Kathryn A. Woolard and Paul V. Kroskrity (eds.), *Language ideologies: practice and theory* (pp. 103–22). New York and Oxford: Oxford University Press.

Kulick, Don, 1992, *Language shift and cultural reproduction: socialization, self and syncretism in a Papua New Guinean village*. Cambridge: Cambridge University Press.

Labov, William, 1966, *The social stratification of English in New York City*. Washington, DC: Center for Applied Linguistics.

Lakoff, Robin, 1973, Language and woman's place. *Language in Society* 2 (1), 45–80.

Lambert, Richard D., 1994, Problems and processes in US foreign Language planning. *The Annals of the American Academy of Political and Social Sciences* 532, 47–58.

1999, A scaffolding for language policy. *International Journal of the Sociology of Language* 137, 3–25.

2002, Review of Joshua A. Fishman, 'Can threatened languages be saved?' *Language Policy* 1 (1), 99–104.

Landau, Jacob, and Kellner-Heinkele, Barbara, 2001, *Politics of language in the Ex-Soviet Muslim states: Azerbaijan, Usbekistan, Kazakhstan, Kyrgyzstan, Turkmenistan and Tajikistan*. London and Ann Arbor, MI: C. Hurst & Co. and the University of Michigan Press.

Lastra, Yolanda, 2001, Otomi language shift and some recent efforts to reverse it, in Fishman (ed.), pp. 142–65.

Laut, Jens Peter, 2000, *Das Türkische als Ursprache? Sprachwissenschaftliche Theorien in der Zeit des erwachenden türkischen Nationalismus.* Wiesbaden: Otto Harrassowitz.

Lee, Tiffany, and McLaughlin, Daniel, 2001, Reversing Navajo language shift, revisited, in Fishman (ed.), pp. 23–43.

Lewis, E. Glyn, 1972, *Multilingualism in the Soviet Union.* The Hague: Mouton.
   1980, *Bilingualism and bilingual education: a comparative study.* Albuquerque, NM and Oxford: University of New Mexico Press and Pergamon.

Lewis, Geoffrey, 1999, *The Turkish language reform: a catastrophic success.* Oxford: Oxford University Press.

Lo Bianco, Joseph, 1987, *National policy on languages.* Canberra: Australian Government Publishing Service.

Lo Bianco, Joseph, and Rhydwen, Mari, 2001, Is the extinction of Australia's indigenous languages inevitable? in Fishman (ed.), pp. 391–422.

Lucas, Ceil (ed.), 2001, *The sociolinguistics of sign language.* Cambridge: Cambridge University Press.

Macias, Reynaldo F., 1997, Bilingual workers and language-use rules in the workplace: a case study of nondiscriminatory language policy. *International Journal of the Sociology of Language* 127, 53–70.

Maher, John C., 2001, Akor Itak – our language, your language: Ainu in Japan, in Fishman (ed.), pp. 323–49.

Malherbe, E. G., 1978, Bilingual education in the Republic of South Africa, in Bernard Spolsky and Robert L. Cooper (eds.), *Case studies in bilingual education* (pp. 167–202). Rowley, MA: Newbury House.

Manase, Bernadette, Luaao, Elisapeta, and Fiamalua, Mataio, 1996, American Samoa Language Arts and Culture Program, in Gina H. Cantoni (ed.), *Stabilizing indigenous languages* (pp. 150–2). Flagstaff, AZ: Center for Excellence in Education, Northern Arizona University.

Marshall, David F., 1986, The question of an official language: language rights and the English Language Amendment. *International Journal of the Sociology of Language* 60, 7–75.

Marshall, David F., 1990, Introduction: China as a linguistic area. *International Journal of the Sociology of Language* 81, 9–13.

Martin, Terry, 2002, *The affirmative action empire: nations and nationalism in the Soviet Union 1923–1939.* Ithaca, NY: Cornell University Press.

Matiki, Alfred J., 2001, The social significance of English in Malawi. *World Englishes* 20 (2), 201–18.

McCarty, Teresa L., 1998, Schooling, resistance and American Indian Languages. *International Journal of the Sociology of Language* 132, 27–41.
   2002, *A place to be Navajo: Rough Rock and the struggle for self-determination in indigenous schooling.* Mahwah, NJ: Lawrence Erlbaum.

McLean, Daryl, and McCormick, Kay, 1996, English in South Africa 1940–1996, in Fishman, Rubal-Lopez and Conrad (eds.), pp. 303–38.

McRae, K. D., 1975, The principle of territoriality and the principle of personality in multilingual states. *International Journal of the Sociology of Language* 4, 33–54.

Mehrotra, Raja Ram, 1993, The first congress of Hindi, in Joshua A. Fishman (ed.), *The earliest stage of language planning: the "First Congress" phenomenon* (pp. 117–27). Berlin: Mouton de Gruyter.

Metz, Helen Chapin (ed.), 1994, *Madagascar: country studies*, Washington, DC: Federal Research Division Library of Congress.

Misra, Udayon, 2000, Sub-national challenges to the Indian state: an Assamese perspective. *Economic and Political Weekly*, 1727–30.

Mohanty, Panchanan, 2002, British language policies in 19th century India and the Oriya language movement. *Language Policy* 1 (1), 57–73.

Mueller, Gerland, 2002, *Rama Indian lands and the protection of Nicaragua's cultural and biological diversity.* Gainesville, FL: University of Florida Levin College of Law.

Mufwene, Salikoko S., 2001, *The ecology of language evolution.* Cambridge: Cambridge University Press.

Murphy, Alexander B., 1993, Linguistic regionalism and the social construction of space in Belgium. *International Journal of the Sociology of Language* 104, 49–64.

Nahir, Moshe, 1988, Language planning and language acquisition: the "Great Leap" in the Hebrew revival, in Paulston (ed.), pp. 275–95.

Nahir, Moshe, 1998, Micro language planning and the revival of Hebrew. *Language in Society* 27, 335–57.

Nekvapil, J., and Neustupný, J. V., 1998, Linguistic minorities in the Czech Republic, in Paulston and Peckman (eds.), pp. 116–35.

Nelde, Peter H., 1996, Language conflict, in Florian Coulmas (ed.), *The handbook of sociolinguistics* (pp. 285–300). Oxford: Blackwell.

Nelde, Peter H., Labrie, Normand, and Williams, C. H., 1992, The principles of territoriality and personality in the solution of linguistic conflicts. *Journal of Multilingual and Multicultural Development* 13, 387–406.

Nettle, Daniel, 1999, *Linguistic diversity.* Oxford: Oxford University Press.

Newman, Stanley, 1955, Vocabulary levels: Zuni sacred and slang usage. *Southwestern Journal of Anthropology* 11, 345–54.

Nic Shuibhne, Niamh, 2001, The European Union and minority language rights. *MOST Journal of Multicultural Studies* 3 (2).

Niedzielski, Nancy A., and Preston, Dennis R., 2000, *Folk linguistics.* Berlin: Mouton.

Niño-Murcia, Mercedes, 2001, Late-stage standardization and language ideology in the Colombian press. *International Journal of the Sociology of Language* 149, 119–44.

Noro, Hiroko, 1990, Family and language maintenance: an exploratory study of Japanese language maintenance among children of postwar

Japanese immigrants in Toronto. *International Journal of the Sociology of Language 86*, 57–68.

Nowak, Martin A., Komarova, Natalia L., and Niyogi, Partha, 2002, Computation and evolutionary aspects of language. *Nature 417*, (6889), 611–17.

Nyati-Ramahobo, Lydia, 2000, The language situation in Botswana. *Current Issues in Language Planning 1* (2), 243–300.

Ó Laoire, Muiris, 1996, An historical perspective of the revival of Irish outside the Gaeltacht, 1880–1930, with reference to the revitalization of Hebrew, in Sue Wright (ed.), *Language and state: revitalization and revival in Israel and Eire* (pp. 51–75). Clevedon, England: Multilingual Matters Ltd.

1999, *Athbheochan na heabhraise: ceacht don Ghaeilge? [Revival of Hebrew: example for Irish]*. Baile Atha Cliath: An Clochohar Tta.

Ó Murchú, Mairtin, 1977, Successes and failures in the modernization of Irish spelling, in Fishman (ed.), pp. 267–89.

Ó Riagáin, Padraig, 1997, *Language policy and social reproduction: Ireland 1893–1993*. Oxford: Clarendon Press.

Ochs, Elinor, 1986, Introduction, in Bambi B. Shieffelin and Elinor Ochs (eds.), *Language socialization across cultures* (pp. 2–13). Cambridge: Cambridge University Press.

Olson, Marie L., and Pearson, Frederic S., 2001, Policy-making and connections to violence: a case study of India, *Working paper of the Program on Mediating Theory and Democratic Systems*.

O'Reilly, Camille C. (ed.), 2001, *Ethnicity and state* (vol. 2: *Minority Languages in Eastern Europe Post-1989*). Basingstoke, England: Palgrave.

Oyama, Susan, 2000, *Evolution's eye: a systems view of the biology–culture divide*. Durham, NC and London: Duke University Press.

Ozolins, Uldis, 1996, Language policy and political reality. *International Journal of the Sociology of Language 118*, 181–200.

Pandit, Prabodh B., 1975, The Linguistic Survey of India – perspectives on language use, in Sirarpi Ohannessian, Charles A. Ferguson and Edgar C. Polomé (eds.), *Language surveys in developing nations* (pp. 71–85). Arlington, VA: Center for Applied Linguistics.

Paul, Herman, 1909, *Prinzipien der Sprachgeschichte* (4th ed.). Halle: Max Niemeyer.

Paulston, Christina Bratt, 1997, Language policies and language rights. *Annual Review of Anthropology 26*, 73–85.

1998, Linguistic minorities in Central and East Europe: an introduction, in Paulston and Peckman (eds.), pp. 1–18.

Paulston, Christina Bratt (ed.), 1988, *International handbook of bilingualism and bilingual education*. New York: Greenwood Press.

Paulston, Christina Bratt and Donald Peckman (eds.), 1998, *Linguistic minorities in Central and East Europe*. Clevedon, England and Philadelphia, USA: Multilingual Matters Ltd.

Pauwels, Anne, 1998, *Women changing languages*. New York: Addison Wesley Longman.

Pavlenko, Aneta, 2002, "We have room for but one language here": Language and national identity in the US at the turn of the 20th century. *Multilingua 21* (2/3), 163–96.

Pecos, Regis, and Blum-Martinez, Rebecca, 2001, The key to cultural survival: language planning and revitalization in the Pueblo de Cochiti, in Leanne Hinton and Ken Hale (eds.), *The green book of language revitalization in practice* (pp. 75–82). New York: Academic Press.

Peicheng, Su, 2001, Digraphia: a strategy for Chinese characters for the twenty-first century. *International journal of the sociology of language 150*, 109–24.

Pennycook, Alastair, 1998, *English and the discourses of colonialism*. London and New York: Routledge.

Phillipson, Robert, 1992, *Linguistic imperialism*. Oxford: Oxford University Press.

Phillipson, Robert, Rannut, Mart, and Skutnabb-Kangas Tove (eds.), 1995, *Linguistic human rights: overcoming linguistic discrimination*. Berlin and New York: Mouton de Gruyter.

Phillipson, Robert, and Skutnabb-Kangas, Tove, 1995, Language rights in postcolonial Africa, in Phillipson, Rannut and Skutnabb-Kangas (eds.), pp. 335–46.

Pickering, W. S. F., 2001, Blasphemy, in Sawyer and Simpson (2001), p. 240.

Pitman, James, and St. John, John, 1969, *Alphabets and reading*. London: Pitman.

Plaza, Pedro, and Albo, Xavier, 1989, Educación bilingüe y planificación lingüística en Bolivia. *International Journal of the Sociology of Language 77*, 69–91.

Poulton, Hugh, 1998, Linguistic minorities in the Balkans (Albania, Greece and the successor states of former Yugoslavia), in Paulston and Peckman (eds.), pp. 37–80.

Pranjković, Ivo, 2001, The Croatian standard language and the Serbian standard language. *International Journal of the Sociology of Language 147*, 31–50.

Quirk, Randolph, and Stern, Gabrielle, 1990, *English in use*. London: Longman.

Raag, Raimo, 1999, One plus one equals one: the forging of Standard Estonian. *International Journal of the Sociology of Language 139*, 17–38.

Rajagopalan, Kanavillill, 2002, National languages as flags of allegiance, or the linguistics that failed us: a close look at emergent linguistic chauvinism in Brazil. *Journal of Language and Politics 1* (1), 115–47.

Rannut, Mart, 1995, Beyond linguistic policy: the Soviet Union versus Estonia, in Phillipson, Rannut and Skutnabb-Kangas (eds.), pp. 179–208.

Ricento, Thomas (ed.), 2001, *Ideology, politics and language policies: focus on English*. Amsterdam and Philadelphia: John Benjamins.

Rodriguez, Cristina M., 2001, Accommodating linguistic difference: towards a comprehensive theory of language rights in the United States. *Harvard Civil Rights-Civil Liberties Review 36*, 133–223.

Rosier, Paul, and Holm, Wayne, 1980, *The Rock Point experience: a longitudinal study of a Navajo school program.* Washington, DC: Center for Applied Linguistics.

Rubal-Lopez, Alma, 1996, The ongoing spread of English: a comparative analysis of former Anglo-American colonies with non-colonies, in Fishman, Rubal-Lopez and Conrad (eds.), pp. 37–84.

Rubin, Joan, 1968, *National bilingualism in Paraguay.* The Hague: Mouton.

Rubin, Joan, Jernudd, Björn H., Das Gupta, Jyotirindra, Fishman, Joshua A. and Ferguson, Charles A. (eds.), 1977, *Language planning processes.* The Hague: Mouton.

Ruiz Vieytez, Eduardo Javier, 2001, The protection of linguistic minorities: a historical approach. *MOST Journal of Multicultural Studies 3* (1).

Sadeghi, Ali Ashraf, 2001, Language planning in Iran: a historical review. *International Journal of the Sociology of Language 148*, 19–30.

Sadiqi, Fatima, 1997, The place of Berber in Morocco. *International Journal of the Sociology of Language 123*, 7–22.

Salmon, Vivian, 1999, Orthography and punctuation, in Roger Lass (ed.), *The Cambridge history of the English language* (vol. III: *1476 to 1776*, pp. 13–55). Cambridge, UK: Cambridge University Press.

Saulson, Scott B. (ed.), 1979, *Institutionalized language planning.* The Hague: Mouton.

Sawyer, John F. A., 2001, General introduction, in Sawyer and Simpson (eds.), pp. 1–3.

Sawyer, John F. A., and Simpson, J. M. Y. (eds.), 2001, *Concise encyclopedia of language and religion.* Amsterdam, New York, Oxford, Shannon, Singapore, Tokyo: Elsevier.

Schegloff, Emanuel, Jefferson, G., and Sacks, Harvey, 1977, The preference for self-correction in the organization of repair in conversation. *Language 53* (2), 361–82.

Schiffman, Harold E., 1996, *Linguistic culture and language policy.* London and New York: Routledge.

Schlyter, Birgit N., 2001, Language policies in present-day Central Asia. *MOST Journal of Multicultural Studies 3*(2).

Sealey, Alison, and Carter, Bob, 2001, Social categories and sociolinguistics: applying a realist approach. *International Journal of the Sociology of Language 152*, 1–19.

Searle, John R., 1995, *The construction of social reality.* London: Allen Lane.

Shraybom Shivtiel, Shlomit, 1999, Language and political change in modern Egypt. *International Journal of the Sociology of Language 137*, 131–40.

Sibayan, Bonifacio, 1974, Language policy, language engineering and literacy in the Philippines, in Fishman (ed.), pp. 221–54.

Sibayan, Bonifacio, and Gonzales, Andrew, 1996, Post-imperial English in the Philippines, in Fishman, Rubal-Lopez and Conrad (eds.), pp. 139–72.

Sims, Christine P., 2001, Native language planning: a pilot process in the Acoma Pueblo community, in Leanne Hinton and Ken Hale (eds.), *The green book of language revitalization in practice* (pp. 63–73). New York: Academic Press.

Sirles, Craig A., 1999, Politics and Arabization: the evolution of post independence North Africa. *International Journal of the Sociology of Language* 137, 115–30.

Skutnabb-Kangas, Tove, 2002, Comment: (North) American ambiguities and paranoias. *International Journal of the Sociology of Language 155/156*, 179–86.

Skutnabb-Kangas, Tove, and Bucak, Sertal, 1995, Killing a mother tongue: how the Kurds are deprived of linguistic human rights, in Phillipson, Rannut and Skutnabb-Kangas (eds.), pp. 335–46.

Spencer, John (ed.), 1963, *Language in Africa*. Cambridge: Cambridge University Press.

Spolsky, Bernard, 1974a, Linguistics and education: an overview, in Thomas A. Sebeok (ed.), *Current Trends in Linguistics* (vol. 13, pp. 2021–6). The Hague: Mouton.

1974b, Navajo language maintenance: six-year-olds in 1969, in Frank Pialorsi (ed.), *Teaching the bilingual* (pp. 138–49). Tucson, AZ: University of Arizona Press.

1975, Prospects for the survival of the Navajo language, in M. Dale Kinkade, Kenneth Hale and Oswald Werner (eds.), *Linguistics and anthropology, in honor of C. F. Voegelin* (pp. 597–606). Lisse: Peter de Ridder.

1989, *Conditions for second language learning: introduction to a general theory.* Oxford: Oxford University Press.

1995a, The impact of the Army Specialized Training Program: a reconsideration, in Guy Cook and Barbara Seidelhofer (eds.), *For H. G. Widdowson: principles and practice in the study of language: a Festschrift on the occasion of his sixtieth birthday* (pp. 323–34). Oxford: Oxford University Press.

1995b, *Measured words: the development of objective language testing.* Oxford: Oxford University Press.

2002a, Norms, native speakers and reversing language shift, in Sue Gass, Kathleen Bardovi-Harlig, Sally Sieloff Magnan and Joel Walz (eds.), *Pedagogical norms for second and foreign language and teaching: studies in honour of Albert Valdman* (pp. 41–58). Amsterdam and Philadelphia: John Benjamins.

2002b, Prospects for the survival of the Navajo language: a reconsideration. *Anthropology and Education Quarterly 33* (2), 1–24.

2003, Reassessing Maori regeneration. *Language in Society 32* (4).

Spolsky, Bernard, and Cooper, Robert L., 1991, *The languages of Jerusalem.* Oxford: Clarendon Press.

Spolsky, Bernard, and Shohamy, Elana, 1999, *The languages of Israel: policy, ideology and practice.* Clevedon, England: Multilingual Matters Ltd.

2001, Hebrew after a century of RLS efforts, in Fishman (ed.), pp. 349–62.

Spolsky, Ellen, 2001, *Satisfying skepticism: embodied knowledge in the early modern world.* Aldershot, UK: Ashgate.

Spolsky, Ellen, and Schauber, Ellen, 1986, *The bounds of interpretation: linguistic theory and literary text.* Stanford, CA: Stanford University Press.

Srivastava, R. N., 1988, Societal bilingualism and bilingual education: a study of the Indian situation, in Paulston (ed.), pp. 247–74.

Statistics New Zealand, 2001, *Provisional report on the 2001 Survey on the Health of the Maori Language.* Wellington: Statistics New Zealand for Te Puni Kokiri.

Stewart, William, 1968, A sociolinguistic typology for describing national multilingualism, in Joshua A. Fishman (ed.), *Readings in the sociology of language* (pp. 531–45). The Hague: Mouton.

Strubell, Miquel, 2001, Catalan a decade later, in Fishman (ed.), pp. 260–83.

Tabouret-Keller, André, 1968, Sociological factors of language maintenance and language shift: a methodological approach based on European and African examples, in Fishman, Ferguson and Das Gupta (eds.), pp. 107–27.

Thomas, Wayne P., and Collier, Virginia P., 2002, *A national study of school effectiveness for language minority students' long-term academic achievement.* Santa Cruz, CA: Center for Research on Education, Diversity and Education, University of Santa Cruz.

Tickoo, Makham L., 1996, Fifty years of English in Singapore: all gains, (a) few losses? In Fishman, Rubal-Lopez and Conrad (eds.), pp. 431–56.

Tollefson, James W., 1997, Language policy in independent Slovenia. *International Journal of the Sociology of Language 124,* 29–50.

Trim, John L. M., 1959, Historical, descriptive and dynamic linguistics. *Language and Speech 2,* 9–25.

Trim, John L. M., 2002, Review of Gabriella Hogan-Brun, national varieties of German outside Germany. *Language Policy 2* (1).

Tsilevich, Boris, 2001, Development of the language legislation in the Baltic states. *MOST Journal of Multicultural Studies 3* (2).

Tuominen, Anne, 1999, Who decides the home language? A look at multilingual families. *International Journal of the Sociology of Language 140,* 59–76.

Varennes, Fernand de, 1997, *To speak or not to speak: the rights of persons belonging to linguistic minorities.* Working paper: UN Sub-committee on the rights of minorities.

2001, Language rights as an integral part of human rights. *MOST Journal of Multicultural Studies 3* (1).

Vavrus, Frances, 2002, Postcoloniality and English: exploring language policy and the politics of development in Tanzania. *TESOL Quarterly 36* (3), 373–97.

Venezky, Richard L., 1970, Principles for the design of practical writing systems, *Anthropological Linguistics 12* (7), 256–70.

Vikor, Lars S., 2000, Northern Europe: languages as prime markers of ethnic and national identity, in Barbour and Carmichael (eds.), pp. 105–29.

Voegelin, Carl F., and Voegelin, Florence M., 1964, Languages of the world: Native American fascicle one. *Anthropological Linguistics 6* (6), 2–45.

Voegelin, Carl F., Voegelin, Florence M., and Schutz, Noel M. Jr, 1967, The language situation in Arizona as part of the South West cultural area, in Dell Hymes and W. E. Bittle (eds.), *Studies in Southwestern ethnolinguistics* (pp. 403–51). The Hague: Mouton.

Votruba, Martin, 1998, Linguistic minorities in Slovakia, in Paulston and Peckman (eds.), pp. 224–54.

Wallace, Mike, and Wray, Alison, 2002, The fall and rise of linguists in education policy-making: from "common-sense" to common ground. *Language Policy 1* (1) 75–98.

Watson-Gegeo, Katherine Anne, and Gegeo, David W., 1986, Calling out and repeating routines in Kwara'ae children's language socialization, in Bambi B. Shieffelin and Elinor Ochs (eds.), *Language socialization across cultures* (pp. 17–50). Cambridge: Cambridge University Press.

Wee, Lionel, 2002, When English is not a mother tongue: linguistic ownership and the Eurasian community in Singapore. *Journal of Multilingual and Multicultural Development 23* (4), 282–95.

Weeks, Theodore R., 2002, Religion and russification: Russian language in the Catholic Churches of the "Northwest Provinces" after 1863. *Kritika: Explorations in Russian and Eurasian History 2* (1), 87–110.

Weinstein, Brian, 1982, Noah Webster and the diffusion of linguistic innovations for political purposes. *International Journal of the Sociology of Language 38*, 85–108.

1989, Francophonie: purism at the international level, in Björn Jernudd and Michael J. Shapiro (eds.), *The politics of language purism* (pp. 53–80). Berlin and New York: Mouton de Gruyter.

White, Dob, 1997, The position and roles of minority languages and their writing systems in China. *International Journal of the Sociology of Language 97*, 47–57.

Wilcox, Sherman, 1999, Deafness and sign language instruction, in Bernard Spolsky (ed.), *Concise encyclopedia of educational linguistics* (pp. 249–55). Amsterdam and New York: Elsevier.

World Bank, 1993, *Indigenous people in Latin America: human resources development and operations policy* (HRO Dissemination Notes No. 8, June 7, 1993). Washington, DC: World Bank.

Wright, Sue Ellen, 2001, Language and power: background to the debate on linguistic rights. *MOST Journal of Multicultural Studies* 3 (1).

Yahya-Othman, Saida, and Batibo, Herman, 1996, The swinging pendulum: English in Tanzania 1940–1990, in Fishman, Rubal-Lopez and Conrad (eds.), pp. 377–400.

Yaowen, Zhou, 1992, News from China: minority languages in perspective. *International Journal of the Sociology of Language* 97, 37–45.

Youguang, Zhou, 1986, The modernization of the Chinese language. *International Journal of the Sociology of Language* 59, 7–23.

Young, Catherine, 2002, First language literacy: literacy education in a multilingual Philippine society. *International Journal of Bilingual Education and Bilingualism* 5 (4), 221–32.

Young, Robert W., 1977, Written Navajo: a brief history, in Fishman (ed.), pp. 459–70.

Zondag, Koen, 1987, "This morning the church presents comedy": Some aspects of Frisian in the religious domain. *International Journal of the Sociology of Language* 64, 71–80.

Index

CPSIA information can be obtained
at www.ICGtesting.com
Printed in the USA
LVHW03s0139150818
586963LV00016B/358/P

9 780521 011754